THE SEXUAL ABUSE OF ADOLESCENT GIRLS

Dedicated to the memory of Declan Curran, 1981-1995

The Sexual Abuse of Adolescent Girls

Social workers' child protection practice

STEWART KIRK
University of York

Ashgate

Aldershot • Brookfield USA • Singapore • Sydney

Published by
Ashgate Publishing Ltd
Gower House
Croft Road
Aldershot
Hants GU11 3HR
England

Ashgate Publishing Company
Old Post Road
Brookfield
Vermont 05036
USA

British Library Cataloguing in Publication Data
Kirk, Stewart
    The sexual abuse of adolescent girls : social workers'
    child protection practice. - (Evaluative research in social
    work)
    1.Child sexual abuse - Great Britain 2.Child sexual abuse -
    Investigation - Great Britain 3.Child sexual abuse - Great
    Britain - Prevention 4.Sexually abused teenagers - Services
    for - Great Britain
    I.Title
    362.7'6'7'0941

Library of Congress Catalog Card Number: 99-72658

ISBN 0 7546 1037 3

Printed and bound by Athenaeum Press, Ltd.,
Gateshead, Tyne & Wear.

Contents

Preface

This book is the result of a study to determine the ways in which a variety of factors influence the actions of social workers in child protection cases involving the sexual abuse of adolescent girls by a family member.

These influences on practice fall into five broad categories. The first category comprises central government legislation, policy and practice guidance, local procedures, local organisational and administrative issues and the availability of a whole series of resources within social services and beyond. The second category comprises those issues arising out of the governmental mandate for interagency coordination and the operation of the child protection network. The third category comprises those issues deriving from the girl and her status, and the form and seriousness of the abuse. This includes the crucial issue of the age of the girls concerned. The fourth category comprises those issues deriving from the girls' families, both non-abusing members and perpetrators. This includes issues both of family structure and familial relationships. The fifth category comprises those issues to do with the skills, limitations and practice preferences of the social workers themselves.

The book has developed out of a doctoral research project based around a research process of in-depth interviews with social workers with reference to recent cases they had dealt with.

The various influences on their practice are considered both in terms of practical enablements to practice and constraints on practice, and in terms of indirect influences on practice. These are considered in terms of issues deriving from specific concrete situations, forms of abuse and the personalities of the various protagonists, mediated through the meanings they hold for practising social workers.

Through the examination of these various themes a number of areas of tension become apparent. The research demonstrates clear tensions between the social workers' perceptions of the therapeutic task of child protection work and the aims of the criminal justice system, the rigidity of certain aspects of the child protection procedures and the aftermath needs of abused adolescent girls, and normative perspectives of risk and client choice.

Deriving from the analysis of the influence of these different factors on practice are recommendations for improved in-service training, including joint training for social workers and police officers, and recommendations for a review of the transitional procedures between child protection and adult services.

Acknowledgements

This study would not have been possible without the help of a great many people. Firstly, I wish to thank all of the social workers and social services managers that were kind enough to give up their valuable time in interviews. Secondly, I must thank Dr. Carol-Ann Hooper for her constructive criticism and intellectual support throughout the project, and Professor Ian Sinclair and Mr Bob Coles for their help in the early stages. I also wish to thank those undergraduate and postgraduate students at the universities of York and Bradford for their good-natured criticism and interest in the project. Thanks also go to my wife, Bernadette, my children, Anne, Catherine and Daniel, and other family and friends (they know who they are) for both emotional support and practical assistance in completing this book. Special thanks go to Mrs Jane Kirk, Messrs. John Manson, Dennis Robertson and Duncan Kirk for transporting a non-driver across the country to conduct interviews.

Series Editors' Preface

Evaluative Research in Social Work brings together research which has explored the impact of social work services in a variety of contexts and from several perspectives. The vision of social work in this series is a broad one. It encompasses services in residential, fieldwork and community settings undertaken by workers with backgrounds in health and welfare. The volumes will therefore include studies of social work with families and children, with elderly people, people with mental and other health problems and with offenders.

This approach to social work is consistent with contemporary legislation in many countries, including Britain, in which social work has a key role in the assessment of need and in the delivery of personal social services, in health care and in criminal justice. It also continues a long tradition which perceives an integral relationship between social work, social research and social policy. Those who provide social work services are acquainted with the complexities of human need and with the achievements and shortcomings of major instruments of social policy. This knowledge was exploited by, amongst others, Booth, Rowntree and the Webbs in their studies of poverty. Politicians and sociologists have also recognised that, together with the people they try to help, social workers can provide a commentary on the human meaning of public policies and the social issues that grow from private troubles.

This knowledge and experience of the recipients and practitioners of social work are not, of course, immediately accessible to the wider community. A major purpose of research is to gather, organise and interpret this information and, in the studies in this series, to evaluate the impact of social work. Here there are many legitimate interests to consider. First and foremost are direct service users and those who care for them. These are the people who should be the main beneficiaries of social work services. Also to be considered are the personnel of other services for whom liaison and collaboration with social work are essential to their own successful functioning. The needs and views of these different groups may well conflict and it is the researcher's task to identify those tensions and describe social work's response to them.

The problems which confront social work are often extremely complex. They may need to be tackled in a variety of ways; for example, through practical assistance, advocacy, counselling and supervision. Outcomes may be similarly varied and studies of the effectiveness of social work must demonstrate the different kinds of impact it can have. These may entail changes in users' circumstances, behaviour or well being. On these changes, and on the kind of help they have received, users' perspectives must be of great significance. Also of central interest to those who provide or manage services is an understanding of their form and content and the relationship between the problems identified and the statutory responsibilities of social workers and the help given. Social work researchers must therefore take care to study what is actually delivered through social work and how, as well as its outcomes, aspirations and objectives. For good and ill social work has an impact on large and increasing number of citizens. A major aim of *Evaluative Research in Social Work* is to increase well-informed understanding of social work, based on knowledge about its real rather than imagined activities and outcomes.

The identification of effectiveness, in its various forms, can also not be the end of the story. The costs of the associated services must be studied, set in the context of their effectiveness, to allow the most efficient use of resources.

These demands present major challenges to researchers who have to use, adapt and develop a wide range of research methods and designs. Ingenuity and persistence are both required if evaluative research in social work is to be pursued in contexts often regarded as beyond the scope of such enquiry. *Evaluative Research in Social Work* intends to make widely available not only the research findings about the impact of social work but also to demonstrate and discuss possible approaches and methods in this important and developing field of enquiry.

The first volumes in this series described studies undertaken in the Social Work Research Centre at the University of Stirling. In 1997, we decided actively to seek proposals from major centres of research for future books in this series. It had become clear from the 1996 UK Higher Education Funding Councils' assessment of research in British universities that both the quality and quantity of social work research were increasing substantially. It was also clear that a priority for many researchers - in this strategic and applied field - is, quite appropriately, to publish digests of their work in books and journals designed particularly for busy practitioners and managers. A consequence of this is that the full context, content and methodology of the research may never enter the public domain. This is a loss for researchers and those with a specialist interest in the subjects under enquiry, especially so in a relatively new and complex field of research when methodological innovation and development are important. Ashgate publications provide an excellent context for books which can explore subjects in depth and also allow exploration of research design, method and technique.

Juliet Cheetham and Roger Fuller   University of Stirling

1 Introduction

Introduction

This book seeks to examine the influences on social workers' practice in cases involving the sexual abuse of adolescent girls. In order to do this one needs to develop an understanding of a number of issues relating to child abuse in general, child sexual abuse in particular, and issues specific to adolescence.

Therefore, firstly, there is a discussion of the various perspectives of child abuse and child protection. This is followed by a review of the relevant parts of the Children Act, 1989, and its place in the historical development of child protection policy and practice. Following this is a discussion of the process of interagency coordination in child protection, and the 'mandated' nature of the relationship between the different agencies in the child protection network.

This leads on to a discussion of the nature of adolescence and the ways in which female adolescence differs from male adolescence, and how adolescence *per se* is different from both childhood and adulthood. This is followed by a discussion of the aetiology and consequences of child and adolescent sexual abuse, and finally a discussion of some of the difficulties that child protection practitioners can face in terms of working with adolescent girls who have been sexually abused.

This gives us the contextual framework for an understanding of the social workers' accounts. The purpose of the study is to gain an understanding of the ways in which social workers take specific actions in their day to day work in child protection cases that involve adolescent girls alleging sexual abuse by a member of the family, including why they act in certain ways rather than others. Crucially, one needs to discover, what is specific to child protection practice with this particular client group that differentiates it from that relating to boys and younger children.

The Contested Nature of Child Abuse

Any attempt to understand the processes of intervention in child protection cases must be founded upon an appreciation of the nature of child abuse.

Before any process of social intervention can take place, a social problem needs to be identified and rendered amenable to administration, registration and control (Foucault, 1977; Donzelot, 1979; Squires, 1990). The nature of any intervention process is predicated upon the definition of certain behaviours as socially or morally unacceptable. Changing social constructions of the nature of childhood itself (Aries, 1962) and variations over time in social mores over what constitutes right behaviour have profoundly influenced the formulation of what constitutes child abuse (Parton, 1991; Corby, 1993).

> It [child abuse] is a product of a particular culture and context and not an unchanging phenomenon...what is considered to be abusive in a particular society alters over time ...[and] ...what is viewed as abusive in one society is not necessarily seen as such in another (Corby, 1993, Pg.39).

In essence, child abuse is best seen as a label given to a series of behaviours towards children that are officially considered abusive, as 'not all harms towards children are considered, by governments anyway, to be child abuse' (Hallett, 1993, Pg.142).

Child abuse is not only a culturally mediated phenomenon, its nature and causation is also highly contested. On the surface the discourse on child abuse and the manner of dealing with it appears unproblematical, dominated by politicians, the members of committees of inquiry and child protection professionals, 'the licensed interpreters of social evidence' (Dingwall *et al*, 1983, Pg.53). It tends to be perceived as a misuse of power against children, and to a lesser extent against women and the poor (Parton, 1985; Campbell, 1988; Parton and Parton, 1989). In reality child abuse forms an arena of contention and debate. Fox-Harding (1991a, 1991b), for example, talks of competing perspectives of child liberation and patriarchy, whilst Gordon (1988) places child abuse within a wider context of domestic violence. The ways of dealing with child and adolescent sexual abuse can also be seen in terms of a series of legitimated utterances and silences (Wise, 1991), that fail to affirm the experiences and complex emotions of the mothers of sexually abused children (Hooper, 1992) and of those children themselves.

Whereas there is some ambivalence amongst the public as to the point at which the appropriate physical chastisement of a child or adolescent crosses over into physical abuse (Briere, 1992), child sexual abuse is almost universally condemned. However, sexual abuse can be difficult to define. Adult behaviour towards children that falls short of penetration may be open to interpretation, and what is regarded as the inappropriate sexual behaviour of adults towards children is mediated through cultural norms of sexual activity, and via the social construction of childhood (La Fontaine, 1990)

When child sexual abuse takes place within the family these issues are compounded by ideological perceptions of privacy, family life and intrafamilial social relations. Although all forms of child abuse comprise the abuse of children by those in a position of power or authority over them, the perception of both the public and of the 'victim' of familial child sexual abuse make it qualitatively different from sexual abuse outside the family and other forms of child abuse. In her analysis of domestic violence in Boston between 1880 and 1960, Gordon (1988) makes clear the similarities and differences in the meaning for the child of physical abuse and sexual abuse within the family.

> In one way incest resembles nonsexual child abuse. The child is treated badly, injuriously by one who is supposed to be a caretaker. The dilemma for the child in both forms of abuse is that her molester is one on whom she must depend for love and sustenance. Nosexual abuse is never pleasant for the child , while incest may be, and may be interpreted as an expression of affection. Yet even very young children know that incestuous sex is, theoretically, forbidden, while nonsexual abuse may develop out of punishment that is accepted as legitimate even by the child. Thus whatever gratification the child gets from parental affection in the incestuous relation is mixed with guilt (Gordon, 1988, Pg.214).

Although they are closely related incest and child sexual abuse are not the same. The familial sexual abuse of children can also be incest if sexual intercourse takes place, but incest can also take place between two adults. Certain forms of incest are subject to legal and moral proscriptions. However, governmental child protection guidance is concerned less with blood relationships than with the misuse of adult power over children. Child sexual abuse is defined as the 'actual or likely sexual exploitation of a child or adolescent' (DoH, 1991c, para.6.40). This is so general as to give little guidance as to what specific practices constitute child sexual abuse. This reinforces the view that something we call child sexual abuse can only exist as a concept within a cultural and ethical firmament that reflects the diversity of contemporary social and moral discourses in respect of children, family life, sexual behaviours and levels of interpersonal violence. Further, child abuse *per se* can also be seen as being constantly mediated through socio-political perspectives of what is an appropriate level of state intervention in terms of protecting children from or within their families.

> What is considered child abuse for the purposes of child protection policy and practice is ...[best] characterised as a product of social negotiation between different values and beliefs, different social norms and professional knowledges and perspectives about children, child development and parenting. Far from being a medico-social reality, it is a phenomenon where moral reasoning and moral judgements are central (Parton *et al*, 1997, Pg.67)

One needs to be very careful, however, from succumbing to any form of relativist fallacy that fails to recognise the material social reality of child sexual abuse. Although definitions of child sexual abuse vary immensely, and change over time, a discourse of child sexual abuse is common currency amongst politicians, child protection professionals and parents, and for those children who have suffered such abuse the consequences can be extremely detrimental. The variability of what exactly can be seen to constitute child and adolescent sexual abuse should not preclude researchers and analysts from recognising the reality of such abuse and the role it plays in determining the whole edifice of child protection systems and processes (Parton *et al*, 1997). It also emphasises the need for child protection practitioners to act on a 'case-by-case' basis, effectively developing definitions of abuse through their work with particular children and adolescents.

The Child Protection Process

One of the consequences of child abuse being identified as a social problem has been the development of institutional processes for dealing with it. These processes are intimately embedded in social, cultural and ideological conceptualisations of childhood, family life, privacy and the legitimate boundaries of state intervention. Further, these child protection processes derive from competing models of child abuse and its aetiology.

Parton (1985) argues that traditionally there have been three basic models of child abuse; the medical model that perceives child abuse as analogous to infectious disease, the social welfare model that sees child abuse as at least partially mitigated by social conditions and material disadvantage, and the legal model that views child abuse as a 'choice' made by individuals to ignore certain accepted rules of social behaviour.

Each model offers a different rationale for child protection intervention. The medical model focuses on the removal of the perpetrator or the modification of his behaviour as the agent of the 'disease'. The social welfare model also concentrates on modifying the perpetrator's behaviour, whilst also looking towards modifying the conditions within which the abuse occurred. The focus of the legal model is significantly different, concentrating principally on the punishment of the perpetrator to deter others from ignoring the 'rules'. Parton (1991) and Parton *et al* (1997) point to the growing influence of the legal model. Along with the resource constraints currently placed on local authority social services departments this presents a disquieting scenario for deprived and disadvantaged children, as social factors of deprivation and disadvantage can be seen to have a direct bearing in cases of chronic neglect and emotional abuse (Wattam, 1992). Social factors are also implicated in physical and sexual abuse. The high number of cases that are 'filtered out' at or prior to the initial investigation stage (Gibbons *et al,* 1995) suggests the need for strict 'gatekeeping' within the process (Wattam, 1997a) due to limited resources for the child protection system in particular (Rickford, 1993) and the financial constraints placed on local government welfare delivery generally.

All three models are individualist models of the aetiology of child abuse, that develop individualist rationales for child protection intervention, reflecting the dominance of individualist explanations for social problems in modern western societies. The nearest one gets to a 'social' explanation of child abuse is Parton's (1991) social welfare model, or what Gough (1993) describes as the 'institutional' model of child abuse and prevention. Even then the proponents of this model believe that:

> ... the state should intervene to assist people disadvantaged by the social system and conceive of this intervention as being applied to individuals and families rather than to changing social structures (Gough, 1993, Pg.213)

Although Gough (1993) concerns himself primarily with those social factors implicated in the capitalist structuring of social relations, the individualist nature of 'explaining' child abuse tends also to take little account of patriarchy. There is a tendency not to confront material features such as the economic dominance of men over women and children, and ideological features such as the patriarchal structuring of familial relations and the male construction of female sexuality, that all contribute towards the sexual exploitation of girls by men, both within and outside the family.

The Background to the Children Act 1989

The principal legal basis for child protection intervention comes from the Children Act, 1989. A stated aim of the government in bring in the Children Bill before parliament was to tidy up the existing legislation relating to children (Eekelaar and Dingwall, 1990), and from a legal perspective this has been achieved (David, 1991). The Children Act is not however a coherent framework for child welfare. Rather, it has drawn together the conflicting strands of child care and child protection provision into a single piece of legislation. By repealing and replacing seven previous Acts such as the Children Act, 1975, and the Child Care Act, 1980, and significantly amending other Acts such as the Children and Young Persons Act, 1969, Parliament succeeded in placing what were a series of contradictions between various pieces of legislation within the confines of a single Act (Fox-Harding, 1991a, 1991b).

Fox-Harding (1991a, 1991b) identifies four competing perspectives within the Children Act:

- 'laissez-faire and patriarchy' – this invokes a principal of minimal intervention and places the rights and dynamics of the family above the rights of the state – this is evident in the non-intervention principal that appears throughout the Act, Care and Supervision Orders, for example, being seen as a last resort (s.31(2)),
- 'state paternalism and child protection' – this grants a prioritised status to the normative values of the state's welfare professionals, and minimises the rights of parents and the civil rights of the child – this is evident in the use of potential harm as a criterion for intervention in terms of Child Assessment Orders (s.43(2)), and Emergency Protection Orders (s.44(1), s.44(6)), for example,
- 'defence of the birth family and parental rights' – this sees the family of birth as the 'natural' location for bringing up children and argues for systems to support the family in that task – this is evident in the provision of family support services in Schedule 2 of the Act,
- 'children's rights and child liberation'[1] – this appears in its moderate form that recognises the rights of children to have their wishes taken into account in any issues to do with their welfare – this is evident in the welfare 'checklist' (s.1(3)).

Fox-Harding (1991a, 1991b) argues that the contradictions within the Children Act go beyond the identification of these four competing perspectives at different points within the text of the Act. She argues that different provisions within the Act are open to competing interpretations. However, although all of Fox-Harding's (1991a, 1991b) perspectives can be seen in some form within the text of the Act, it is the 'state paternalism and child protection' perspective that she sees as dominant.

Freeman (1992) accepts Fox-Harding's (1991a, 1991b) analysis to a point, but contends that although the position of the state is strengthened by giving the right 'of prognosis by social workers' (Pg.4) in the concept of 'likely significant harm', the concept of 'laissez-faire' is the dominant theme.

> The presumption of non-intervention (s.1(5)), keeping compulsory intervention to a minimum, both in public and private matters, is the clearest example of laissez-faire. It is the keynote to an understanding of the whole Act (Freeman, 1992, Pg.3).

Parton (1991) takes a somewhat different line. He sees the public law elements of the Children Act as representing a major refocusing of concern in child welfare onto child abuse to the relative exclusion of other elements of child care. He also sees the Act as affirming his contention that legalism is becoming the dominant theme in child protection, arguing that the Act has aimed,

> ...to remove much of the previous discretionary paternalistic power of social workers and make them more accountable to the courts (Parton, 1991, Pg.191).

Parton's (1991) contention that a medical model of child abuse has been replaced by a legal model can be seen to have transformed child protection practice

> Whereas previously the concern was with diagnosing, curing and preventing the 'disease' or syndrome, increasingly the emphasis has become investigating, assessing and weighing 'forensic evidence' (Parton *et al*, 1997, Pg.19).

This has led to a changing role for child protection social workers. Parton *et al* (1997) stress the ultimate authority of the court and its capacity to overrule the expertise of other professionals. Issues relating to the best interests of the child tend to be interpreted in terms of rights and duties rather than in terms of therapeutic intervention. This makes plain that an understanding of the legislation and the workings of the court may have become more central to the social worker's role than issues of counselling and therapy.

Parton (1991) further argues that due to the low priority given to resourcing preventative measures, the family support services in the Act may have little meaning, and that a clear divide may emerge between parent led child welfare services and legalistic child protection systems. Merrick (1996) in similar vein argues that the Children Act can be seen as a form of 'authoritarian familialism', in that the state will only intervene in the family and in partnership with parents when there is a perceived risk of significant harm to the child. Within this framework Parton (1991) visualises the displacement of the role of social services away from child care, which will become the province of the voluntary sector, towards a legalistic role in child protection under the gaze of the court. David (1991) takes a similar view, seeing the Act as reinforcing the privacy of the family and social work effort being almost entirely focused on child abuse cases.

The increasingly legalistic framework for child protection brings serious problems, as the force of law may be the least appropriate tool for solving the real problems of child abuse (Wattam, 1992). The impact of adversarial proceedings on children and families traumatised by child abuse may cause further damage to already fractured familial relations.

> Whilst this is so, making a case in child protection may still present practitioners and children with the dilemma of a 'no-win' situation (Wattam, 1992, Pg.198).

The concept of a 'no-win' situation is familiar to child protection social workers. When physical abuse is alleged, if social workers intervene too readily they are seen as the agents of a repressive state illegitimately interfering in the private workings of the family, yet if they do not intervene and a child is injured or killed, they take the brunt of the blame (Freeman, 1989). There are similar problems for social workers over intervening when sexual abuse has been alleged. They work within a wider social environment that maintains contradictory sets of values. Child sexual abuse is seen as abhorrent and needing vigorous intervention, yet social workers and other professionals are seen 'discovering' sexual abuse where no abuse has taken place and illegitimately persecuting innocent families.

Although there is evidence to suggest that social workers view care proceedings as an admission of failure (DHSS, 1985), and that the Children Act 1989 and governmental guidance (DoH, 1991a, 1991b, 1991c) emphasise partnership and voluntary arrangements, the overriding focus of the governmental guidance is on the 'best interests of the child'. This recognises that in some cases care proceedings may offer the best approach.

> Where a local authority determines that control of a child's circumstances is necessary to promote welfare then compulsory intervention, as part of a carefully planned process, will always be the appropriate remedy. Local authorities should not feel inhibited by the working in partnership provisions of the Children Act from seeking appropriate court orders. Equally, the existence of a court order should not of itself impede a local authority from continuing its efforts at working in partnership with the families of children in need. Each has a role to play, often simultaneously, in the case management of a child at risk (DoH, 1993, para.2.21).

The problems of internal contradiction within the Children Act 1989 can partly be explained as a result of administrative attempts to develop an holistic approach to child care and protection. Referring to the Short Report (DHSS, 1985), Parton (1991) points out that,

> ...it emphasised the essential connection between children, their families and the circumstances in which they lived (Parton, 1991, Pg.29).

The Short Report (DHSS, 1985) was followed by a working party review and finally a White Paper (DHSS, 1987). The parliamentary debate on the White Paper took place in an atmosphere of great concern for social services child protection practice. Inquiry Reports throughout the 1970s and 1980s had identified two contradictory significant issues. The deaths of some children were attributed to social workers paying too much attention to the needs of parents and not applying the sanctions of the law available to them to adequately protect the child. Other children were seen to have died despite the best efforts of social workers, as the law had failed to provide them with the powers necessary to fully discharge their child protection duties. One of the key findings of this period came from the Beckford Inquiry (1985). The Report clearly stated that the primary task of social work was to protect children, and that, where necessary, the full force of the law should be used to ensure this.

This period also saw significant changes in the ways in which child abuse was characterised. The child protection debate had traditionally been located around concerns over physical abuse. Throughout the 1970s and 1980s this was increasingly being displaced by a concern over sexual abuse. This concern was reflected in practice as growing numbers of children were being placed on child protection registers because of sexual abuse, although they continued to be outnumbered by those placed there because of physical abuse (Creighton, 1984; DoH, 1990b; DoH, 1992; DoH, 1994). The key event in this refocusing of concern was the 'Cleveland Affair' in 1987. This was precipitated by the taking into care of two hundred and four children in Cleveland suspected of being sexually abused. It escalated into a political scandal. Middlesbrough M.P. Stuart Bell claimed that consultant paediatrician, Dr Marietta Higgs, and Cleveland Social Services child abuse consultant, Mrs Sue Richardson, had 'colluded and conspired' to place the children in care by deliberately not involving the police or any other agencies (Hansard, HoC, 29 June, 1987, Col.255). An hysterical attack on the role of paediatricians and social workers 'interfering' in families ensued. Tim Devlin, M.P. for Stockton South likened the actions of social services to those of the S.S. (Hansard, HoC, 29 June, 1987, Col.257). A media frenzy followed and the Cleveland Affair became the focus of a moral panic. The medical/social work intervention was seen as the actions of 'the insensitive representatives of the authoritarian state' (Parton, 1991). The Inquiry (Cleveland, 1988) which followed focused on the problem of defining a precise legal framework for social work intervention in a particularly sensitive area. It marked the beginning of a shift of focus in official thinking about child abuse.

> ...up to this point the priority in policy and practice had been to improve and refine our systems for *identifying child abuse*, subsequently the focus was to refine and improve the *systems of child protection* themselves (Parton *et al*, 1997, Pg.28).

The Cleveland Inquiry (1988) emphasised the need for a form of legally specified rights and responsibilities for parents.

It was into this context that the Children Act 1989 came into being. In some ways the Children Act can be seen as the legislative embodiment of a shift in emphasis by the state on how to cope with 'dangerous children' and 'children in danger'. It marked the culmination of shift in service values towards a concept of partnership (Packman, 1993). The emphasis on partnership, and the all-encompassing, comprehensive nature of the Act, marked it out as significantly different to all previous legislation for or about children and young people.

The Children Act and Child Sexual Abuse

The bringing together of the majority of public and private law pertaining to children in one Act appears to affirm the claim that the Children Act is 'a charter for children' (DoH, 1993, para.1.6) that seeks to promote and protect children's welfare by means of a 'practical and consistent code' (ibid.). However, in reality, the Children Act does not constitute a charter for children. It is better seen in terms of a collection of various pieces of legislation that are in parts complementary and in parts contradictory, reflecting 'the perennial ambivalence of the state', regarding interventions into the family (Corby, 1993). In practical terms, a whole series of established concepts around which child protection practitioners worked have been replaced by new concepts such as 'partnership', 'parental responsibility', and a battery of new orders such as 'emergency protection orders', child assessment orders' and 'family assistance orders'.

Parental responsibility is a central feature of the legislation. It is defined in the Act to mean,

> ...all the rights, duties, powers, responsibilities and authority which by law a parent of a child has in relation to the child and his property (s.3(1)).

Parental responsibility cannot be relinquished short of adoption. If a Care Order is in place the local authority assumes parental responsibility for the child but the parents do not relinquish it. The local authority does, however, have the power in that situation to determine the extent to which a parent may exercise his/her parental responsibility (s.33(3)). The Act also provides mechanisms whereby an unmarried father can acquire parental responsibility (s.4). Important consequences flow from this. An unmarried father can acquire a status equivalent to that of a mother or married father. This includes the right to remove a child being 'looked after' by the local authority (s.20(8)). However, the mother, the child him/herself, or the local authority if the child is subject to a Care Order, can make application for the father's parental responsibility to be brought to an end (s.4(3)). This provides a useful mechanism in cases of familial sexual abuse if the father/perpetrator is unwilling to accede to voluntary arrangements to detach himself from the child.

An important aspect of parental responsibility is that the emphasis is on parents' responsibility for their children's welfare rather than parents' rights over their children. It also emphasises the role of parents rather than the children themselves in making decisions in children's lives. Crucially, it gives a clear message to parents that it is they, rather than the state, who have responsibility for their children. This is reiterated in the 1993 Report.

Central to the philosophy of the Act is the belief that children are best looked after within the family with both parents playing a full part and without resort to legal proceedings (DoH, 1993, par.1.8).

Fundamental to the Act is the paramountcy of the child's welfare (s.1(1), DoH, 1991a, para.1.7). [2] Within this context runs the guiding principle of partnership. [3] The purpose of intervention is not to replace the family but to assist it in its primary duty of caring for children. [4]

> *The development of a working partnership with parents is the most effective rout to providing supplementary or substitutive care for their children.* Measures which antagonise, alienate, undermine or marginalise parents are counter-productive. For example, taking compulsory measures over children can all too easily have this effect though the action may be necessary in order to provide protection...*if young people have to live apart from their family of origin, both they and their parents should be helped to consider alternatives and contribute to the making of an informed choice about the most appropriate form of care* (DoH, 1990a, Pg.8).

Although Care and Supervision Orders are seen as sometimes necessary, the governmental guidance stresses minimal intervention.

> ...a care or supervision order will be sought only when there appears to be no better way of safeguarding and promoting the welfare of the child suffering, or likely to suffer, significant harm (DoH, 1991a, para.3.2).

The need for workers to be able to use professional judgement within the potentially conflicting principles of child protection and minimal intervention is spelled out.

> The balance needs to be struck between taking action designed to protect the child from abuse whilst at the same time protecting him or her and the family from the harm caused by unnecessary intervention...(DoH, 1991c, para.5.11.3).

The key to care proceedings is 'significant harm', yet exactly what this means is far from clear. The Short Report (DHSS, 1985a) contends,

> Having set an acceptable standard of upbringing for the child, it should be necessary to show some substantial deficit in that standard. Minor shortcomings in the health and care provided or minor defects in physical, psychological or social development should not give rise to any compulsory

intervention unless they are having or likely to have, serious and lasting effects upon the child (DHSS, 1985a, para.15(15)).

Governmental guidance (DoH, 1991a, para3.19) suggests that significance can rest either in 'the seriousness of the harm or in its implications'. This vagueness is clarified to some extent in the text of the Act itself.

> ...'harm' means ill-treatment or the impairment of health or development; 'development' means physical, intellectual, emotional, social or behavioural development; 'health' means physical or mental health; and 'ill-treatment' includes sexual abuse and forms of ill-treatment which are not physical (Children Act, 1989, s.31(9)(b)).

This still leaves the concept of significant harm open to interpretation, and is not made any clearer by the 'definition' of significant harm given in the Act. A child's health or development is to be compared with 'that which could reasonably be expected of a similar child' (s.31(10)). The question remains, what is a similar child?

Nevertheless, the basis of significant harm is made clear in governmental guidance (DoH, 1991c). It defines four categories of abuse for the purposes of registration and statistics (para.6.40):

- neglect,
- physical injury,
- sexual abuse,
- emotional abuse.

Sexual abuse is referred to in terms of the actual or likely sexual exploitation of a child or adolescent. The material practices that constitute sexual abuse are not defined. This can have a profound effect on the principle of partnership between social services and parents. Issues raised by Freeman (1992) about the ambivalence of the boundaries between 'normal' physical discipline and physical abuse, resonate with aspects of sexual abuse in a multi-cultural society with disparate norms of familial behaviour and sexual conduct.

> We cannot tell parents in advance that their conduct is 'moderate and reasonable'. But they may discover after the event that it is not so considered (Freeman, 1992, Pg.105).

There are also serious difficulties with sexual abuse in obtaining proof of harm. The increasingly juridical model of child protection the Act represents (David, 1991; Parton, 1991; Parton *et al*, 1997) brings with it the problem of 'proof', exacerbated by the fact that forensic evidence of sexual abuse is rare.

Other, more general problems, are evident in the legislation. Despite the various statutory duties the Children Act 1989 places on local authorities to provide services for children in need and to include children at risk and their parents in decision-making within the child protection process, the legal basis for any intervention is tenuous. The Court of Appeal has ruled that:

> A child may not maintain an action for damages for negligence or breach of statutory duty against a local authority for steps taken or not taken in relation to the child by that authority as the responsible social services authority...The duties imposed on local authorities were framed in terms too general and unparticular and that they accorded too large an area for the exercise of subjective judgement (Law Report, *Independent*, 24.2.94).

The court further ruled that local authorities had no common law right or duty to interfere in the lives of children in their areas. This makes clear that the Children Act cannot be construed as a diminishment of the professional powers of social workers, and nor does it in any legally binding sense embody a concept of social services-parents-child partnership.

Some of the provisions of the Children Act are also in potential conflict with the criminal law. Under the Criminal Justice Act 1991 convicted persons under the age of eighteen can be sentenced to be placed in secure accommodation, yet the Children Act (s.1(3)) declares that the court must take into account the welfare of the child. This is of particular significance for the intervention processes relating to girls below the age of sixteen who have become involved in prostitution. Are they to be prosecuted for soliciting or are they to be made subject to child protection interventions? This is a clear area of conflict as such girls will simultaneously be committing criminal acts whilst being the victims of sexual abuse and exploitation.

The potential conflicts between the Children Act 1989 and the Criminal Justice Act 1991 need to be addressed (Dawson and Stevens, 1993). The need for clarification has been stressed in the Utting Report (DoH and Welsh Office, 1997), especially in terms of the need for the criminal justice system to recognise the problems with its interface with child protection. The Utting Report calls for action in terms of changes to court procedures when dealing with child sexual abuse. The Report calls for child abuse cases to be heard more quickly, an informal courtroom atmosphere and a more flexible approach to the forms of evidence allowable from children, considering modifying the concept of 'beyond reasonable doubt' to something akin to the civil law 'balance of probability' test in child abuse cases. The Report also suggests that 'there is a strong case' (Pg.196) for child abuse trials to become a specialism for judges and barristers with special training to enable them to modify their 'normal' courtroom behaviour.

Child Protection and 'Mandated' Coordination

The theme of poor interagency communication and cooperation tended to dominate a number of child abuse Inquiries (DHSS, 1982; Cleveland, 1988). Little account appears to have be taken of either the massive numbers of child protection cases that were successfully resolved, or of the severe logistical problems inherent in interagency and multidisciplinary cooperation between groups of professionals working within different timescales, with different priorities and different knowledge bases (Hallett, 1993). Since the Colwell Inquiry (1974) social services departments have tailored their child protection intervention procedures in accordance with the recommendations of public inquiry reports and government guidelines. Corby (1993) argues that this has led to a growth of systems and management led social work to the detriment of discretion on the part of front line workers. These systems have increasingly been based on interagency, multidisciplinary procedures.

The Children Act 1989 stresses the duty of the local authority to cooperate with other relevant agencies in the pooling of information (s.47 (9-11)), and governmental guidance (DoH, 1991c) makes plain that the Children Act's assumption of cooperation and partnership between parents and local authorities must be based on 'a concerted approach to interagency working' (para.1.8).

> ...it is essential that Area Protection Committee procedures provide a mechanism whereby, wherever one agency becomes concerned that a child may be at risk, it shares its information with other agencies (DoH, 1991c, para.1.11).

The principle of interagency partnership manifests itself in the forum of the Child Protection Conference, a multidisciplinary body charged with the single duty of determining whether or not to place a child on the child protection register. Government guidance also makes clear that social services (or in some cases the NSPCC) occupy the lead role within the interagency child protection network (DoH, 1991c, para.5.15.2).

The notion of partnership or coordination between agencies for the provision of welfare has been 'a continuing refrain' as a way of providing 'efficient, comprehensive and holistic services' and avoiding 'fragmentation and overlap' (Hallett and Birchall, 1992, Pg.2). Wistow (1982) reveals that the idea of coordination can be traced back as far as the establishment of the Charity Organisation Society in the mid 1860s. The development of the concept in terms of British child protection practice can be seen to derive from two roots.

- The creation of unified social services departments as a result of the Seebohm Report (1968)
- The results of clinical research in the USA that concluded that multidisciplinary teams provided the best way of confronting the problems of child abuse (Helfer and Schmidt, 1976; Steele, 1976; Benjamin, 1981).

The key role played by clinicians, especially paediatricians, in defining and evaluating the problem led to a medicalisation of child abuse and the patterns of multidisciplinary intervention (Pfohl, 1977; Nelson, 1984; Parton, 1985). It is this combination of a medical model of child abuse and a perceived need for inter-agency coordination, that has informed official constructions of child protection systems ever since. The key role of doctors, especially paediatricians, in the child protection system, cannot be underestimated. They are the only professional group sanctioned to make an assessment on the medical conditions that could signify sexual or physical abuse, failure to thrive or emotional disorder.

Inter-agency coordination is not unproblematic, however. As Hallett and Birchall (1992) make clear, there is a potential for conflict at the very heart of coordination.

> In everyday practice, the protection of children is negotiated by a multitude of individuals with varied beliefs and technical skills, located in a wide range of agencies with very diverse functions and priorities (Hallett and Birchall, 1992, Pg.2).

This diversity can manifest itself in terms of a conceptual gap between professions (Norton and Rogers, 1981) and differential desired outcomes (Challis *et al*, 1988). Different agencies and different professionals may also exhibit levels of acceptance and different capacities to resist any injunction to cooperate (Hallett, 1993). Skinner *et al* (1983) contend that:

> ...the fundamental question for all interagency collaboration is for what purpose and for whose benefit (Skinner *et al*, 1983, Pg.33).

This is given a further twist in that the development of particular interagency systems of coordination, although realised differently in different areas, is not entirely voluntary, but delineated and constrained by government policy and legislation.

> The policy developments in respect of child abuse from the late 1970s onwards in the UK constitute mandated coordination (Hallett and Birchall, 1992, Pg.33).

The concept of various professionals from a multitude of agencies 'working together' in child protection, appears, at first, to be both a laudable aim and an obvious approach to a serious social problem. It also fits into a long established trend in the UK of seeing public policies as interdependent and coordination as delivering real welfare benefits (Wistow, 1982), with Inquiry reports repeatedly highlighting the shortcomings of interagency coordination in failures of the child protection process (DHSS, 1973; Clyde, 1992, for example).

Although the messages from Inquiries are often oversimplified in the media and in some of the professional literature, they do serve to highlight the shortcomings of interagency coordination   (Dingwall, 1986; Hallett, 1989; Hill, 1990). This concern with coordination can also be seen in terms of a wider concern with coordinated welfare services within the developed world (Duckett, 1977; Westrin, 1987).   However, despite a widespread reorganisation of welfare service delivery in the UK in the 1970s, it was not until the Children Act 1989 was implemented in October 1991 that finances were identified (Children Act, 1989, section 20) for collaborative interagency work in child protection, although exhortations to different agencies to coordinate practice were by then well established (DHSS and Welsh Office, 1988).   However, the concept of interagency working relationships in child protection is not unproblematic.

Despite the idea of 'working together' being well established, there are considerable difficulties in understanding what it means.   There is a problem of terminology in distinguishing between coordination, collaboration and cooperation. A great deal of the literature from the 1970s and 1980s   (Warren *et al*; 1974; Aiken *et al*, 1975; Hall *et al*, 1977;

Mulford and Rogers, 1982; Challis *et al*, 1988) tends to give mutually exclusive definitions of the process of coordination variously defined in terms ranging from interorganisational awareness to maximised interagency cooperation. This confusion is compounded by a lack of agreement in respect of the terminology itself. Some authors view coordination and collaboration as synonymous (Armitage, 1983; Williams, 1986), whereas others clearly differentiate. Booth (1981, Pg.25), for example, defines coordination as 'working independently but in harmony', and collaboration as 'working together'. Westrin (1987, Pg.7) further complicates the issue by introducing the term 'cooperation', defining it as 'all conscious efforts of agencies or individuals to direct their work towards common goals'. The lack of agreement over terminology cannot be dismissed as simply an academic exercise in semantics. Governmental encouragement to social services and other agencies in the 1970s and 1980s to coordinate service delivery in child protection were seriously hampered as it was unclear what the term meant (Aiken *et al*, 1975; Weiss, 1981; Mulford and Rogers, 1982; Challis *et al*, 1988). The difficulties in defining coordination were, if anything, made worse in the 1980s, with the development of the concept of a hierarchical continuum of coordination (or cooperation) (Armitage, 1983; Bond *et al*, 1985; Gough *et al*, 1987; Westrin, 1987). It needs to be borne in mind that such difficulties can never be fully overcome. Any complex social process such as, for example, cooperating with others, or implementing a particular policy, will always be open to processes of negotiation, amendment and redefinition as part and parcel of the ebb and flow of the power relations between specific individuals involved in the process (Foucault, 1977, 1980).

This highlights two paradoxes in child protection. Firstly, despite the serious difficulties in defining coordination and despite the failures of coordination highlighted in various Inquiry reports, a great deal of interagency coordination takes place, with much apparent success. Secondly, although this routinised coordination appears in general to be very successful, the continuation of failings of coordination that the Inquiry Reports highlight need to be offset against decades of almost universal advocacy of interagency coordination in the professional literature allied to governmental and local administrative requirements for such coordination. The real problem has always been one of definition. The question raised almost a decade ago by Olive Stevenson still remains:

> Why has it been so difficult to achieve the cooperation necessary to protect children at risk? (Stevenson, 1988, Pg.5).

Despite difficulties of definition, clear forms of coordination have been observed in a wide ranging corpus of research. Basically coordination can be seen to take two forms.

- Routinised coordination; that is the coordination of practices that is so deeply embedded in the operational rules and day-to-day routines of an organisation that it is taken for granted (Webb, 1991). In child protection one can see the operation of such routinised coordination in that both governmental guidance and ACPC manuals of procedure can be seen as operational rules that contain within them clearly defined coordination processes. An ongoing criticism of routinised coordination (Warren, 1973; Benson, 1982; Webb, 1991) is that it tends to be inherently conservative, reinforcing existing policies and practices and serving to inhibit heterodox thinking and innovative responses to specific situations.
- Radical coordination. As a modality of service delivery this is altogether more risky (Dartington, 1986), as it implies change and contains within it the potential to disturb the contours of established practice and existing professional boundaries (Webb, 1991). For a variety of reasons, most notably the role of central government in the development of coordination in child protection, there is little evidence of radical coordination in child protection in the UK.

One needs at this point to develop an analytical framework for the understanding of interagency coordination and the impact it has on social workers' child protection practice. To begin with one needs to recognise that following the 'discovery' of child physical abuse and subsequently child sexual abuse child abuse rapidly assumed the status of a 'social problem', whose nature and solution were defined in organisational and interorganisational terms (Parton, 1985). Organisational theory has moved on from a position in the 1960s and 1970s that focused on single organisations and their intraorganisational processes, through a focus on the interface between organisations and their external environments, to the study of interorganisational relationships. In a review of coordination in child protection Hallett (1995) discusses that as far as public policy in general is concerned, this reflects a growing awareness of the complex networks within which public policy is achieved (Benson, 1975; Rhodes, 1990). Earlier work on interorganisational relationships tended to be framed within the 'exchange' perspective as developed by Levine and White (1961), wherein organisations were seen to develop relationships with other organisations with a view to the mutual benefits to be gained from such relationships. This perspective exhibits two major problems. Firstly, it assumes that organisational decision-making is always rational and seeks to gain maximum benefit for the organisation, and secondly, it fails to pay sufficient credence to the structured imbalances of power between different organisations within specific policy fields. This is compensated for, to some extent, in more sophisticated analyses deriving from the work of Aldrich (1972, 1976, 1979) and Benson (1975) who developed a 'power/dependency' perspective that focused on the strategies employed by organisations to reduce their levels of dependency on other organisations within the context of interorganisational competition for scarce resources (such as public funding). Schmidt and Kochan (1977) argue that organisations do not routinely engage in mutually exclusive exchange or power/dependency relationships, but in both according to the circumstances they find themselves in. They thus recommend an integrated approach to the study of interorganisational relationships, a view that is echoed by Cook (1977). One also notes the potential for serious psychodynamic problems in interagency coordination, especially in terms of collaborative or joint working. Woodhouse and Pengelly (1991), drawing upon psychodynamic theory, point to the ubiquitous nature of triangular relationships, making the point that,

> ...the dynamic forces they generate exert a powerful influence on human interaction (Woodhouse and Pengelly, 1991, Pg.217).

Woodhouse and Pengelly (1991) further suggest that such relationships are inevitable in collaborative situations, arguing that a 'triangle of collaboration',

> ...is made manifest whenever two practitioners, or coalitions of practitioners, have to deal with each other in relation to clients or patients (Woodhouse and Pengelly, 1991, Pg.217).

They see this leading to a general anxiety amongst professionals that is likely to inhibit any collaborative efforts. Clearly, different aspects of coordination will provoke different levels of anxiety; the most significant difficulties being likely to arise in areas such as Child Protection Conferences and joint police/social services investigations and interviews. For Woodhouse and Pengelly (1991) the significance of the psychodynamic barriers to collaborative work cannot be overemphasised, arguing that collaborative work can threaten the ways of understanding of different professionals and thus their professional identities. They argue that personal, professional and institutional boundaries are utilised to protect them. They further argue that joint training of professionals from different agencies in terms of coordination and collaboration is relatively ineffective if not preceded by learning systems within the specific agencies that encourage practitioners and managers to understand their task related anxieties and moderate their use of defensive boundaries.

It needs to be made clear, however, that interagency coordination in child protection as a process cannot be analysed entirely from any single perspective. This is principally because coordination in child protection is not something that derives solely from the internal imperatives of the specific agencies involved. Rather, the mechanisms of coordination in child protection, at least at a formal level, are clearly set out in legislation (Children Act, 1989) and central government policy directives (DoH, 1991a, 1991b, 1991c). Interagency linkages are forced upon the various agencies (social services, education, police etc.) by a third party in a position of legitimate authority over those agencies (central government). In other words, interagency coordination in child protection is 'mandated' coordination (Hallett, 1993), and any analysis of the impact of the actions of other agencies/professionals on the child protection work of social workers must recognise this. Elements of the exchange perspective and of the power/dependency perspective, however, remain useful in any analysis:

• Governmental policy directives, the mandate for interagency coordination, emerged from situations where interagency linkages already existed. The governmental imperative to mandated coordination in child protection in the UK developed out of an understanding of the child protection process in the UK and the USA that was based upon voluntary interorganisational and interprofessional relationships.

• Legislation and policy directives are interpreted by the specific agencies subject to the mandate (Hjern, 1982; Barrett and Hill, 1984; Rhodes, 1981, 1986, 1988), and consolidated within already existing interagency and interprofessional patterns of coordination, in ways that enable practitioners to meet their own professional ends (Lipsky, 1980).

A comprehensive and useful conceptual model of interagency coordination in child protection can be derived from the work of Benson (1982). Following this model, child protection can be perceived as a policy sector within an overall political economy of welfare. The child protection policy sector comprises a complex of different organisations and agencies interconnected by a whole series of resource dependencies. The sector operates at two levels.

- The first level comprises three elements; the division of labour within child protection to different agencies (social services, police, NHS etc), the contours of what exactly constitutes child abuse and child protection, and the interagency dependencies within the child protection policy sector.
- The second level limits the operation of activities in the first level. The second level comprises interest-power structures and the rules of structure formation. The rules of structure formation are twofold:
  - i)   Negative rules which define the limits or boundaries of the policy sector,
  - ii) Positive rules that actively go towards forming the structure.

In child protection both these processes are clearly at work. As far as interest-power structures are concerned Benson (1982) identifies five as being of primary importance:

- Demand groups - the users or recipients of a set of services - in child protection this would be abused children and perhaps non-abusing members of their families.
- Support groups - those providing financial and political resources - in child protection this would mean the government and elected members of local authorities.
- Administrative groups - those in administrative control within organisations - in child protection this would be social services managers, senior police officers, education officials etc.
- Provider groups - those engaged in service delivery - in child protection this would be social workers, police officers, GPs, teachers etc.
- Coordinating groups - those engaged in rationalising programmes and services between sectors - in child protection this would mean governmental agencies such as the Audit Commission.

Some commentators suggest that the problems of coordination go beyond potential conflict and can actually work towards an unacceptable level of social control (Davies, 1977; Dingwall *et al*, 1983; Westrin, 1987; Domoney *et al*, 1989). There is also a very real danger that coordination *per se* as a policy can become reified to the detriment of other policy goals

(McKeganey and Hunter, 1986). This becomes apparent in the paradoxical nature of the political debate surrounding the idea of interagency collaboration in the social welfare generally. Although there is a general degree of pessimism over the results of collaboration, the idea is still vigorously promoted as a means of investing service delivery with a greater measure of rationality   (Hudson, B., 1989). Nevertheless, although there are real difficulties in respect of differential professional knowledges and different agency purposes, the value of case conferences as a procedural mechanism in dealing with the issues surrounding child protection cases is 'highly valued by many participants' (Hallett and Birchall, 1992, Pg.295).

The Client Group: Adolescent Girls

Adolescence is a very difficult notion to theorise. At one level it can be seen as a developmental period in the life-cycle that occurs between childhood and adulthood (Coleman, 1976), and is seen broadly to coincide with the teenage years (Phoenix, 1991). This developmental aspect is recognised in legislation as various legal rights, responsibilities and entitlements are acquired in stages throughout the teenage years. It is seen as a period of maturing, although this involves a series of temporal displacements. The age of menarche for girls in the United Kingdom, for example, is around the age of thirteen, yet the minimum age for consensual sexual relations is sixteen and the age of legal majority eighteen. The age at which the adolescent is thought to have achieved social maturity is far less well defined, but it is certainly perceived of as being later than that for biological maturity.

As a period of social and biological development, adolescence has been conceptualised as a time of potential crisis (Anderson and Clarke, 1982; Coleman and Hendry, 1990) epitomised by intrafamilial conflict (Cohen, 1986), and as a time of identity development (Erikson, 1968), and a general rise in self-esteem (Coleman and Hendry, 1990), that itself can be critically undermined by external pressures (Coleman and Hendry, 1990). Coleman   (1976), however, argues that although profound biological, emotional and social changes may occur during this period, there is little evidence to suggest that the psychological development that takes place at this time is qualitatively different from that at any other time in an individual's life. Murcott (1980), in a discussion of the social construction of teenage pregnancy, argues that a key feature of adolescence is that adolescents are primarily thought of by adults as children. Yet, adolescence is qualitatively different from childhood. It is a period within which the individual moves from having his/her roles ascribed by parents and other adults to a choice of roles and role interpretation that is synonymous with adult life (Ollendorf, 1972; Coleman and Hendry, 1990; Mitterauer 1992).

Adolescence, however, is not the same for boys and girls. The same patriarchal ideologies, opportunity structures and familial expectations that act to maintain children as dependent non-citizens also serve to render women as significantly different to men. The adult world that the adolescent boy confronts is one wherein he is expected to assert himself, and be competitive and ambitious (Sharpe, 1976). He is expected to express his individuality. It is a very different world for the adolescent girl. It is in adolescence, as they move into womanhood, that girls are confronted on a day-to-day basis with definitions of themselves, not in terms of their aptitudes, abilities, capacities, or even primarily in terms of their social class, but in terms of their sexual reputation (Lees 1986; Lees, 1997). They are brought face to face with an adult culture that diminishes their individuality, categorising them as 'respectable' or as 'whores'.

> Defining girls in terms of their sexuality rather than their attributes and potentialities is a crucial mechanism in ensuring their subordination to men. It means that girls live in a very different social world to boys - one where being a girl determines everything they do. Girls are depicted as nude pin-ups in the gutter press, as sex objects, as appendages of men, as objects of male lust or as victims of male violence (Lees, 1986, Pg.15).

In much of the clinical and psychological research literature adolescence itself is seen as a highly sexualised concept (Griffin, 1993). Adolescence is also perceived of as a time of potential delinquency, male delinquency being characterised by aggression, female delinquency in terms of sexual deviance. The fear of a deviant, predatory adolescent female sexuality is 'embedded in the heart of contemporary British welfare practice' (Hudson, A., 1989, Pg.197). Sexually abused girls are categorised as 'the problem', whereas the real difficulty lies within the realms of male sexual violence. Kersten (1989) argues that the displacement of the problem onto the behaviour of adolescent girls can act as a strategy for avoiding serious investigation of particular families.

Although throughout the history of child protection practice in the UK there have been competing perspectives on the rationale for intervention (see Fox-Harding, 1991b, for example), in general terms the family has been perceived of as a 'safe haven', the optimum location for a satisfying personal life. Feminist work in recent years in respect of child sexual abuse and domestic violence (Driver and Droisen, 1989; Gordon,

1988; Griffin, 1993) has made abundantly clear that families can also be the sites of oppression, exploitation and abuse. The heuristic force of familial discourses and the equally powerful ideology of virtuous innocent femininity can form a double bind for teenage girls who are sexually abused within the family (Gordon, 1988), with the consequence that the girl will almost inevitably experience confusion and guilt whether she acquiesces and keeps quiet, or refuses and discloses the abuse. Abusers will use threats and coercion to prevent disclosure. These serve to place the responsibility for the maintenance or break up of the family onto the girls, which adds to their 'internalised feelings that they are guilty and responsible for the crimes of adult men' (Hudson, A., 1989, Pg.205). Roberts and Taylor's (1993) review of the research findings implies that these strategies enjoy some success.

Despite the efforts of abusers to prevent disclosure the self-referral of sexually abused adolescent girls to the authorities has always been of a higher degree than self-referral for any other form of neglect or abuse (Gordon, 1988; Hudson, A., 1989). One reason for this may be located in the structuring of female adolescence. Although girls' peer groups are as significant to them as boys' peer groups are to them they are more transient (Salmon, 1992), and female adolescent culture is far more likely to be based around the family home than is that of boys (Griffin, 1985; Salmon, 1992). The patriarchal structuring of society tends to see adolescent girls belonging to the family in a way that boys do not, leaving them with no other avenue of escape than referral to social services (Hudson, A., 1989).

There are elements within the child protection process that fail to recognise the specificity of abused adolescents. The Children Act 1989 can be seen as an 'infantilising' document in that it characterises all persons from birth to eighteen (and in some cases beyond) as children. This is offset, to some extent, however, in that the Act also contains a 'maturity principle' in terms of dealings before the courts, which tends towards paying greater attention to the wishes of older children than to those of younger ones. There remains, however, the vexed question of who judges the maturity of the child and on what criteria?

The Aetiology of Child and Adolescent Sexual Abuse

The Department of Health (DoH, 1991c) classifies child abuse as falling into four distinct categories; neglect, physical injury, sexual abuse and emotional abuse. Although the definitions given by the Department of Health (DoH, 1991c) for each type of abuse are general and perhaps simplistic, they are of analytical value as they serve to render particular sets of behaviours visible through their clarification in official discourses. The official purpose of the classifications is to form categories of abuse for the purpose of placing individual children on the child protection register. With the exception of the category of emotional abuse, the Department of Health classifications articulate closely to definitions of abuse emerging from research. There are logistical problems in the use of the emotional abuse category, principally deriving from the difficulties in defining or describing such abuse, and there are problems arising for research in attempting to assign any causal link between emotional abuse and any adverse development for the child concerned (Hallett and Birchall, 1992). The problems that arise in terms of emotional abuse highlight a serious issue in terms of child protection policy and practice in general; the paramount importance of definitional issues, as these 'determine when intervention into the privacy of the family is permissible' (Haugaard and Repucci, 1988, Pg.14).

After the Maria Colwell Inquiry (1974) and the 'discovery' of the 'battered baby syndrome', by Dr Henry Kempe in the USA, the specific problem of child abuse began to be more widely recognised (Eekelaar and Dingwall, 1990). Corby (1993) argues that Kempe's ideas of the parental abuse of children as a consequence of a psychological syndrome articulated well with the relatively affluent period of the 1960s. It seemed more acceptable than relating child abuse to poverty or deprivation, and, crucially, it allowed the state to intervene in certain dysfunctional families without threatening the sanctity of family life *per se*.

> By giving child abuse a medical label and seeing it as a treatable condition, the new forms of intervention into family life were not seen as a threat to the independence of families in general because they were only aimed at the families that had the illness (Corby, 1993, Pg. 27).

Although, as Parton (1991) and Parton et *al* (1997) have described, the medical model of child protection has been displaced to some extent by firstly a social welfare model and latterly a legal-juridical model, official child protection discourse and professional practice still retain individualist explanations of the aetiology of child abuse that pathologise not only the behaviours themselves but also those families within which it occurs, to the relative exclusion of recognising different forms of child abuse as deriving from deeply embedded material and ideological structures in contemporary society. Governmental policy and guidance (Children Act, 1989; DoH, 1991a, 1991b, 1991c), and professional practice, although giving some regard to social factors, tend to remain focused on an individualist aetiology for all instances of child abuse. However, it is clear that the causation patterns of neglect, physical abuse and sexual abuse are not the same.

The research into physical abuse and neglect tends to show relatively close correlations between social class, deprivation and such abuse (Gil, 1970; Becker and Macpherson, 1988; Crittenden, 1988; Moore, 1992), although how much this is a function of the economic and psychological stresses of poverty (Brown and Madge, 1982), and how much simply to the fact that poorer families are already the subject of welfare surveillance, as recipients of income support and other welfare benefits (Gil, 1970; Roche, 1989; Parton, 1991) is problematic. A similar ambivalence in understanding is clear in the disproportionate numbers of physical abuse referrals from single parent households (Sack et *al*, 1985) and amongst ethnic minorities (Corby, 1993). Evidence also suggests (Creighton, 1984; Creighton and Noyes, 1989) that there is very little gender bias in the makeup of physical abusers; fathers being somewhat more likely statistically to physically abuse their children than are mothers. Given the gendered structuring of the labour market and the culturally assigned division of responsibility within families, which leaves mothers spending considerably more time with their children than do fathers, this suggests men are more likely to physical abuse their children than are women.

The research into child and adolescent sexual abuse establishes a very clearly gendered aetiological pattern. The evidence points to perpetrators as being overwhelmingly male and the victims being predominantly, though not entirely female (Russell, 1984; Kelly *et al*, 1991). Research also suggests that a significant proportion of perpetrators are known to the victim; family friends, step-fathers and male co-habitees being especially implicated (Gordon, 1989; Conte, 1990), and a there is a higher level of registration for child sexual abuse of children from one-parent families (Creighton and Noyes, 1989).

Benedict and Zautra (1993), working within a social psychological perspective, have concluded that family dysfunction in terms of parental absence or parental conflict are the key criteria for creating an environment conducive to child sexual abuse. However, along with all attempts at prediction this fails to take account of the majority of families that function badly in those ways that do not form a locus for the sexual abuse of children. Their research is also problematic in that their findings are based upon the reports of college students recounting past rather than current experience. A model of explaining sexual abuse that has a relatively high degree of heuristic force is that developed by Finkelhor (1984). For Finkelhor, four preconditions have to be met for child sexual abuse to occur. Firstly, the abuser must become motivated to commit the abuse. Secondly, he must overcome his internal inhibitions. Thirdly, he needs to overcome various external inhibitions, and fourthly, he needs to overcome the child's possible resistance. The analytical sophistication of Finkelhor's four precondition model lays in its capacity to incorporate psychological and sociological research findings with arguments deriving from meta-theoretical feminist arguments in respect of the cultural patterns of patriarchy.

This degree of sophistication is apparent within every element of the four precondition model. The first precondition, the motivation to sexually abuse is seen by Finkelhor (1984) to comprise three elements - i) emotional congruence: the individual finds that relating sexually to a child satisfies some important emotional need, ii) sexual arousal: the child then becomes the potential source of sexual gratification for that individual, and iii) blockage: alternative sources of sexual gratification are either not available to the individual or he does not find them satisfying. Finkelhor (1984) argues that at least one of these elements needs to be present for the first precondition to be satisfied. The second precondition, the overcoming of internal inhibitors, draws together psychological and cultural factors. Finkelhor (1984) argues that society places certain specific inhibitions on sexual relations with children, and for an individual to sexually abuse a child the lack of such inhibitors needs to be explained. This suggests that it should make it possible in practice to determine the appropriateness of various therapies for men who have sexually abused, in that part of the explanation of the lack of inhibitors would be to determine whether their absence was permanent or temporary, perhaps as the result of traumas or emotional problems the individual was suffering at the time. Importantly, though many men may lack the inhibitors to sexual relations with children they will not sexually abuse unless they have already met the criteria of the first precondition.

Even when both of these preconditions have been met, however, Finkelhor (1984) is clear that abuse may well still not occur. Two further preconditions have to be met that are outside the individual psychology of the potential perpetrator. Firstly, a whole range of external inhibitors come into play. The opportunities to be alone with the child, and the level of supervision from family members and the wider community the child enjoys are seen by Finkelhor (1984) as the principal external inhibitors.

A crucial element in this aspect of Finkelhor's model is that the mother-child relationship can impact upon the level of the child's vulnerability, but '*is not of itself causal*' (Hooper and Humphreys, 1998, Pg.7). The mother-child relationship has some bearing on the vulnerability of the child to sexual abuse, as does the quality of the child's social network (Smith, 1995), but the responsibility for the abuse remains entirely with the abuser. The role of mothers as non-abusing parents in cases of child sexual abuse has been the focus of a lively debate. Early family systems theorists (Justice and Justice, 1979; Giaretto, 1982; Furniss, 1983) developed the concept of circular causality for family dysfunctions involving all family members. The abuse by the father, for example, was seen as a secondary problem, a response to poor communications. A forceful feminist critique of family systems therapy that characterised the orthodox family systems perspective as 'mother-blaming' (Breckenridge and Bereen, 1992), developed in relation to child sexual abuse in general (Macleod and Saraga, 1988), father-daughter incest (Nelson, 1987) and the position of mothers whose daughters had been sexually abused (Hooper, 1992). This critique highlighted the invidious position of mothers in families wherein child sexual abuse occurred, making the clear point that whatever mothers did or did not do the principle of circular causality implicated them in the abuse, whilst simultaneously minimising the degree of blame to be attached to the perpetrator. There is very persuasive research evidence that mothers play little if any active part in the sexual abuse of their children (Williams and Finkelhor, 1990; Hooper, 1992; Birns and Meyer, 1993). Research also suggests that it is simplistic to characterise mothers as either knowing or not knowing about the sexual abuse of their children. Rather, mothers' knowledge of any abuse is best seen in terms of a whole range of levels; not knowing until told by professionals, knowing something is wrong but unsure exactly what, suspecting sexual abuse but being unable to prove it, and mothers who are aware that sexual abuse has occurred but believe they have acted to stop it only to find it has recurred (Hooper, 1992; Humphreys, 1992). Hooper and Humphreys (1998) make clear that the mothers of sexually abused children inhabit a world of great cognitive and emotional complexity, involving intense and often conflicting relationships with the child, the offender, and other members of the immediate and extended family. Hooper and Humphreys (1998) point to the fact that many women in their earlier research (Hooper, 1992; Humphreys, 1992) spoke of holding quite contradictory positions simultaneously, certain of the truth of the abuse one day, only to gravely doubt it the next. Hooper and Humphreys (1998) point to a complex process of discovery, centred on difficult and often ambiguous information, such that mothers' degree of belief would fluctuate over time. In other words, it would be inappropriate to simply label a particular mother as protective or non-protective; rather

her degree of protectiveness is best seen in relation to the complexities of 'finding out' that she is confronting.

The final precondition in Finkelhor's (1984) model is that the potential perpetrator needs to overcome the resistance of the child. This takes into account the variable capacity of children to resist sexual abuse, such as the degree to which the perpetrator believes the child will keep the abuse secret. This again, brings the role of mothers and other family members and friends into the child sexual abuse scenario. The more vulnerable or unsupported the child, for whatever reason, or the more ignorant she is in terms of sex and sexual abuse, the greater the likelihood of the abuser overcoming her resistance. This precondition can be seen to articulate closely with the empirical research findings that point to sexual abuse rarely being short term (Gordon, 1988; Waterhouse and Pitcairn, 1991). In contrast it tends to develop into a deep-seated behavioural pattern. Boon (1984) suggests that the perpetrator indoctrinates or 'grooms' the victim into perceiving of the abuse as 'normal' behaviour.

Although girls from working class backgrounds appear disproportionately on child protection registers under the category of sexual abuse, this can be seen as relating far more closely to more general issues of the welfare surveillance of poorer families (Parton, 1991) than any intrinsic class bias in the prevalence of child sexual abuse. The research does not point to any degree of correlation of either class or ethnicity with child sexual abuse.

> ...other than gender, there are no easily identifiable common characteristics of [child sexual] abusers. They can be of any age, any cultural background and come from all walks of life from dockers and farm labourers to doctors and judges (Hevey and Kenward, 1989, Pg.211).

Child sexual abuse can be seen to some extent as a function of the construction of masculinities and male sexuality. Both object relations theory and general psychoanalytic theory point towards the development of masculine identities as a separation from the mother leading to an exaggerated contempt for women that leaves men with a propensity to objectify women and girls and with a desire to dominate others (Jagger, 1988). It is also clear that deeply embedded within western culture is the notion that within heterosexual relationships men will choose someone who is younger, smaller and weaker then themselves. Many children and adolescent girls fulfil this role better than real adult women. In many men's magazines adult women are portrayed in a childlike way and in much pornography children are shown in a sexualized manner (Kelly *et al*, 1995).

One can thus see child and adolescent sexual abuse as a function of male sexuality deriving from patriarchal ascriptions of gendered behaviour that attribute sexual conquest as legitimate masculine behaviour and objectify women as the locus of uncontrollable male desire (Lees, 1986). In other words, the sexual abuse of girls and young women can be seen as residing within a continuum of male defined sexuality and 'normalised' heterosexual activities ranging from consensual sex through pornography to sexual harassment, abuse and rape.

It can also be argued that under the cultural conditions of capitalism, and particularly since the massive rise of privatisation and consumerism in all spheres of life since the early 1980s, with the consequent weakening of ties of community, there is an increased commodification of the self generally. Individuals increasingly seek personal, immediate gratification of their consumption needs. Amongst those needs are those concerned with sexual activity. As masculine sexualities can be extremely objectifying, once any sense of the other is lost, it can become relatively easy to commit abusive acts.

Finkelhor (1991) suggests that men are both socialised into a limited modality of expressing emotion that revolves around sexual relationships and are placed in a hierarchical position to children (as they are to women). Corby (1993, Pg.149) contends that this 'creates the climate in which such abuse can happen'. He further suggests that gender socialisation gives male abusers an opportunity to evade responsibility for their actions.

Although the specific practices that constitute child sexual abuse remain open to question, the importance of recognising it as a serious form of child abuse lies in the realms of the consequences such abuse can hold for the victim. One of the main features of being an abused child is inconsistency of care (Steele, 1986), leading to a general sense of insecurity and low self-esteem. Research suggests that neglected children (Erickson *et al*, 1989; Oates *et al*, 1985), and sexually abused children (Browne and Finkelhor, 1986; Bagley and Ramsey, 1986) appear to have a greater and more ongoing sense of low self-esteem than physically abused children. This would suggest that outside the obvious factors of acute or chronic injury occasioned by episodes of physical abuse, the psychological effects of child sexual abuse might be more serious than those of physical abuse.

The Prevalence of Child Sexual and Adolescent Sexual Abuse

Some research (Oliver, 1993) suggests that patterns of child abuse are passed on through generations, although this position has been increasingly critiqued (see Hooper, 1995, for example) in the light of prevalence studies (Russell, 1984; Kelly *et al*, 1991) that show child sexual abuse as relatively commonplace and locate it within a more general critique of patriarchal social relations. This suggests that the evidence for the generational transmission of familial patterns of abuse could be interpreted not in terms of the psychological or social psychological factors specific to particular families, but in terms of the adverse social conditions experienced by particular families through the generations.

The statistics on the incidence and prevalence of child abuse are contradictory, to some extent depending upon the theoretical framework adopted. If, however, official statistics, in the form of the number of children on child protection registers, are used as a marker, then not only is child abuse a very serious social problem, it also one that is escalating. Between 1984 and 1991 there was a fourfold increase in the number of children on registers (DoH, 1992). They are now four per thousand of the population under the age of eighteen. Prevalence studies (Kelly *et al*, 1991, for example), however, suggest that registration figures for sexual abuse represent only a small minority of incidents of sexual abuse.

The Consequences of Child and Adolescent Sexual Abuse

Research (Briere, 1984; Russell, 1986) suggests that one of the long-term consequences of child or adolescent sexual abuse is that it socialises girls into the role of victim, something that plays itself out in later life. Corby (1993), in reviewing the literature points to short-term consequences ranging from depression, withdrawal and low self esteem to sexual precociousness, absconding and poor school performance. Herman (1994) collapses the distinction between short-term and long-term consequences to some extent. Drawing upon the similarities of effect of different types of trauma experience, she sees the consequences of child and adolescent sexual abuse in terms of Post Traumatic Stress Disorder, arguing that:

> Traumatic events produce profound and lasting changes in physiological arousal, emotion, cognition and memory (Herman, 1994, Pg.34).

She sees the symptoms of Post Traumatic Stress Disorder as falling into three main categories:

- Hyperarousal: The self-preservation system of the individual becomes permanently alert, leaving the individual easily startled, easily provoked and irritable, and unable to sleep well.
- Intrusion: The individual constantly relives the past trauma as if it is in the present in the form of flashbacks and nightmares, with memories of the trauma lacking narrative content. The individual is often impelled towards repeating the moment of terror, sometimes in a disguised form, to the point that she can place herself in further danger.
- Constriction: Individuals in extreme danger can become very angry or terrified. However, they can equally become detached and extremely calm, perceiving the experience as either happening to someone else or as a bad dream. This reaction is closely associated with the profound passivity displayed by some individuals when they give up all semblance of resistance. This can be a very beneficial reaction at the time, but its persistence after the original trauma is maladaptive and constrains normal functioning.

For Herman (1994) the aftermath of trauma of any kind can be seen in terms of an oscillation between intrusion and constriction. The victim is perpetually unable to find the balance between reliving the trauma and seeing it as having happened to someone else, of being angry and impulsive and being totally passive, of extreme feelings and extreme lack of feeling. This degree of instability of feeling is seen by Herman (1994) as the defining feature of Post Traumatic Stress Disorder and one that serves to exacerbate the individual's sense of unpredictability and helplessness. She also makes the point that although individual differences can influence the exact form the Post Traumatic Stress Disorder will take, the most powerful determinant is the nature and severity of the trauma. She further argues that the effects of trauma are greatest on those who are already vulnerable or disempowered, particularly children and adolescents, and is especially severe when the perpetrator of the trauma is one who ought to be the caregiver.

> The experience of terror and disempowerment during adolescence effectively compromises the three normal adaptive tasks of this stage of life: the formation of identity, the gradual separation from the family of origin, and the exploration of a wider social world (Herman, 1994. Pg.61).

In the specific case of familial child and adolescent sexual abuse the trauma is multiplied in that the abuse is not a single traumatic event, but takes place within a 'familial climate of pervasive terror' (Herman, 1994, Pg.98), often involving patterns of totalitarian control, enforced secrecy and destructive intrafamilial relationships. This tends to leave the victims of the abuse hypervigilant, always alert to the warning signs of assault, a lowering of self-esteem, and sense of safety, through the individual's realisation that she does not have control over what happens to her body. The child or adolescent may also feel betrayed by others in the family who failed to protect her. Herman (1994) notes that the victims of chronic familial child or adolescent sexual abuse often develop highly dissociative states to the point that they are often able to ignore serious physical pain. This dissociation often leads to the child or adolescent shutting off that part of her life from her day to day experience. When dissociation is not possible the consequences can be even worse. She may try to justify the abuse, rationalising that she has been punished because she is bad, and this can be exacerbated by constant scapegoating. If she also finds some degree of physical pleasure from elements of the abuse this can become proof to her that she was the initiator and bears the full responsibility. This can lead the girl to seeing herself as being innately wicked.

> The child entrapped in this kind of horror develops the belief that she is somehow responsible for the crimes of her abusers. Simply by virtue of her existence on earth, she believes that she has driven the most powerful people in the world to do terrible things. Surely then her nature must be thoroughly evil. The language of the self becomes a language of abomination (Herman, 1994, Pg.105).

The disruption of normal bodily states by chronic sexual abuse can lead to confusion, agitation, emptiness and a sense of being utterly alone. Herman (1994) refers to this as dysphoria. This can lead to both suicide attempts as an effort to regain control and self-harming as a way of relieving intense emotional pain. A whole range of self-damaging behaviours, from compulsive risk-taking to purging and vomiting can also be seen as forms of regulation of internal emotional states.

Finkelhor (1996) warns against 'discovering' a history of child or adolescent sexual abuse as a standard answer for adult psychopathology. Although he does not refer to Herman's (1994) Post Traumatic Stress Disorder formulation in terms of the consequences of child sexual abuse, he is clearly not in full agreement. One of the implications of Herman's

(1994) formulation is that the negative consequences of child or adolescent sexual abuse, though they may differ in each individual and according to the severity of the abuse, automatically flows. Finkelhor (1996) adopts a more empirical approach, making the point that over three-quarters of those with a history of sexual abuse have no current psychiatric diagnosis. This is not necessarily in complete contradiction to Herman (1994), as those who are seen to be psychologically healthy may well have 'recovered' from a psychiatric condition. An important point that Finkelhor (1996) does make is that practitioners may well be placing the blame for current psychiatric problems on the individual's history of sexual abuse, whereas the problems could equally be attributable to events prior to the sexual abuse, making the point that the children who suffer from sexual abuse tend to be emotionally deprived or abused.

The Difficulties for Practitioners

The problem for practitioners is to identify both actual abuse and the likelihood of abuse occurring. All forms of abuse are more likely to occur to children who are fostered out to non-relatives (Zurvain *et al*, 1993). Intervention in cases of child sexual abuse can be particularly problematic. A primary attribute of child sexual abusers is denial or displacement of the blame for their actions (Gordon, 1988; Berliner, 1991; Dobash et *al*, 1993), often drawing upon concepts of a predatory female sexuality (Hudson, A., 1989) that inverts the abuse in terms of a Lolita syndrome whereby the man becomes the victim of seduction by the sexually precocious girl (Gordon, 1988).

As in most cases the only people who are aware that the abuse has taken place are the perpetrator and the victim (Berliner, 1991), the child's disclosure is of paramount importance. The Cleveland Report (1988), however, contended that the social workers and clinical psychologists in that case had been too uncritical of children's testimony. This has led to some scepticism on the part of the courts in respect of social work evidence emanating from disclosure interviews. The arena of sexual abuse throws up other problems for practitioners. Although the framework for intervention is exceptionally child centred, practitioners have to be aware of the needs of women coming to terms with the sexual abuse of their children, often at the hands of their own partner. They may require a great deal of emotional and other support (Dempster, 1993). The need to take into account the needs of the victims and the needs of the carers in cases of child physical abuse and neglect is highlighted by Wolfe (1993). Corby (1993) argues further that traditional forms of social work practice that focused on the parents (usually mothers) in physical abuse cases, and on the child in sexual abuse cases, need to be superseded by an holistic approach that:

> ...responds to the emotional needs of all abused children and all members of a family in which abuse occurs...(Corby, 1993, Pg.148).

There are also difficulties in child protection practice in terms of the operation of the procedures that derive from the legislation. Although the Children Act makes provision for a series of different orders, Education Supervision Orders and Child Assessment Orders tend not to be used to any great extent (DoH, 1993), and of those applications made to the court for all types of order, over ninety per cent result in an order of no order or are withdrawn or refused.

A particular problem with Care Order proceedings is that they tend to take a minimum of around ten to twelve weeks to complete, leaving the courts sometimes making use of the private law elements of the Children Act (Section 8 Orders) 'as a preferred alternative' (DoH, 1993, para. 2.12). The comprehensive nature of the Children Act 1989 makes it easier for the courts to operate with a deal of flexibility in terms of dealing with applications for specific orders; an application for a Care Order, for example, may result in a Supervision Order or a Residence or Contact Order under Section 8 of the Act.

The minimal intervention principal in the Children Act 1989 and governmental guidance (DoH, 1991a, 1991b, 1991c) has resulted in a lower level of court activity than prior to implementation of the Act, one consequence being a noticeable reduction in the number of children being looked after by local authorities (DoH, 1993, para. 2.28), reflecting an 'increasing cooperation with parents and decreasing recourse to the courts as the Act intended' (DoH, 1993, para. 2.36).

The relatively low numbers of Emergency Protection Orders issued by the courts compared to the level of emergency interventions prior to the implementation of the Act has caused concern to some local authorities (SSI, 1992). They are concerned that the courts are taking too long to grant the orders to be effective as an emergency measure, and that once granted the duration of EPOs is too short to facilitate the parents right of challenge (i.e. less than seventy two hours). These complaints are countered by the Department of Health (DoH, 1993) by reiterating the centrality of the interests of the child in all provisions made under the Children Act 1989.

The making of an EPO and its duration should always be governed by what is in the best interests of the child - including allowing the local authority sufficient time to carry out its investigation - so that a child at risk is afforded the proper protection through the appropriate court order...(DoH, 1993, para. 2.26).

Child protection practitioners also have problems in terms of under-reporting of actual abuse and over-reporting of children showing signs of being at risk (Wattam, (1997). This derives directly from the legislation in that for the first time intervention criteria include,

...a prediction of what may or is likely to occur in the future (Parton *et al*, 1997).

This has led to many professionals outside social services, such as teachers and GPs becoming more likely to report the signs of possible physical and sexual abuse or to social services and to refer children to social services they perceive as being at risk. The child protection process thus has to operate a filtering system that removes seventy five per cent of children from the process at some stage prior to registration (Gibbons *et al*, 1995; Wattam, 1997a). That is, the vast majority of children reported to social services as being abused or at risk of abuse are eventually seen not to be at risk of significant harm. However, alongside this problem of over-reporting is the gross under-reporting of actual harm. In terms of sexual abuse it is impossible to be clear what proportion of those children that are abused ever come to the attention of social services or the NSPCC, but prevalence studies (Kelly *et al*, 1991, for example) suggest that only a tiny proportion of all sexual abuse episodes ever come to the attention of the relevant agencies.

Summary

Several significant themes emerge from the literature. The child protection system, in terms of legislation and governmental policy, albeit with some emphasis on the participation of the child and its family in the decision-making process, tends to conceive of children from birth to sixteen as some form of homogeneous group. The greatest prevalence of sexual abuse is towards children between the ages of eleven and fifteen (in terms of referrals to social services) and the vast majority of those who are abused are girls. Serious short-term and long term psychological and emotional consequences flow from being a victim of child or adolescent sexual abuse, and these consequences maybe substantially different for older girls than they are for boys or younger girls, due to the specific stage of emotional, sexual and cognitive development they are at. There are, therefore, serious issues to be addressed in terms of the potential for the legislative procedures to fail to take adequate account of those aspects relating to the age of the child concerned.

It is also clear that child and adolescent sexual abuse is problem for girls of men, and that the vast majority of perpetrators tend to be well known to the victim through blood ties or ties of allegiance. The problem of a predatory male sexuality may actually be worse than is recognised in the research in that although men form the majority of the perpetrators of child and adolescent sexual abuse, the environmental opportunities to abuse are more open to women than men. The patriarchal structuring of both paid employment and domestic labour suggest that women spend much more time alone with children than do men, yet there is little evidence of them taking this as an opportunity to abuse.

One also needs to note that a disproportionate number (in comparison with other types of abuse and other age/gender groups) of sexually abused girls from this age group voluntarily disclose the abuse (often as self-referrals to social services), perhaps, at least in part, deriving from the home-centred socialisation patterns of adolescent girls that leave them with little alternative in the way of established extra-familial peer groups to utilise in times of familial crisis.

It is also apparent that governmental policy and legislation stresses inter-agency coordination as being in the 'best interests' of the child. This clearly carries both benefits and disbenefits. The concept of coordination as a method of removing duplication of effort and of sharing information is clearly of profound importance. However, mandated coordination can lead to inter-professional resentments and 'defensive' behaviours that may not necessarily be in the best interests of the child. Further, the insistence on an almost entirely child-centred approach may not be of as much long-term benefit to the child as a more holistic approach that deals with issues involving other family members, most notably the emotional and practical difficulties endured by the mothers of sexually abused girls.

Finally, although not entirely prescriptive, the legislation and government guidance is legalistic and laden with procedures, with implications for the exercise of professional judgement by social workers. One also notes that child and adolescent sexual abuse can be extremely difficult to describe in terms that render it amenable to legal-juridical intervention.

2 Methodology

The Research Framework

The themes arising from the literature review raise several issues. Firstly, there is a gap in the literature. There is a well established body of research surrounding issues to do with the prevalence of child sexual abuse, its causes and its effects upon those who have 'survived' it. There is also a growing body of literature concerned with social services implementation of child protection procedures, and a smaller body of literature concerned with the analysis of social work practice. There is very little research, however, that specifically focuses on social workers perceptions of the operation of the child protection process in respect of familially sexually abused adolescent girls, and how those perceptions work to organise their practice. This book, therefore, is an attempt to confront one basic question.

How do social workers perceive of the child protection process in respect of familially sexually abused adolescent girls, and how do various factors of the process influence their practice?

Any attempt to gain an understanding of social workers' perceptions of the child protection process, and the ways they see various elements of the process impacting on their practice for a particular client group, can only succeed on the basis of a thorough grasp of what those elements might be. Preliminary discussions with social workers and social services managers identified five broad areas of influence:

- The organisational structure and procedures of the social services department
- Issues relating to the girl herself and the abuse she has suffered
- The behaviour and attitudes of the girl's family
- The actions of other agencies involved in the case
- The personal and professional capacities of the worker.

In order to be able to conduct an analysis in these terms, certain contextual information was required. It was imperative that a detailed understanding be gained of the legislative framework for child protection.

This forms a major part of the literature review. It is also important that local procedures and the organisational structure be known. This required the reading of local documents of procedures for the local authorities from which the sample of social workers was drawn, complemented by semi-structured interviews with managers with a strategic responsibility for child protection in each of those authorities.

The importance of relating social worker perceptions to aspects of legislation and local administrative and policy statements can be seen in that different legislative and administrative texts or statements do not alone constitute 'policy', as it is not organisations that 'act' in the sociological sense, but people. 'Policy', is better seen as the concrete outcomes of specific agencies, and in this case it is individual social workers that actually intervene in families. However, they do not act as free agents (Marx, 1968; Perrow, 1979; Giddens, 1993). Rather, their actions are continually mediated by the context of legislative, organisational and professional concerns. Hallett and Birchall (1992) make clear the importance of considering this complex interplay when looking at issues of coordination in child protection, referring to the work of Rhodes (1981, 1986, 1988) on the relationship between central and local government. They make the point:

> There is an increasing awareness of the problematic nature of central control in complex societies and awareness of the power of local agencies to resist and subvert policy initiatives or engage in delaying tactics (Hallett and Birchall, 1992, Pg.36).

Even this point is perhaps too simplistic. Rather, it is the 'techniques and tactics' (Foucault, 1980, Pg.102) of domination, negotiation and resistance at both institutional and individual levels that determine specific practical outcomes (policy) in specific cases.

Access, Confidentiality and 'Usefulness'

In conducting research in this area certain practical and ethical factors needed to be taken into consideration. From a practical aspect, there was a need to gain access at two distinct levels:

- Access to the relevant local authority documentation. Some of this, such as statements of policy and public access to specific provisions, is in the public domain, and thus posed no practical problem. Other aspects of documentation, such as local practice guidance, were internal either to the local authority as a whole or to the social services department and of a private nature. Access to such documentation had to be granted by the local authority.

- Access to the social workers for interview. Clearly, I would have been in no position to interview social workers about their child protection cases unless I had been allowed into the Area Office for that specific purpose. In this context the Office Manager, or other person from the management structure of the social services department, acted as 'gatekeeper'. The consent by a 'gatekeeper' of access to potential respondents, in this case social workers, did not however automatically constitute consent to conduct the interviews (Homan 1991).

> Gatekeepers are those who control access to data and to human subjects. Whether or not the granting of access implies consent to conduct research varies according to the gatekeeper and situation (Homan, 1991, Pg.82).

In order to gain that access it was imperative that the 'gatekeepers' were made aware of both the credibility and the potential usefulness of the research. The credibility of the research was demonstrated in that it was using well-established social research methods. Although this is strictly not a piece of evaluation research, the usefulness of the project to child protection work was made clear in that the purpose behind the research is an attempt to investigate the relationship between legislation, local policy formulation and social work practice. This has a clear articulation with the enterprise of managing social services departments, and any policy implications that can be drawn from the results could well prove 'useful' to social services managers. An additional safeguard for the local authorities concerned was a commitment that any local authorities that participated would remain anonymous. This should have removed any fear that managers had of their authority being exposed as a repository of 'poor practice'.

Official access to social workers within the local authorities working in child protection was only a first step. It was not a guarantee that any particular social worker would agree to be a part of the research programme, as agreement or refusal to such participation was clearly a personal decision made by each potential participant. In an area as sensitive as child abuse and child protection there are many legitimate reasons for social workers to refuse to participate.

- The concern that the dissemination of information about particular cases may breach aspects of client confidentiality.
- The concern on the part of the social workers that the results of the research could be for the use of management as an attempt to expose less than optimum working practices (Barnes, 1979).

It was therefore made clear to those social workers invited to participate that the object of the study was not people as named individuals, but the process of child protection intervention. Traditionally those individuals that have been the object of social research have had their integrity protected by processes of 'confidentiality, anonymity and disguise' (Barnes, 1979, Pg.41). The anonymity of the client and the worker was therefore guaranteed. In other words, my examination of the processes undertaken by social workers in individual cases did not require me to know the identity of the children or families concerned. It was made clear that it would be appropriate if cases were presented to me in an anonymous form. Some of the social workers preferred to do that, others found it easier to leave real names in and leave the anonymising to the researcher.

Just as it was important at the organisational level for the purpose of the research to be made clear, it was equally imperative that the rationale and purpose of the research be made clear to practitioners. Firstly, there was the need to negotiate my presence and the expectations I had of my role, and clarify the limitations the social workers felt must be placed on my intercession (Kimmel, 1988). Secondly, the more informed the interviewees were as to my purposes the greater the likelihood of willing cooperation and reliable information (Barnes, 1979). As well as the practical benefits of gaining the confidence of the social workers, there are also fundamental ethical reasons why they had to be informed of the reasons and purposes of the research. Social work invests its practitioners with a degree of personal autonomy in their working practices. As such, social work needs to be considered as something which social workers themselves, at least in part, define and control. They, therefore, had to retain the right to allow or deny the researcher access to knowledge of their working practices.

> If individuals are to control access to their own private domains they must know who are those who approach them and what is their purpose. This in turn requires that researchers declare their interests. So it is that the ethical principles of informed consent and openness rest upon the concept of privacy (Homan, 1991, Pg.42).

In other words, the interviews could only be conducted within the parameters of 'informed consent', with the implication that the participants could either agree or refuse to participate, and could terminate participation at any time. Kimmel (1988) stresses the importance of informed consent in research into social welfare programmes:

> ...primarily because individuals may be strongly and/or immediately influenced by the research...(Kimmel, 1988, Pg.69/70).

He also acknowledges the practical unattainability of 'fully informed consent'. In addition to the fact that it would require the researcher to explain endless technical details to each participant, often the researcher does not know all of the answers pertinent to the research (Kimmel, 1988, Pg.69). Both social services departments and social workers were therefore given the following information:

- The reasons for the research
- A description of the basic methods of research
- An acknowledgement of the right not to participate and the right to withdraw from participation
- The reasons why this authority/worker/client was included in the research sample.
- An acknowledgement of anonymity and confidentiality

In practice access proved to be very difficult. The search for respondents began with a trawl of the eight nearest local authorities with responsibility for social services. In the first instance a brief questionnaire was sent to the Director of Social Services in each of the authorities, requesting copies of local procedures and other child protection documentation, registration figures, and access to the manager responsible in the authority for child protection. A typical response was refusal to participate, with the reason most often cited being the pressure of work on social workers' time. Some of the local authorities cited policies that refused access to all research requests apart from those sponsored by the Department of Health or other governmental agencies. The research itself suggested that the pressure of work on social workers' time may well have been a legitimate reason to refuse research access, although it also seemed probable that in an atmosphere of surveillance, where social services departments are under constant scrutiny from a variety of sources there may well be a understandable resistance to yet another piece of research. The search for participating authorities continued until two northern local authorities granted access. The two authorities were both primarily rural, with area offices in rural areas, small industrial towns and small to medium sized market towns. In neither local authority was there an ethnic minority population of noteworthy size, although the population served by one area office did contain a significant number of people of Chinese ethnic origin. The general lack of ethnic diversity was reflected in the fact that all the social workers in the sample and all the girls in the cases they discussed were white.

The next stage was to work through social services managers with child protection responsibilities to find social workers willing to participate. One of the problems encountered in respect of gatekeeping was that social workers in some of the authorities that refused to participate were willing to take part, but management blocked their participation. The sample was thus limited by two factors;

i)   the effects of gatekeeping by   senior social   services managers   that served to limit   the   sample   to social workers of only two local authorities, and,

ii)   the choices in respect of participation by individual social workers within those two authorities.

In effect, within the constraints set by the managers of the various local authorities, a self-selected sample of social workers from two local authorities emerged. The fact that the sample is a self-selected one carries some implications. For example, in various ways the respondents proved to be relatively critical of their departments and of the process. One needs to remain aware of the possibility that their willingness to participate may have been predicated upon a desire to anonymously criticise their employers without any personal or professional risk being attached. Therefore, although this in no way invalidates their accounts, the experiences they recalled in their accounts may not be typical for social workers in this field. Those who agreed to participate stated that they wished to assist in research that would enhance the understanding of child protection work. Although at the level of 'gatekeeper' the constraints of time were evoked as the primary reason for non-participation, it was not possible in those departments that agreed to participate to find out why a significant proportion of social workers refused to take part. The issue of not having time to participate was not altogether convincing, as it emerged from the accounts of those who did take part that the workloads of all social workers in their area offices were relatively similar.

Most importantly, the sample was small. As the research was not quantitative, in one sense that was not an issue. Nevertheless, the smaller the number of respondents, the less opportunity for the process to *explore* the *variety* of opinions, perceptions and meanings, social workers attached to the process. The sample size was large enough and the quality of the material good enough, however, to develop an analysis of some of the ways in which this aspect of child protection was perceived by social workers.

Both in terms of organisational practice and individual social worker preference, not all the social workers in the sample could be said to be specialists in dealing with child sexual abuse. Some of the social workers had caseloads where sexual abuse cases formed thirty per cent or less of the cases they dealt with. Others seemed to specialise in sexual abuse, and their caseloads were dominated by sexual abuse cases. As far as the interviews were concerned, the social workers referred to their most recent case, which may or may not have been a current case. Those social workers who had more than one case current discussed the one that had travelled furthest within the child protection process. None of the social workers had more than two cases current that fitted the age and relationship framework for the research.

Interviewing the clients in specific cases in order to contextualise the social workers' accounts was considered, but on balance it seemed that the degree of enhancement to the depth and quality of the study to be gained from the girls' accounts was not sufficient to justify the intrusion of a male researcher discussing with them, even obliquely, anything at all to do with their abuse. It was decided instead to review the literature in respect of 'survivors' to help contextualise the social workers' accounts.

The Sample

Twenty-one social workers, across seven different sites, agreed to participate. All of them were qualified, and all but one had qualified in England and Wales. The one exception had qualified in New Zealand, although she had since worked in England for over twenty years. The social workers ranged in age from twenty-seven to fifty-four, and a significant proportion (thirteen) were graduates. Some of them were more experienced than others. The times when they qualified ranged from 1974 to 1994, and for the least experienced of the social workers in the sample the case she discussed in her account was her first experience of working with sexual abuse. The small number of respondents did not allow me to attempt to gain a gender balance in the sample, the final sample comprising two male social workers and nineteen female social workers. All the social workers were white.

Of the twenty-one cases discussed, five involved the prosecution of the perpetrator, only two of which resulted in conviction. One of those cases that resulted in conviction was complicated in that both the principal perpetrator (the mother's boyfriend) and the girl's mother were convicted. He was imprisoned, she received a suspended sentence. The other conviction was not for sexual abuse but for cruelty and resulted in a fine for the perpetrator. The social workers also reported the co-presence of emotional abuse in six cases, but in only two cases were the girls names placed on the Child Protection Register under Emotional Abuse. Five cases were also placed on the Register under the category of Physical Injury, one of which was under that category alone. All twenty-one girls had their names placed on the Child Protection Register under the category of Sexual Abuse. The relationship of the girl to the perpetrator varied somewhat. All were abused by men in a position of care and authority over them. In ten cases the perpetrator was the natural father, in eight the perpetrator lived with the mother but was not the natural father, in two cases the perpetrator was the mother's boyfriend but not residing in the family, and in one case the perpetrator was the adoptive grandfather of the girl. The ages of the girls at disclosure varied. One was eleven, five were twelve, twelve were fourteen, and three were fifteen. In eighteen cases the abuse had been of two years duration or less, in one case the girl reported the abuse commencing four years earlier, and in two cases the abuse had been of more than five years duration. The form of sexual abuse ranged from inappropriate touching through clothes to full sexual intercourse and involved varying degrees of physical coercion.

Social Workers' Accounts

Once access had been gained to a sample of social workers and they had agreed to participate in the research project the central element of the research programme began. This aspect of the research clearly divided into two distinct yet intimately configured methodological phases, with a great deal of overlap between them. These were the collection of data from the social workers, and the analysis of that data.

Collecting the Data

As the key objective in acquiring data from social workers was to try and gain some understanding of their perceptions of the child protection process and the meanings they attached to various elements within that process, a qualitative approach to both data collection and analysis was indicated. A variety of approaches were considered. These included a form of participant observation which would entail spending time in particular area offices and with particular social workers during their execution of their child protection tasks, group interviews with social workers, and interviews with individual social workers. For a variety of reasons it was decided that the data collection phase should comprise semi-structured interviews with individual social workers in respect of specific cases that they were currently dealing with or had recently closed. The reasons for that particular choice of data collection method were as follows:

- Participant observation was not possible, as those social workers that had agreed to participate were dispersed across a number of different area offices.
- Group interviews were discounted for both analytical and practical reasons. Although it would have been possible for social workers to give their accounts of what they had done in specific cases within the context of a group interview, in practical terms the recording of their responses may have proved difficult, and there may have been problems in terms of the respondents amending their responses in respect of various aspects of the cases in order to show collegial solidarity.

It was therefore decided that the best way to obtain the data was to interview social workers individually in depth in respect of specific cases.

Blaikie (1993) makes clear that the basic access the researcher has to the social world of another (in this case the social worker's world of child protection) is through their accounts. These will feature the concepts they use to structure their world and the 'theories' they utilise to account for what goes on. This follows from the theoretical precepts of interpretivist sociology (Weber, 1964; Schutz, 1972; Giddens, 1993) that make clear to any social researcher in this context the importance not only of ensuring that the respondent's account is explanatory in terms of what (s)he has done, but also why (s)he did it.

Some research (Pithouse, 1987) suggests that although there is a degree of mutual referentiality within the Area Office in respect of confirmation of professional practice, social work is almost entirely conducted on an individual basis with little open discussion of cases or procedures. It was therefore appropriate that individual interviews with workers in the area of child protection formed the fulcrum of the research. This did not preclude, however, eliciting information from individual workers about any process of Area office group discussions of child protection cases; indeed such questioning is implied in investigating the resources they draw upon to make specific decisions. The method used was that of very loosely structured interviews, conducted on an open-ended basis with a clear topic guide which was referred to ensure that key points were not overlooked. Writers on research methods (Bryman, 1988; May, 1993) tend to differentiate between more formal semi-structured interviews, which seek elaboration and clarification around a set of pre-ordained questions, and focused or unstructured interviews, which are entirely open-ended. In practice this proved to be something of a false dichotomy as the interviews would seem to cut across such categorisations. The interviews focussed on a number of issues, but these issues were located within the actual practices of the workers concerned. In other words, the interviews focussed on specific cases, in terms of what social workers had done and why, rather than a series of abstract issues. Within this context, this follows the work on woman abuse undertaken by Dobash and Dobash (1979, 1992), who stress the role played in gaining an understanding of the topic through the accounts of the experiences of those in the 'front line'. However much specific child protection cases can be typologised and allocated categories, each interaction between worker and child or worker and parent will be different, and in circumstances subtly different from all other cases. Therefore the workers interviewed needed to be able to express their views and feelings around all aspects of those interactions. This pointed towards an open-ended approach, which led some interviews to go in directions that were not anticipated. Bryman (1988) argues that this should be seen in a positive light, in that 'rambling' can reveal concerns and perspectives that the researcher was not previously aware of.

The interview schedule thus developed was then tried out, as a form of pilot exercise, on social workers known personally to the researcher. This gave the opportunity to amend some of the key questions and the prompts before engaging in the data collection process. In practice, each interview served to amend the schedule for subsequent interviews if and when respondents gave account of issues that had not been previously considered.

It is worth consideration here that the research topic, adolescent sexual abuse and child protection practice, is a very sensitive area, both in terms of the state intruding into the family and the moral outrage attached to aberrant sexuality. It was important to be aware that certain issues of gender and power may have presented themselves in the interview situation. The male gender of the researcher could have acted as a barrier to the acquisition of information from female social workers or the responses given could be intrinsically different to those that would have been given to a female researcher. No evidence emerged from the interviews that the gendered interactions of the researcher and the respondents had any impact on the accounts given, although it is clearly impossible to be absolutely sure. It was also important to confront the issue that social workers aspire to professional status and, as social work is a 'discursive' occupation, they are skilled at interview techniques. It was important to be aware of their capacity to control the interview situation. The importance of a topic guide cannot be overemphasised here in that it proved to be of great value as a reminder of what topics had not been covered in interviews within which the interviewee had shown highly developed discursive skills.

Each of the interviews lasted between one and a half and two hours and was tape-recorded. In each case the interviewee was asked if (s)he consented to the taping of the interview and none of the respondents refused. The tape-recording of the interviews was absolutely crucial. It obviated the need for detailed note taking, and thus allowed for a relatively 'naturalistic' interaction between the respondent and the researcher.

The final element of the data collection process that linked it to the process of analysis was to transcribe the recording in full and add notes as to the atmosphere of the interview and the researcher's perceptions as to the degree of candour in the respondent's account. This was seen as an important part of the data collection process as the quality of the interaction between the interviewer and the interviewee can have a bearing on the quality of the data to emerge from the account. Goffman (1971) contends that the status of the audience and the social actor's perception of that audience mediate the accounts given by an individual. The justifications or rationale given by an individual for his/her actions are thus located within a 'vocabulary of motives' appropriate to that particular interaction (Mills, 1940; Gerth and Mills, 1954). It was thus apparent that the situation of the interview itself and the language utilized within that particular interaction formed an important aspect of the data to be interpreted and analyzed.

The process of transcription was a laborious one, each interview taking at least two full working days to transcribe, but an essential one in that it then provided printed material from which to develop the analysis.

Data Analysis

Prior to conducting the first batch of interviews there was no predetermined framework for analyzing any of the accounts. This framework developed in response to the data generated by the interviews. Each of the interviews was transcribed in full and summarized with notes as to the attitude of the respondent and the ambience of the interaction. Miles and Huberman (1984) suggest that a coding framework is a necessary part of preliminary analysis whilst in the field, as it makes more clear both exactly what the research question is, and helps to refine the process of ongoing data collection. Therefore each transcript was coded and as the interview schedule developed some codes were discarded and new ones developed. Miles and Huberman (1984) warn against using numerical codes as these are completely abstract. Therefore the coding framework was developed in the form of abbreviations rather than numbers. This process continued after the completion of interviews until a final coding framework emerged. The codes were clustered into groups that referred to the major themes of each chapter of the book. The analysis was thus developed along the lines of a series of themes to emerge from the data.

The key point is that the analysis was data driven. In other words the analysis was inductive in that it was developed out of patterns and processes found in the accounts social workers gave of their actions and perceptions in specific cases:

...without presupposing what the important dimensions will be (Patton, 1990, Pg.44).

This process of induction is carried to its ultimate end in the concept of 'grounded theory' by Glaser and Strauss (1967), who argue that the generation of theory is intimately involved in the process of research, and constantly evolves through the use of continuing comparative method. In some ways this gives little guidance for the researcher as to how to arrive at an end point for a particular piece of research. Clearer guidance is given by Strauss and Corbin (1994). Following Glaser and Strauss (1967) they argue that the interpretations of their data that qualitative researchers arrive at must include the 'perspectives and voices' (Strauss and Corbin, 1994, Pg.274) of those being studied, but that such interpretations must go beyond merely giving voice to those individuals. Rather their voices and perspectives need to be located within some form of theoretical framework. The purpose of theory for Strauss and Corbin (1994) is that it can act to translate the results of qualitative research from the particular of the individuals/organisations studied into some form of general social scientific rule. In other words, theory derived from empirical research data can act as a method of predicting that given similar conditions for a similar respondent group similar consequences will flow. 'Grounded theory' thus gives qualitative research results 'scientific' validity. The benefits of 'grounded theory' can be seen in terms analogous to those utilized by natural scientists and quantitative researchers in the social sciences. Whilst remaining fixed to an interpretive conceptualisation of the social world, 'grounded theory' can be seen to fit into the Popperian 'sophisticated methodological falsificationist' view of science (Lakatos, 1970), in that theories are seen as always temporary, capable of being falsified by the development of new theories that can account for the results of previous research and new apparently irreconcilable data within new theoretical frameworks. In other words 'grounded theory' emerges from the researcher developing 'plausible relationships' (Strauss and Corbin, 1994) between concepts and sets of concepts deriving from her/his empirical data, and examining the ways in which these relationships fit or do not fit within existing theoretical frameworks. In practical terms it becomes clear that grounded theory is not a methodological prescription. Rather, the concept of grounded theory alerts the researcher to the need to develop analytical themes and perspectives within his/her interpretation of the research data, and to grasp the relationship of those themes and perspectives to already existing theoretical frameworks .[1]

The process of developing the various themes and perspectives through the mechanism of coding elements of the workers' responses was not a discrete process carried out after the completion of data collection. Rather, the process of analysis was ongoing from the moment of transcription of the first interview, and the various themes and patterns to emerge were continuously tested and amended in the light of 'new' evidence.

The Impact of the Research on the Researcher

I began this research project under the erroneous belief that it would remain within the confines of 'work' and would have little personal impact on me. However, as the interview schedule developed I began to realise that this was impossible. Three factors were to have a bearing on this. The perpetrators of the abuse in the accounts given by the social workers were ordinary men, who seemed little different to me. The girls who were subject to the abuse were ordinary teenage or adolescent girls, little different from my own daughters. The problems social workers spoke of, especially in terms of the interplay between child protection and the criminal justice system, served to constantly remind me of the teenage son of family friends who suffered immense psychological trauma after being sexually abused by a neighbour. His parents constantly sought counselling for him but this was refused on the advice of the police. After an unsuccessful suicide attempt he eventually succeeded in hanging himself in the family home. In a sense, throughout the research programme I had to confront a series of emotions that perhaps led me to an unhealthy degree of hypervigilance in terms of my own children.

Moran-Ellis (1996), as a female researcher in child sexual abuse and the mother of young children, reports a similar sense of exaggerated concern for her children. Our situations, however, are somewhat different. As the working mother of young children living with a male partner, her realisation that it is 'ordinary' men who sexually abuse, caused her significant anxieties in terms of her male partner looking after her children, although neither he nor they gave any indication that any abuse had occurred or was likely to occur. Moran-Ellis's (1996) understandable concern reflects her realisation that the empirical evidence on child sexual abuse (Macleod and Saraga, 1988; Hearn, 1990, for example) showing that it is 'normal' men that abuse, can be interpreted as locating child sexual abuse as one of the elements within a paradigm of male dominance fixed into deeply embedded structures of patriarchy. Moran-Ellis's (1996) concerns were not alleviated by her experiences of male academics in the field of child sexual abuse research, some of whom she saw as perceiving of the subject either defensively in trying to attribute the perpetration of child sexual abuse to a group of men that were 'other' to 'normal' men (i.e. deviant) or in terms of a perceived salaciousness in their responses to knowledge of the sexual acts involved in cases of abuse.

My own emotional response to the work was somewhat different. Although sharing much of Moran-Ellis's (1996) sense of disgust and horror at what child sexual abuse in particular and male violence towards females in general entails, much of my disgust was self-directed. I was at one and the same time, a father of three children, two of whom were teenage girls, and a man, knowingly capable of being as sexually titillated by such things as salacious tabloid journalism as any other man. One of the great benefits I derived from the research, difficult as it was to deal with, was a greater awareness that perhaps all men are capable of child sexual abuse and that one's male sexuality may well contain dangerous and oppressive elements that need to be carefully self-regulated.

It also made me realise that although I had intellectually grasped the patriarchal and unpleasant nature of the portrayal of femininity as adolescence by the fashion industry and others, I had failed to fully comprehend how insidious and dangerous this could be. I began to comprehend that not only were such portrayals distasteful, but they could also serve to legitimate some of the excesses of male power and control over adolescent girls that the research was examining. Thus to some degree I was unable to conduct the research without some degree of anger at myself for my ambivalent attitudes, at the child protection system for not being more efficient than it is, and at the perpetrators for symbolically depriving my daughters of their adolescent innocence. Feminist researchers (Stanley and Wise, 1983; Kelly, 1988; Kirkwood, 1993; Moran-Ellis, 1996) argue that the personal response of the researcher is intrinsic to the research project itself, and that it is neither possible nor desirable to attempt to distance one's ethnographic self from one's personal identity and emotions. This has become abundantly clear to me, and is succinctly expressed by Lincoln and Denzin (1994) in terms of analysing the data and writing it up:

> The false division between the personal and the ethnographic self rests on the assumption that it is possible to write a text that does not bear the traces of its author. Of course, this is not possible. All texts are personal statements (Lincoln and Denzin, 1994, Pg.587).

The Structure of the Book

The coding framework went beyond simply providing the framework for the development of specific analytical themes and perspectives from the raw data. Each of the specific 'codes' fitted within a cluster or 'family group' of codes that could be seen to form a meta-code or overarching theme. The coding framework thus provided a structure for the presentation of the findings, each chapter being primarily a discussion of a specific 'family group' of codes. The chapters are variously concerned with procedural and organisational issues, inter-agency coordination, the abused girls themselves, their families, and the social workers' skills and practice preferences. The order in which the five substantive chapters are presented should not be read as any form of prioritisation of the findings.

3 Procedure and organisation

Introduction

The social workers' child protection practice was not accomplished in a vacuum, rather it was always both enabled and constrained by the structures of welfare service organisations and the procedures or systems of social work delivery.

The social services departments of the local authorities were charged with delivering child protection services in accordance with central governmental legislation and policy. However, those social services departments were also answerable to a locally elected council. Saunders (1984) contends that modern western democracies can be characterised as 'dual states', comprising two analytically distinct components:

- Central government with a general duty towards investment in infrastructure and the funding of services,
- Local government and its bureaucracies with a duty of delivering services

This accurately describes the split between the roles of central and local government regarding the personal social services. In the delivery of child protection the interplay between these two elements can be complex. Central government furnishes social services departments with a comprehensive series of duties and powers in respect of child care and protection, principally deriving from the Children Act 1989, but those duties and powers are executed within a series of locally developed procedures that take into account issues such as the geography, and demography of particular local authorities. Social Services departments have lines of accountability in terms of child protection to both the local authority and central government, tending to place the senior personnel of social services departments in a key position in terms of the implementation of policy and the development of particular procedures. Within the services they provide for children and their families Social Services departments develop a series of priorities that reflect local political considerations, although social services managers stressed that the influence of elected members tended to be less in the area of agenda setting than in terms of taking decisions based upon agendas set by senior social services officers. The key position held by officers at the interface of central and local governmental policies, enhanced by membership of national professional bodies and specialist training granted them a legitimated knowledge (Foucault, 1979, 1990; Dunleavy, 1980) and 'expertise' that afforded them a powerful influence on local child protection procedures. It therefore becomes clear that one needs to gain an understanding of the organisation of child protection in each of the local authorities and the ways in which the policies and procedures that have developed impact upon the child protection practice of social workers. Social work *per se* is relatively difficult to define and cannot be understood in isolation from its structural location and its political and procedural systems. Pithouse (1987), in his research into the ways in which social work is accomplished in area offices, places great emphasis on the role of management structures, informal networks and organisational procedures:

> ...while the lay person may view success in social work as 'solving' the individual or family problem, the practitioner may be more concerned with following legal procedures or completing records and applying specific resources or routines (Pithouse, 1987, Pg.49).

The purpose of this chapter is to examine the ways in which the structural and procedural elements of child protection were mediated into the specifics of the social workers' practice in cases involving the intra-familial sexual abuse of adolescent girls. This aspect of the social workers' practice needed to be broken down into a series of discrete factors that each dealt with particular aspects of the structuring of local authority child protection work, the organisational and policy-led systems or procedures of local authority child protection work, and the culture of local authority social work teams. At this point there is a need for a degree of circumspection, as it was not actually possible to entirely divorce the structural, the systemic and the cultural one from another; cultural elements impinged on structural and systemic elements, for example, but the factors as developed can be seen each to be **primarily** structural, systemic or cultural.

Structural Factors

Social work can be seen variously in terms of a middle-class profession within a class-structured society or as a semi-professional 'trade' delivering techniques of care within a patriarchally structured society. In both formulations it is imbued with a function of legitimation and social control and is seen as an agency of the state that seeks to ameliorate rather than challenge class and/or gender inequalities. A significant proportion of social workers are female, implying at some level an extension into the professional arena of the 'natural' caring skills attributed to women. In all aspects of social work there is a structural-cultural gap between the practitioners of social work and their clients (Heraud, 1970). The development of social work and the statutory agencies within which it is practised can be seen as an integral element of the development of the 'social' (Squires, 1990); a space that intersects the public and the private as an arena within which issues such as deprivation, poverty and unemployment are constructed as social problems. As social services form an integral part of the web of welfare, the problems of poorer families are much more likely than those of more affluent families to be visible to the social work 'gaze', despite the clarity of research findings (Russell, 1984; Kelly, 1988, Kelly *et al*, 1991, for example) that sexual abuse is principally perpetrated by men on women and children, with no significant correlation to social class. Social workers, however, tend to be professionally qualified and many are university graduates, suggesting that they tend to be middle-class either by birth or education. The construction of child sexual abuse as a social problem over the past twenty years (Parton, 1991; Parton *et al*, 1997) has ensured that it clearly occupies a space within the 'social' that renders it visible to social work agencies.

These macro-structural features of social work are important in contextualising both child sexual abuse and child protection. However, those structural elements of social work that were explored as central to the research project were the organisational and management structures of social services child protection, and the availability of resources social workers could draw upon to accomplish their child protection tasks. These structural factors were examined from the point of view of the ways in which social workers understood them as shaping their child protection tasks in terms of both enablement and constraint, and in terms of an analysis of the ways in which they influenced their child protection practice.

Organisational Structure

Both the authorities that took part in the research process were non-metropolitan County Council authorities, with social work teams covering both urban and rural areas. As non-metropolitan County Councils they delivered child protection services through the organisation of a social services department. Unlike the situation in some unitary authorities the organisation and management structure in these two authorities was dedicated to the delivery of social services without any distractions in terms of other aspects of welfare delivery.

The organisational structure of the child protection 'system' within the two authorities was very similar. The specific division of managerial duties and the titles given to particular strategic managers differed, but, in terms of child protection, they both operated what was basically a three-tier management system. In each authority there was a central manager responsible for services for children and families. The individuals holding these positions were keen to emphasise their own backgrounds in child protection work, and stressed that this experience gave them the capacity to understand the day-to-day child protection problems confronted by social workers, and, perhaps more significantly, it gave them the capacity to understand the implications of government guidance and legislation for the development of policy. The next tier down was that of service manager, responsible for a single aspect of children and families such as child protection, and the final tier of management was that of team manager, a role that appears universally in social work to act as a conduit between central management on the one hand and social workers on the other.

The social workers saw the team manager's role as crucial to their practice. They stressed the importance of the team manager in respect of formal and informal supervision, and advice. This was a particularly significant issue in one authority as the social workers were very anxious over proposals to reduce the number of team managers by 'sharing' them between teams, in effect halving their access to their team managers. This highlighted the social workers' concerns over staffing levels in general. This general unease was compounded by increased levels of reporting that placed extra pressure on diminishing staff resources, and in one area there were serious misgivings over staffing levels that failed to compensate for the growth in clientele due to recent demographic changes. The importance of the team manager from the perspective of the worker and his/her practice resided primarily in his/her role in worker supervision. Both authorities had very similar structures of supervision in place although actual supervision arrangements varied widely across all teams and appeared to be tailored to local circumstances and levels of worker experience. The process of supervision was valued not only by the social workers but also by senior management, in that they felt it could highlight practice and training deficits and could also bring to light problems both of individual practice and, more importantly, of the 'system' itself that were hitherto unknown.

The senior child protection managers of each of the authorities saw policy development to some extent as 'bottom-up', deriving in part from information gleaned from the supervision process. The overall development of child protection policy in both authorities involved some external inputs and a variety of inputs from various levels within the organisation. One manager identified the key components of policy development as the results of internal inquiries, the conclusions and recommendations of Child Protection Conferences, which he constantly monitored, and the deliberations of the Child And Families Management Team, comprising team managers who would take cognisance of what their supervisees had told them. In the other authority policy development was more systemised and more hierarchically organised in that dedicated small groups of managers would look at research and legislation and then write a short paper for examination by the Children and Families Group, before presentation to the Social Services Committee. The key point would be that although the processes differed, both managers stressed the line management approach to information gathering from the bottom up as essential to policy development, laid on top of legislation and governmental policy, inquiry reports and the monitoring of important issues.

The importance of the management structure and its operation in terms of the ways in which child protection social workers understand various cases and give 'meaning' to their task revolves around attempting to gain some analytical understanding of the degree to which their work is shaped by those structures (Howe, 1986), and the degree to which they act with professional autonomy in determining the day-to-day practice of their departments (Lipsky, 1980). The social workers in both authorities saw their department as having open and accessible structures, in that senior management made themselves available to social workers for advice and decision-making, and that social workers felt that management supported them in their work. This view was mediated to some extent in ways similar to those found by Pithouse (1987, 1990) in that social workers also tended to distinguish very much between the team manager, who was seen as being part of the team, someone who shared their perceptions and understood their needs, and senior management, who were seen as out of touch and preoccupied with efficiency savings and procedures.

The official organisation of support systems was seen as very important. In one team the senior social worker had been relieved of her caseload to enable her to act as support and trouble-shooter in other cases. Although this meant the absorption of her cases by other workers in the team without any additional workers being employed, the workers saw the overall changes as beneficial. They felt guaranteed of back-up when they went on 'difficult' visits, and the senior social worker became the central actor in an organised process of de-briefing for workers who had been on stressful cases. In other teams organisational changes were seen as beneficial for very different reasons. The department had scrapped family resource centres and redeployed the family workers in the area teams. The social workers saw this as releasing them from the additional paperwork that had come in the wake of the Children Act.

In both authorities there were clear lines of management responsibility for child protection policy and practice, that involved to some extent a principle of subsidiarity. Decisions were taken at as low a level as possible in terms of practice, by social workers supported by team managers. The concept of support was the most important aspect of structure in terms of enabling the social workers in their task. The social workers thus viewed with misgivings any resource driven amendment to the management structure, such as the reduction in the number of team managers in one of the authorities, that could reduce their capacity to access support.

Outside Resources

The social workers' child protection tasks were clearly circumscribed by the availability of therapeutic and other services they could access on behalf of their clients. There were a multiplicity of resources from the private, the statutory and the voluntary sectors, including resources from social services, but they are best seen as outside resources in that they are resources external to the child protection team. The key external resources the social workers utilised when working with sexually abused adolescent girls were therapeutic services in the form of psychological and psychiatric services in the statutory sector and girls/women's survivors groups in the voluntary sector. The child protection practice of individual social workers was shaped to some extent by the presence or absence of locally accessible girls' sexual abuse survivor groups or perpetrators groups, and by the length of psychiatrist's and psychologist's waiting lists.

Social workers saw a role for therapy for perpetrators, that accorded with the cautious proposal put forward by Dobash *et al* (1993) that some perpetrator intervention strategies may help to minimise future abusive behaviour, [1] although the social workers were of the view that success rates in perpetrator therapy were poor, and thus felt that such initiatives would always have a very low priority in the allocation of child protection resources and would thus be unlikely to become available.

The social workers constructed their practice in respect of adolescent sexual abuse cases to some extent in terms of geography. Both the authorities in this study comprised in part medium sized market or industrial towns, although they were predominantly rural and geographically large. Although the impact of geographical issues was different between the teams that were located in the towns and those which were located in the rural areas, they experienced similar problems in respect of the provision of both statutory and non-statutory resources. The provision of services by the health service and the voluntary sector, for example, tended to centre around the more urban centres of population, leaving those social workers in the rural areas with real difficulties of access that rotated around two distinct issues. Firstly, there was the problem of cost in terms of both money and time in transporting clients substantial distances (round trips of over 50 miles were not uncommon), and secondly there was the problem of expecting clients to travel those distances in order to receive a service. This caused the social workers some concern, as they did not see it as always being in the client's interests.

Amongst those areas of statutory provision that were seen by social workers as being particularly significant to the long-term prognosis for sexually abused teenage girls were mental health services. Access to these services appeared to be very difficult in both authorities, and to a great extent was dependent upon where in each authority the client lived. Those in the more urban areas definitely had a greater degree of access to these services than those in the more rural areas. Not only were psychological and psychiatric services concentrated in the more densely populated parts of the counties, but the social workers felt that the overall level of provision was fairly poor and certainly worse than would be the case in metropolitan areas. One social worker in a rural team compared her practice now with the ways in which she operated when working for a London authority. Within the London area social workers could refer their clients to a variety of specialist services on a London wide basis. To provide a similar level of opportunity choice in the non-metropolitan counties would require additional resources of a very high order. This interplay between geography and general resourcing emphasised the problems for child protection in rural areas over and above any general debate in respect of resourcing. Many resources were relatively inaccessible due to the distances social workers and their clients needed to travel to avail themselves of them. In effect this precluded the development of resources on a county wide basis, leaving provision at an *ad hoc* relatively low level. To develop services beyond this point would necessitate the provision of a great many more localised services, which may only serve a handful of people, and thus not be justifiable within the budgets of social services and the NHS. It would also be difficult to imagine this niche being filled by the voluntary sector, as exactly similar problems of the economies of scale would apply to them.

The problem of access to psychological services was clearly illustrated by a social worker from a team in a small market town, who reported that the team was visited once a fortnight by one of the two psychologists for their half of the county to meet with clients that the team referred to him, but he didn't deal with any sexual abuse referrals. The psychologist that dealt with sexual abuse referrals didn't travel away from her base in a town twenty-four miles away, where she took individual consultations and ran groups for sexually abused girls. The social worker further reported that both psychologists had waiting lists for referrals of about three months, something that appeared quite usual throughout both authorities. In one area social workers were concerned at what they saw as a complete lack of both psychological and psychiatric support; a psychiatrist that set one day a week aside to deal with any social work referrals and a nine month waiting list for referrals to the psychologist.

The need for mental health services generally for sexually abused adolescent girls cannot be overemphasised, yet clearly the interplay of geography and economics in these particular areas meant that the capacity of social workers to access such services for girls they were working with was severely constrained. The response of psychological and psychiatric services to social worker referrals of sexually abused adolescent girls varied between cases, as did the outcome for the girls. The way in which they perceived of the mental health services seemed to be in direct relationship to the outcomes for their clients. All the social workers made some criticism in terms of the difficulty in initially accessing such services. One manager suggested that access would be improved if social services took the lead in the provision of psychological services in respect of child abuse and employed psychologists attached to Family Centres or Children and Families Teams. To carry this idea a little further one could suggest that if any emotional or mental problem associated with the abuse was thought to be present the social worker should always make the referral to the 'in-house' psychologist.

The provision of therapeutic services by the statutory sector, however, was only part of the story. As one social worker pointed out, without the voluntary sector child protection would be in severe difficulties. The bulk of voluntary sector provision as far as child protection is concerned tends to be concentrated around issues of neglect and physical injury and assistance and advice to parents in respect of the key tasks of physical care. It also tends to be involved in work related to the care and protection of the under fives, perhaps reflecting the greater degree of public sympathy for younger children [2]. The social workers were very aware that the voluntary provision of services and resources for sexually abused teenage girls was poorer than that for other groups of abused or disadvantaged children.

The most significant resource provided by the voluntary sector for sexually abused girls is that of survivors' groups, although provision varied immensely from area to area within the two local authorities, with little provision in the rural areas. As one manager pointed out, the voluntary sector are the major provider of such groups, as social services simply don't have to money to run such groups themselves. This view was reinforced by one social worker who used to run a girls' group along with another social worker. She reported that when they requested social services support in terms of time they had it refused due to lack of resources.

At the most basic level survivors groups, by their very existence, can give sexually abused girls hope, by showing that women have come through the aftermath of abuse. Survivors groups and the voluntary organisations involved with them can do far more, however [3]. One of the area teams in the study had made a number of referrals of sexually abused teenage girls to the local Rape Crisis Centre, who ran specific groups for sexually abused teenage girls and were actively working on the problems associated with girls who had been subject to incest. One of the social workers in the team saw the Centre's work as very beneficial to some of her clients. She also saw then as plugging a serious gap in the provision of services for this particular client group, that of continuity of contact and therapy through the statutory age limit of child protection into adulthood, as the group would continue to work with girls beyond the age of eighteen. It is important, however, not to over-emphasise the role of survivors groups as some form of therapeutic panacea. The key activity within groups such as that run by Rape Crisis was that of talking through one's feelings, and the value and importance of such activities and the benefits derived from them may well differ considerably between individuals, and could, among other things, be impacted upon by social class. One social worker referred to two seemingly similar cases of familial sexual abuse, whose key difference was the social class of the participants. This class difference seemed to affect many aspects of the case, not least the reactions to and benefits derived from referral to the Rape Crisis group. The girl from the middle-class background got a great deal out of the group, talked through her feelings, and picked up the pieces of her life, and began to develop 'normal' adult social relations. The worker was satisfied that the girl's prognosis was good. The girl from the working-class background, however, found the Rape Crisis group intimidating and gained little from it. Surprisingly, the worker also felt that her prognosis was good, in that she has now settled down with a caring young man. It would be disingenuous to suggest that social class does not to some extent determine the impact various therapeutic interventions will have on an individual; class is a crucial factor in the shaping of an individual's psyche. In this instance, however, it is difficult to determine if the social class of the girls concerned had a direct impact on the value of particular therapies, or if there was a high degree of mediation in terms of the professional's expectations of the differential benefits of specific therapies for differently 'classed' individuals. This does not preclude the probability of genuine class differences in the ways in which individuals approach issues relating to health and well-being. It may well be that certain types of therapy could be inappropriate for many working-class girls. Cornwell (1984) makes the point that working-class women are likely to see the recovery from illness as a personal responsibility, and further they are likely to have very strong inhibitions in terms of whom they can speak to and what they can speak about in respect of sexual issues. In effect, there may well be problems with some forms of group therapy for working class girls who have been sexually abused in that their class and gender socialisation would tend to dispose them towards a stoical view of their abuse and a reluctance to express their feelings in public.[4] Hooper *et al* (1997) point out that although there are both benefits and drawbacks in terms of both short-term and long-term groups, in general long term groups offer the most therapeutic value. However, due in the most part to resource constraints the statutory agencies are far more likely to initiate short-term groups. The social workers in the sample reinforced this view in that what services were available to them in terms of therapeutic groups tended to be of a short fixed-term nature.

The social workers' references to issues relating to the availability of outside resources shows that they varied widely and tended to be concentrated in the towns. This then suggests a very real gap between an 'ideal' of therapeutic intervention and the realities of what is possible. Social workers in different teams developed different strategies due to the availability and accessibility of different resources, to the point that in many areas the vast majority of therapeutic work was done by social workers themselves or not at all. These differences in practice tended primarily to represent the different degrees of constraint on access. However, some developments, such as the development of the incest work at the Rape Crisis Centre could perhaps represent some form of therapeutic development in the armoury of social workers that goes beyond what they would in the abstract have thought of as an 'ideal' solution, and also represents a partial solution to the problem of the intersection of the length of time for recovery from sexual abuse and the upper age boundary of the child protection process[5]. Novel forms of outside resources could thus be visualised as enabling mechanisms that could improve this aspect of child protection work.

Systemic Factors

Social work is not only dependent upon the structures within which it takes place, but also via the operation of systems of welfare delivery. Child protection work is accomplished through a whole series of policies and procedures, that embody the priorities of the organisation and the availability and deployment of internal resources. These policies and procedures are not however simply sets of rules by which to operate, but are infinitely negotiable and are mediated through the perception and experience of those involved within them. Furthermore, the 'meanings' attached to specific priorities and procedures are to a greater or lesser extent open to interpretation. For example, the priority given to protection over prevention by social services departments is to some extent dependent upon the 'meaning' attached to the concept of prevention. It was necessary to examine the ways in which social workers saw these various aspects of 'system' as impacting on or shaping their practice.

Organisational Priorities

Managers suggested that at the departmental level children's services were prioritised over services for adults. The mechanisms identified by the managers for setting priorities within children's services seemed a little vague. Recommendations from research were mentioned as being important but not to be slavishly followed. Rather they were to be taken into consideration in the light of other locally derived knowledges, although exactly what these were was difficult to discern. It was, however, clearly evident what those priorities were. Within children's services in both authorities, as far as the deployment of resources was concerned, child protection rated as the highest priority. Child protection was seen as the most sensitive and the most important aspect of children's services, and within child protection the managers identified a hierarchy of priorities. The tasks given the highest priority were those associated with the first stage of the child protection process, from referral through initial investigation up to the Initial Child Protection Conference and registration. Hallett (1995) reports similar findings. The managers also indicated that a similar prioritisation of this stage was evident in all the other agencies involved in the process. Older ongoing cases were granted a lower priority, unless they were particularly crisis-ridden, and the lowest priority of all appeared to be given to organising services for sexually abused girls (and boys) who were coming up to eighteen, stemming from the lack of agreed procedures for dealing with clients at the age boundary of the child protection process[6].

Social workers tended to confirm this hierarchy of priorities and saw it as an important organising feature of their practice. They saw the initial investigation stage as being stressed at the expense of other aspects of the work. One worker put it very succinctly:

> If you are working with someone when you've already done the investigation and the child is safe and then another one comes in then that becomes the priority. (SW).

The social workers saw this as relating directly to chronic understaffing. Their concern centred on what they saw as a crisis management approach to child protection that concentrated on setting the process in motion and then actually did less and less for the girls as time went by. This led many of them to feel the service they provided for sexually abused adolescent girls was relatively poor and not of a professional standard. They also worried that the simple prioritisation of the initial stages at the expense of long-term work could sell the girls short in that without fully dealing with the issues and taking full account of the girls' broader welfare and care needs (Farmer and Owen, 1995), and the possibilities were greater that the girl could return to the attention of social services at a later date with worse problems than ever. They also saw this as implying a cost to social services. This is not to say that long-term work did not take place, but it appears that the space was rarely there. One worker, who had been involved in some long-term work on the aftermath of sexual abuse said that it felt like 'swimming against the tide' (SW), and that one had to constantly justify the work in terms of crisis prevention. She reflected a widely held view amongst the workers in the study by complaining that the performance of child protection teams seemed to revolve around statistics concerned with the number of children on the register rather then the number of children receiving beneficial therapeutic work. This perhaps indicates a significant problem in terms of assessing the efficacy of child protection interventions. There is no reliable method for linking social workers' child protection inputs to any specific child protection outcomes for the girls concerned. For any two sexually abused girls, one may be adequately protected and make a full recovery, whilst the other may be reabused or remain emotionally or psychologically damaged, even with identical social work intervention. Similarly, a girl who is sexually abused and does not come to the attention of social services may become adequately protected and make a full recovery. In other words, although the child protection intervention practices of social workers are predicated on legislation, procedures and training that is in itself derived from compelling evidence that such interventions are beneficial, it is not possible to make a causal link between intervention and outcome for any individual client. However, as the child protection work of social services social workers is funded by public money there is a powerful imperative to attempt to measure the efficiency and effectiveness of their work. In the absence of other quantitative indicators registration figures assume a significance that is to a large extent unjustified, as an attempt to measure the unmeasurable. The social workers also felt that the initial investigation stage was stressed at the expense of what they actually saw as social work, and that a form of crisis management had developed, with the consequence that they felt constantly hurried and doubtful of the quality of the work they were doing.

The Concept of Prevention

The concept of prevention in child protection is a slippery one. At one level it is difficult to envisage any area of social work that cannot be said to preventative (Fuller, 1992). Prevention, at this level, in child protection simply implies the prevention of future harm to children and young people. There is no indication of exactly what harm is going to be prevented from occurring to which young people. Any specific child protection intervention can thus come under the rubric of prevention, as can any initiative to attempt to prevent children and young people in generally from falling into risk of significant harm. The concept is given more clarity by borrowing from the vocabulary of health care (Parker, 1980; Jones, 1985), and making a distinction between primary, secondary and tertiary levels of prevention, although that leaves a great deal of debate over what exactly constitutes each particular level. A primary level of prevention could be visualised as efforts to confront the social-structural features of poverty and deprivation that produce the environment for physical abuse and neglect, or the gendered structuration of power and issues of masculine aggression that create the possibilities for sexual abuse. However, traditionally, child care and protection work has never been totally committed to that role. The genesis of modern child protection in the nineteenth century placed great emphasis on 'saving' children from abusive environments by removing them (Squires, 1990), although the NSPCC also made efforts to reform parents. The balance has now shifted more towards the concept of reform in that social work seeks to initiate change in 'problem' families or to remove the abuser. Despite the development of 'anti-oppressive' practice and the recognition in both training and practice of the complex interaction between the societal and the individual levels, the evidence points to child protection work remaining located in the realm of the personal rather than the societal. Although the social workers expressed concern at the lack of preventative programmes and acknowledged the role of wider social structural dynamics in the development of child sexual abuse, they saw their task, in general, in terms of 'saving' individual children from specific situations and the abusive activities of particular aberrant or deviant men. This may have less to do with social workers' being unconvinced of the societal element in the aetiology of child sexual abuse, and be more closely linked to the role of social work *per se* of trying to devise individual solutions to difficult and often intractable problems through work with individuals and families.

This is not to suggest that the preventative model is without value. Hardiker *et al* (1991) suggest that, in an analytical sense, there are four distinct levels of prevention. The primary level of prevention comprises the provision of services that will prevent the child protection process from being triggered and thus prevent individuals from falling into client status. They suggest that this would include such things as day care for pre-school children and outreach work with adolescents. This conceptualisation appears to make some sense as far as the prevention of physical injury and neglect is concerned, but the aetiology of sexual abuse suggests that primary prevention thus visualised may be of only very limited effect.

Finkelhor (1986) argues, however, that useful primary prevention programmes can be developed in respect of child sexual abuse. From a review of such programmes in the USA, he discusses the rationale for primary prevention and suggests that the need derives from three basic facts. A significant proportion of children will suffer sexual abuse, most victims of sexual abuse are not identified, and many victims of child sexual abuse could be spared much suffering if armed with information about their right to refuse sexual advances, and the inappropriateness of some adult behaviours. The basic thrust of Finkelhor's (1986) argument is that children from a very young age should be given information to make them aware that even men they like could abuse them and to broaden their awareness of what behaviours towards them are inappropriate. He further suggests that children should take action when they have been abused, primarily by telling someone, repeatedly if necessary, until they are believed. Finkelhor (1986) also points to programmes aimed at parents and professionals, arguing that professionals need to be aware of the signs of sexual abuse and report it early to prevent further abuse, and that parents need to be helped to overcome their embarrassment and anxieties about talking to their children about sexual abuse. Finkelhor (1986) further argues that specific programmes ought to be aimed at high risk children and their parents. Through a review of the relevant research and his own findings (Finkelhor, 1979), Finkelhor (1984) has developed a checklist of risk to assist in this task. This high risk checklist appears in various forms (Finkelhor, 1979; Finkelhor, 1984; Finkelhor and Baron, 1986), with seven basic risk factors:

i)   Having a stepfather,
ii)   Living without the mother for any length of time,
iii)   Not being close to the mother,
iv)   The mother being significantly less educated than the father,
v)   No physical affection from the father,
vi)   Low family income, and,
vii)   The child having two or less friends in the neighbourhood.

Those preventative programmes in the United States that Finkelhor (1986) reviewed have tended to concentrate on empowerment programmes for children and adolescents, in the form of teaching them what is and what is not appropriate behaviour towards them. Gilbert (1992) criticises this policy as it tends to place the responsibility for her/his wellbeing almost entirely onto the young person, arguing that primary prevention programmes should be designed to increase the vigilance of parents and teachers, qualitatively displacing the responsibility for the well-being of the young back onto society at large. Gilbert's (1992) conceptualisation serves to illustrate how confusing the concept remains. His perception of primary prevention programmes seems to accord to some extent with Hardiker *et al*'s (1991) concept of secondary prevention in that it assumes the beginnings of abuse. Hardiker *et al* (1991) see a secondary level of prevention as comprising work with individuals who have just acquired client status; principally intervention at an early stage to prevent the need for more high profile intervention later; such things as child and family counselling.

The tertiary level of intervention put forward by Hardiker *et al* (1991) comprises casework to avoid the worst effects of chronic family difficulties. In essence this is the predominant mode of child protection work in that it perceives of the family as dysfunctional and seeks to initiate change either in the structure of the family (the removal of the perpetrator or the victim) or in the family patterns of behaviour (to end the abuse). Hardiker *et al* (1991) also put forward a quaternary level of prevention. This occurs when a child has been removed from home and involves intensive intervention in the family to create the conditions that will enable the child to return home. However, Hardiker *et al* (1991) make clear that it is not always possible to locate any specific intervention exactly within one of these categories. Fuller (1992) makes the telling point that practitioners have a specific view of prevention that routinely places it in opposition to statutory work. He goes on to argue that not only do practitioners see prevention and protection as dichotomously opposed, but they also feel that prevention is routinely pushed off the agenda through the pressure of crisis protection work. The implication is that if only more attention was paid to prevention then less children would be in need of crisis interventions. The findings of the current research tend to reinforce this view. Although there was some ambivalence as to what was seen as prevention, the social workers tended to draw upon cyclical models of adolescent sexual abuse that revolved around concepts of maternal failure to protect. Within this context the social workers were critical of their departments for being primarily reactive to child protection crises, rather than being proactively involved in preventative work. They placed great emphasis on the need for the provision of adequate aftermath services as a form of prevention of sexual abuse to the next generation and argued that resources ought to be made available. The rationale they gave for additional resources to be provided for aftermath work clearly illustrates two distinct points. Firstly, the social workers felt their practice to be under-resourced and felt that all aspects of the work other than crisis intervention needed to be 'justified' in terms of economy and effectiveness. In this case the implication is that such 'preventative' aftermath work will produce long-term cost benefits to the organisation through the future reduction of workloads, within the context of a child protection benefit of fewer girls from the next generation being sexually abused. Secondly, the social workers perceptions were located within a concept of 'cycles of abuse' that ascribes a specific role of protection to mothers. This conceptualisation also implies the normality of the generational replication of heterosexual reproductive relationships, which immediately questions the value of aftermath work for those girls who are lesbian, infertile or otherwise unlikely to form such relationships.

A more ambivalent response was gained from social services managers. They saw prevention in two ways. Firstly, they expressed a view similar to that of practitioners, except that unlike the practitioners they had little idea of exactly what measures would constitute prevention.

> In reality what they [social workers] are doing is putting out fires, so prevention is always taken as second best as it were...I think we've probably got it the wrong way round...because if you put in preventative resources at a very much earlier stage...it can go some way to alleviate some of the problems that you find later on. (Manager).

The alternative management view remained closer to Hardiker *et al*'s (1991) rejection of the dichotomy between prevention and protection. One manager saw one role of child protection being the prevention of further harm. Parton (1991) contends that there has been a gradual divorce between child care processes and child protection systems. The manager, however, saw child care and child protection as occurring on a continuum with preventative measures occurring at various points. His main emphasis was that if you protect a child from harm you are caring for that child, whilst simultaneously preventing that harm occurring.

The major problem with any discussion of prevention is that different individuals locate the concept at different points in the processes of child care and child protection. The official policy of both the authorities in the sample was a reactive one of crisis management, despite the fact that a strategic manager in Children and Families in one of them was particularly in favour of developing primary prevention programmes. In other local authorities[7], primary prevention programmes have been developed to a greater extent. The social workers, however, were highly critical of their departments' policies and felt that the resourcing of preventative programmes ought to be prioritised to a far greater extent, although their conceptualisation of prevention conflated notions of reduction of risk for children and adolescents in the present and the reduction of risk for future generations of girls, and appeared to be embedded in concepts of 'cycles of abuse'[8] that are shown to be relatively difficult to sustain (Hooper, 1995).

The Resourcing of Child Protection

The discussion of resourcing in terms of child protection, needs to be seen in the light of the resourcing of public services generally. It can be argued that child protection is resourced from a multiplicity of points within the statutory and voluntary sectors. However, within the context of social worker perceptions and practice the resourcing of particular aspects of child protection from sources other than social services departments is only of oblique interest. For example, the ways in which the voluntary sector resources specific initiatives is of interest only in the ways in which it shapes the provision of external resources the social worker can draw upon to accomplish her/his child protection task. Therefore, the discussion of the resourcing of child protection at this point will confine itself to a discussion of the impact of the direct resourcing of social services child protection on the practice of social workers dealing with specific child protection cases involving the familial sexual abuse of adolescent girls.

The managers understood that social workers' child protection practice was circumscribed by resource constraints in the sense that resources were meagre and there was not enough money in the system, a situation they saw as continuing to worsen as Standard Spending Assessments were constantly being squeezed by central government. Some social workers concurred with that analysis, seeing under-resourcing as a chronic problem that severely constrained their practice in a myriad of ways:

> Not enough money, not enough workers, not enough manpower, not enough training, not enough facilities, not enough buildings, everything. (SW).

Others gave more specific examples of the ways in which they saw under-resourcing as limiting their practice. In essence, they felt that a lack of resources meant constant pressure on their time. One part-time social worker, for example, had done some research for Barnado's in her own time and it was recognised by her department as of value to them, yet they were not in a position to grant her any time off to write it up.

Similar issues emerged when the social workers were asked about the time and space allowed them within the work environment for reading such things as research reports. One worker felt that social workers tended to give lack of time as an excuse for not reading up on relevant research, arguing that if a piece of research was relevant to a case you were dealing with then you ought to read it, although she acknowledged that the opportunity to do so depended to a great extent upon the knowledge that such research existed. She further argued that it was useful to have an individual employed solely to gather together research and other useful material to make it available to workers. Although this view was a little more sophisticated than those offered by most of the social workers in that it suggested a remedy, it nevertheless served to illustrate the lack of prominence given to reading in social services offices. The concept of reading as part of the enterprise of social work appeared almost non-existent, and social workers reported that any research they read up on was done almost entirely in their own time. This articulates closely with the findings of Fisher (1995), who found little evidence of social workers across all aspects of child protection reading research literature, despite the injunction in the guidance to keep up to date with current research (DoH, 1988; section 4.3), and the assumptions inherent in government guidance (DoH, 1991c, para.5.16) that social workers will be able to acquire a complete understanding of the child and family situation. Fisher (1995) also found that little of the workers' knowledge base derived from their qualifying training. Rather it came to some extent from their in service training but primarily through their own practice, including their supervision, and from official governmental and departmental guidance. He identifies certain problems accruing from this, notably that the official guidance can tend to distil research findings in ways that can tend towards oversimplification. For example, government guidance (DoH, 1991d, Pg.56) states that there is no known cure for sexually abusive behaviour, whereas the multiplicity of research findings do not offer such a conclusive view. Among the principal reasons Fisher (1995) argues that social workers do not read research literature was the overwhelming pressure of heavy caseloads that simply did not leave time within the working day for reading. He also found that social workers tended not to read very much academic material relating to child protection in their own time. Arguments well documented elsewhere in terms of the emotional stress of the work would suggest that child protection social workers need their time away from work to remove themselves entirely from all aspects of the work. In the current research something of an exception to this apparently general rule of a non-reading office culture emerged. One area team had in place an arrangement to spend one hour per week in a team seminar. The seminar was used by those who had been on courses or had come across a difficult problem to share their views with the team as a whole. This was seen as a positive thing by the team members, but as a rather haphazard way for improving practice knowledge.

The social workers also saw resource constraints as impacting upon more practical aspects of their work. Both local authorities had initiated strict mileage allowances upon staff of around eighty miles per week, leaving them unable to claim back the costs of any further distance travelled. Those workers in predominantly rural areas found it difficult to fit their initial investigations and other day-to-day visits within the allowance, although some of them suggested it encouraged them to make more efficient use of their cars. Those social workers in a particular area that contained a large military establishment found the interplay between the mileage allowance and the transitory nature of military populations problematic. In many of the cases they dealt with extended family support networks were geographically widely dispersed and thus suitable placements for the young people were often a considerable distance from the area office, even at the other end of the country. Statutory visits to these young people, if made by car, used up a considerable proportion of a worker's annual mileage allowance. The workers in such situations thus had to negotiate with the department for a special mileage allowance for those journeys. Similar problems were experienced in terms of foster placements in rural areas, in that suitable families were few and geographically widespread. This often meant that when a social worker applied for a Care Order the only suitable foster placement was many miles both from the young person's home and the area office. The social worker, in first visiting the potential foster family, then escorting the young person there and later making statutory visits, would make a massive incursion into her/his mileage allowance, yet it would be a situation of little choice. In some of the rural areas this led to the seemingly bizarre situation that young people from one area were being accommodated in foster homes in another, whilst young people from the second area were being accommodated in the first. Although there are sound arguments that in some cases it is preferable to place some considerable distance between a sexually abused teenage girl and her abuser, [9] from a resource only perspective it would appear logical to move the clients between placements to cut down on social worker travelling distance, but as one social worker said:

> ...you can't just suddenly do a reshuffle just for the sake of the social workers (SW).

The principal problem the social workers encountered with strict limitations on mileage allowances was that they felt their autonomy in terms of defining their own work schedules was significantly compromised. The same limitations applied to management, and the managers felt a similar constraint on their autonomy, in that they saw mileage allowance limitations curtailing their capacity to attend meetings with each other and with front-line staff, reducing the level of support they could offer to workers in the field.

The social workers were also concerned over the closely related issue of 'dead time', the time spent travelling between sites. Although they recognised that central management saw the necessity of such travel, to and from home visits etc., they felt that councillors were constantly pressuring their departments to reduce the amount of time individual social workers spent travelling. One social worker saw travelling time as beneficial in that it gave her time to assess the case she had just been dealing with and to prepare for the next one, although her view was atypical. Most of the social workers felt that far too much time was spent travelling from place to place and not enough time spent actually dealing with cases, although none of them saw how this could be avoided, especially in rural areas. In respect of 'dead' time the social workers clearly saw elected members following an agenda that failed to fully appreciate the complexities of the social worker-client relationship. In one team, for example, two workers had ongoing cases in a town about twenty-five miles from the area office. Councillors saw it as more sensible to have one worker deal with both families, but in each case the Initial Case Conference had designated the preferred gender of the worker, one female and one male, thus precluding a change of worker for either family. The social workers felt that councillors failed to appreciate issues of client choice and participation, making clear that unless the client requested it, it would be difficult to justify a change of key worker.

The social workers found other problems arising out of long distance visits. If a social worker was making a statutory visit to a placement at the other end of the country, it could well mean that (s)he would be absent from the office for up to two days. As all the time spent both on the visit and travelling to and from the visit counted as time spent at work, this would leave her/him with one or two days lieu time. One consequence of this would be to temporarily reduce staffing levels for up to four days because of a single statutory visit. In the area office that covered the military establishment, the social workers felt that the relatively high numbers of such visits and the consequent temporary staff shortages were not matched by an enhanced establishment of social workers. They felt that the social services department refused to acknowledge the specific temporal-geographical problems associated with child protection work in an area containing a high proportion of military families.

The questions of mileage, travelling time and finding foster placements were seen as a greater constraint on practice in rural areas than in the more urban areas. One resource issue, however, seemed to cut across any rural-urban divide; that of caseloads. Most social workers felt that caseloads were too high, and several pointed out that they were working well above agreed caseload limits. The research (Dingwall, 1989; Hallett, 1995) suggests this is a widespread and enduring problem detrimentally affecting practice. The principal effect this seemed to have was that of impacting upon the time that could be spent on specific cases. The social workers variously commented 'it would be nice to have time to plan each visit properly' (SW), 'we all work well over hours' (SW), and:

> I never think anything that I'm doing has enough time actually, so this case is not unusual (SW).

Not all the social workers felt that caseloads were perennially too high. Some saw them in terms of peaks and troughs, the development of their own time management skills, and techniques of ordering their routine work to leave spaces for emergencies. Most of the social workers, nevertheless, thought that caseloads were too high, placing them under constant pressure in terms of the time they could spend on any individual task.

The social workers' response to having one particular resource demand met was one of ambivalence. In one area team, they had pressured management to provide them with mobile phones to enable them to maintain contact with the office when out in difficult situations such as removing young people from the family home. The provision of the phones created some problems. Social workers who were duty workers for the day began to be expected to go out on routine visits as they would remain contactable via the mobile phone. This was seen as an added pressure that one worker concisely summarised as seriously damaging her capacity to concentrate on the routine case visit as she was constantly anticipating the next emergency.

One area that caused concern to both social workers and managers was the reduction within social services departments of support staff for front-line workers. Managers saw this as an attempt by councillors to meet budget requirements without cutting back on the numbers of social workers, but both managers and social workers saw the impact of a reduction in support staff along with the increased amount of paperwork involved with child protection procedures post-Children Act reducing the amount of time social workers were able to spend with their clients.

A small number of the social workers felt that child protection was not underfunded, rather it was the deployment of resources that was sometimes at fault. One social worker said that in his team resourcing was not a problem. He felt that the staffing of teams ought to take into account gender issues, and that the team he worked in was a good team, partly because there was a gender mix, that allowed the option of a female or a male key worker as appropriate for individual cases. He did go on to admit that on occasions cases simply had to be given to individuals regardless of gender simply due to caseload levels, and when discussing a particular case it became apparent that resource issues did impact upon it at several points. His client, a girl who self-referred, had to be asked to return to the area office the following day to see the duty officer as when she first came in the duty officer was busy on another investigation and there was no-one available to see her. Also, although he was the key worker most of the work done with the girl was done by an (unqualified) family worker, both for reasons of gender and the fact that he did not have time. The form and duration of therapeutic care that the girl received involved protracted arguments within social services and beyond in respect of its cost. This suggests that even those social workers that did not see resource limitations as a particular issue found that their practice was to some degree shaped by resource constraints. Most of the social workers believed that the resourcing of child protection had worsened in recent years. Many of them pointed to a reduction in the level of in-service training from professional development courses to a more simple skills training [10] as a prime example of increasing resource constraints.

The discussion of the resourcing of child protection clearly involved the deployment of resources and is thus to a greater or lesser degree inextricably entwined with issues of organisational priority. It is also clear that the impact of resource deployment on specific cases varies a great deal. The discussion of mileage allowances, for example, illustrated the role that could be played by the team manager in subverting instructions from the department's centre. The degree to which that particular team manager influenced the issue, however, cannot be known for sure. It appeared in the account of one social worker in that team, and may in part reflect an attitude that emerged in many places in the research; that social workers saw the team manager as an individual who understood and supported what they were trying to do, whereas central management were seen as out of touch and more interested in policies and procedures than in the actualities of child protection work and the needs of familially sexually abused adolescent girls.

Above and beyond any issues of the deployment of resources was a genuinely felt sense of (worsening) underfunding. Social workers saw the opportunities for post-qualification training being diminished, saw themselves as having caseloads that precluded them spending as much time as they would wish with individual clients and saw restrictions on mileage allowances as undermining their capacity to make home visits on the basis of the client's best interests. There seemed to be a sense in which they felt besieged through a lack of funding. One social worker made clear that however you dress it up resources means only one thing:

I think anybody who is naive enough to believe that resources don't equal money is living in cloud cuckoo land. (SW).

The current research shows there are particular consequences of underfunding. The social workers in the study felt that their ongoing training needs were not being met as well they ought to be and that they were not given the time and space to acquaint themselves with the results of contemporary child sexual abuse and child protection practice research. This is a significant problem in child protection work in the area of child sexual abuse as it is a rapidly changing field both in terms of understanding of the issues and in terms of practice. Ongoing training is thus essential if the girls who are the victims of the abuse are to get the best possible quality of service. Fisher (1995) found that child sexual abuse was to some extent the most problematic area of child protection for social workers in respect of their knowledge base. There was little time and space for them to read the relevant research literature, yet official guidance (DoH, 1988; DoH, 1990a; DoH, 1991a, 1991b, 1991c) was seen by workers as being more relevant to physical abuse and neglect than sexual abuse. What guidance there was (DoH, 1991d) was often seen to offer advice that appeared at odds with their own practice experience, leading to some degree of confusion as to how best to proceed in some cases. Fisher (1995) also found that amongst some other members of the professional network, there was a lack of knowledge even of the governmental guidance and official procedures. The need for training in terms of enhancing professionals' understanding of the causes and signs of child sexual abuse, the benefits and disbenefits of specific intervention practices, and an intimate knowledge of the procedures is thus of paramount importance.

The central issue for the social workers in terms of resources was the limitation on the time they were able to spend with their clients. Two distinct but inter-related consequences flow from this. Firstly, the morale of these social workers dealing with sexually abused adolescent girls was not good; they seemed to have something of a siege mentality, and secondly best practice was not always possible or even known. This is a strong indication that girls in this situation may not be getting the service they deserve from social services departments.

Child Protection Procedures

At one level child protection procedures must be seen as the principal enabling factors for child protection to take place, as without any officially recognised procedures the whole concept of a child protection process would collapse. The child protection procedures currently in place derive from the Children Act 1989, and associated government guidance (DoH, 1991a; DoH, 1991b; DoH, 1991c; DoH, 1991d), and are mediated via local procedures and practice guidance as determined by social services departments and Area Child Protection Committees. The procedures comprise both legal requirements of social workers in terms of action and paperwork at various points in the process, and practice guidance. The purpose of any set of welfare procedures is that they should lead to satisfactory outcomes (Galligan, 1992), although one needs to be aware that some procedures may be followed by some workers 'more in the letter than in the spirit' (Farmer and Parker, 1991, Pg.189). The stated purpose of child protection procedures is that they:

> should provide appropriate training and guidance to ensure that all professionals can recognize signs of abuse and respond accordingly. (DoH, 1991c, para. 5.11.12).

Howe (1986, 1991a, 1991b) sees the primary purpose of procedures as providing an embodiment of the purposes and values of the department that the worker becomes inculcated within, arguing that if workers were completely autonomous without the constraining action of procedures then the department would lack control of the social work task. In this sense the role of procedures can be seen to be 'disciplinary' (Foucault, 1977, 1979). The development of more and more procedures is indicative of a contemporary shift in the definition of social worker from practitioner to manager, illustrated to some extent by the insistence of public inquiries to consistently support administrative practices rather than independent, autonomous, professional judgement (Howe 1991b), as child protection becomes increasingly driven by legislation (Parton, 1991; Parton *et al*, 1997). The consequence is that:

> When social worker meets client, the broad shape of her practice...is defined by statutes, designed by administrators, and driven by managers (Howe, 1991b, Pg.220).

One of the criticisms in respect of child protection procedures prior to the Children Act 1989 was that they were too general (Stevenson, 1989) and thus relatively unhelpful in guiding practice. This begins to question social worker claims to professional status. One of the key defining elements of a profession is that its members make judgements in the course of their work with reference to an accepted body of theory, with only minimal reference to organisational procedures (Greenwood, 1966), professionals being self-regulating rather then managed. Toren (1972) defines social work as an 'heteronomous' profession in that social workers do work in accordance with a whole series of internalised norms or professional ethics, but they are also subject to statutory and administrative procedures and work within an hierarchically designed management structure. Within this overall 'semi-professional' rubric, child protection work is best characterised as 'regulated improvisation' (Farmer and Parker, 1991). Procedures clearly underpin the whole child protection enterprise, with particular significance at a number of points in the process. The first significant point comes immediately after referral, at the point of initial investigation. Government policy (DoH, 1991c) makes clear that:

> ...all referrals, whatever their origin, must be taken seriously and must be considered with an open mind (DoH, 1991c, para.5.11.1).

All the social workers stated that their teams complied, although one of them suggested that some teams in her county ignored anonymous referrals in order to cut down on workloads. The social workers saw the initial investigation as particularly stressful, as it could involve them stepping into the unknown when visiting a girl and her family for the first time. To some extent their anxieties were exacerbated by changes in police procedure. The police have become increasingly reluctant to accompany social workers on initial investigations[11]. The social workers also felt that the criminal justice element of child protection impacted negatively on their capacity to deliver therapeutic services[12], especially in respect of joint video interviews. These two issues, though very different, illustrate the capacity of the criminal justice system to define its own role within child protection.

There were critical points in the process beyond the specific requirements of the criminal justice system where procedures influenced social worker practice. The initial investigation was also the point from which the duty social worker prepared a report and a decision was made as to whether or not there was a child protection case. If it was decided that there was a child protection case, the next step, the final element of the initial stage, was the Initial Child Protection Conference. This was a defining point (Birchall, 1989) at which a suspicion of, or referral for, child abuse became a fully fledged child protection case (Dingwall *et al*, 1983), although this does not take into account the various decisions taken between the initial investigation and the conference by practitioners (Birchall, 1989). This multi-agency forum makes a single decision, whether or not to place a young person's name on the child protection register and under what categories. Both the initial investigation and the Initial Child Protection Conference act as 'filters' (Wattam, 1997a) as far as the child protection process is concerned. The vast majority of initial investigations do not result in registrations. NSPCC estimates for 1993, for example, suggest that only around one in seven investigations for all forms of child abuse result in a child's name being placed on the register (*Times*, 24.3.94). The Initial Child Protection Conference also makes recommendations as to how the child protection intervention is to proceed and appoints a key worker (DoH, 1991c, para.5.15.4). In the cases discussed by the social workers the recommendations ranged from very general to relatively specific instructions to key workers and individuals from other agencies on exactly how to proceed. During the lifetime of the various cases there were periodic Case Reviews, whose principal task was to decide whether or not to alter the young person's registration status and to make further recommendations. In the cases under discussion these reviews took place at intervals of around six months in accordance with government guidelines (DoH, 1991c, para.5.18.1). The decisions of all the conferences and reviews were primarily based on the reports presented to them by the relevant social worker.

The social workers found most initial registrations fairly unproblematic. This seems to contradict some research findings (Dingwall *et al*, 1983; Dale *et al*, 1986; Corby, 1987; Higginson, 1992) that suggest anomalies in registrations with a tendency for conferences to underestimate risk leading to under registration in marginal cases. One manager felt that registration was problematic especially in terms of emotional abuse and to a lesser extent sexual abuse. She also felt that sexual abuse had the added handicap of the need to be sensitive to false allegations, although research does not bear out her fears (Jones and McGraw, 1987; Everson and Boat, 1989). Research in both the United States (Jones and Seig, 1988) and the United Kingdom (Bentovim *et al*, 1988) has shown that a number of false allegations can emanate from custody and access disputes following family breakdown, but in terms of the overall numbers of referrals for sexual abuse these false allegations are not significant enough to warrant concern as far as individual social service departments are concerned[13]

Social workers were less satisfied in respect of decisions taken at later reviews, feeling that some young people were being removed from the register sooner than they ought to be. Statistics seem to bear out this concern. Across all areas of child abuse the research has shown that around a quarter of children removed from the register are reabused (Barth and Berry, 1987; Gibbons *et al*, 1993; Cleaver and Freeman, 1993). The reason for placing a child's or young person's name on the register has traditionally been because they have suffered or are likely to suffer significant harm, although present government guidelines are that the register should not simply contain a list of names of children who have been abused, rather it should list only those children with current child protection needs that are unresolved, and for whom an inter-agency plan has been formulated (DoH, 1991c). Research (Tilley and Burke, 1988; Cann, 1989), however, has shown that different authorities have used different criteria for registering children; registrations also fluctuate widely from area to area, indicating very localised policy differences even within single authorities. One manager suggested this was a consequence of the historical development of registration procedures, although it also suggests that it may have something to do with the differential availability of resources in different areas and does seem to suggest that there is some relationship between registration and resources. Fisher *et al* (1995), in a survey of 138 cases in a single local authority, found that child protection conference decisions to place a child on the register or not, revolved around the judgements they made in four broad areas of concern: those associated with any actual or suspected abuse, the characteristics or social circumstances of the child's carers, perceptions of poor parenting, and the degree of unwillingness of parents to cooperate and work with social workers or doctors. They found these various areas of concern assumed differential degrees of importance in different types of child abuse. In terms of sexual abuse, only two factors appeared to have any significance; evidence of the abuse and the presence/absence of a known abuser (of that child or any other). They also found that some social workers referred to the mother's inability to protect the child, but this would appear to be subsumed to some extent within the issue of ongoing contact between the child and the abuser. One factor that they found was completely ignored in any registration decisions was the wishes or feelings of the girls themselves. Corby and Mills (1986) and Jones *et al* (1987) found that registration was used as a means of procuring extra resources for particular cases. Corby (1987) found that registers were used as an aid to ranking cases in order to ration resources. Although not all social workers shared the view, several accepted that their reports sometimes needed to be creatively constructed to ensure registration even if the worker felt that the risk of abuse had passed. It was for similar reasons that social workers sometimes felt young people were removed from the register too soon.

> You have to manipulate the system and make sure the child stays on the register, because often it is the only way they are actually going to get a service from you (SW).

This perceived need to manipulate the register in some ways questions the role of the register, and questions the significance of registration figures, which have traditionally been seen as an indicator of future risk to specific children (Browne *et al* 1988). It is also in direct contradiction to Government policy, which states that:

> Provision of services should not be dependent on registration (DoH, 1991c, 5.15.4).

Hooper (1992) argues that despite the benefits in terms of an inter-agency child protection plan, placing a young person's name on the register can be detrimental. She argues that registration can act in some instances to erode mothers' confidence in their abilities to protect their children and can leave them with a sense of stigma. She further argues that such negative impacts could be minimised by keeping mothers clearly informed at all times and adopting an holistic view of registration as taking place within a network of social relationships.

The social workers generally found the recommendations of Initial Conferences and Reviews both helpful and sensible, although they indicated several cases where the recommendations had been less helpful. In one area a social worker made the point that all Initial Child Protection Conferences seemed to have a recommendation to carry out a family assessment, yet access to families was often circumscribed by a variety of factors such as the refusal of families to have contact with the social worker, or, that the father was living away. [14] Social workers vary in their capacities and interests and to some extent it was also felt that this is not taken into account either in appointing key workers or in making recommendations.

The Child Protection Conference and Child Protection Register are clearly the procedural pivot of child protection and as such play a significant part in shaping social workers' practice. One manager, however, pointed to a further purpose of Conference recommendations and decisions in that they were used as monitoring devices of such issues as parental drug or alcohol abuse, in an attempt to refine the risk assessment factors available to social workers in future cases.

A series of more general procedural issues also impacted upon social workers' practice. The most straightforward of these was the increase in paperwork since the implementation of the Children Act and the procedures that derive from it. More experienced social workers saw the increase in paperwork in the wake of the new procedures as leaving them able to spend only two thirds the time with clients compared to prior to the Children Act, although other, less experienced, workers saw the procedures as ensuring that they did not forget things. One social worker suggested that the procedures could act to deflect the blame from the victim. Taking the view that families often blame the victim of abuse for the break-up of the family she saw the child protection procedures as providing the authorities as a focus for blame, thus taking some of the pressure off the girl.

A major problem area the social workers encountered in working with sexually abused adolescent girls surrounded the configuration of procedural requirements and the age of the girl. Firstly, the outcome of any application to the courts for a Care Order or Supervision Order tended to bear some relationship to the wishes of the girl. Social workers felt that if a teenage girl didn't want to be accommodated, for example, the courts would tend to comply with her wishes, something that was less likely in the case of a younger child. This reflects the incorporation of the 'Gillick' principle into the Children Act 1989. The Gillick principle derives from a decision of the House of Lords in the Gillick v. West Norfolk and Wisbech Area Health Authority Appeal (1986). The Gillick decision limited the power of parents to make decisions for their mature children. Its embodiment in the Children Act can best be seen in terms of a maturity principle, whereby in any court case affecting the welfare of the child his/her wishes are to be taken into account 'in the light of his age and understanding' (Children Act, 1989 s.1(3(a))), and any child who is sufficiently competent can refuse a medical of psychiatric examination ordered by the court (Children Act, 1989 (s.38(6),s.43(8), s.44(7)). Although not stated in the Act a 'Gillick competent' child may also refuse any medical or psychiatric examination required by a local authority. In such a case the child's right to refuse derives directly from the Gillick decision. Although Freeman (1992) notes that the official guidance (DoH, 1991c) fails to fully confront the issue of competence, especially in the area of familialy sexually abused adolescent girls, the social workers found that the courts tended to equate competence with age, with few other considerations. [15]

The social workers were very concerned in terms of mechanisms to deal with the aftermath of abuse for girls reaching the age of eighteen and beyond. Although if the girl had been subject to a Care Order the social services department had a responsibility to assist and befriend her until the age of twenty one, there was no set of procedures operating in either department for continuity of social work input once girls reach the statutory age limit of the child protection process. They were automatically removed from the register and no process existed in either authority for a transfer across to adult therapeutic services[16].

The social workers stressed the uniqueness of each case, and made it clear that in some ways every client was a guinea pig. They saw the value of the procedural element of child protection in providing an organisational framework for their child protection activities. They also saw the procedures as limiting the actions they could take. They saw procedures as guiding practice, but without providing them with all the answers on how best to proceed.

Cultural Factors

The whole enterprise of child protection work with sexually abused adolescent girls is located within discourses of family, motherhood, and appropriate sexual behaviour. Furthermore, the social workers in the sample came from a variety of backgrounds, but could generally be seen as middle-class, either from families of origin or because of their professional training and education. One thus needs to bear in mind that their interpretation of specific elements in particular cases and their consequent construction of those cases would in some way be mediated through their class and professional norms and expectations. In effect, their practice could be seen to be shaped to some extent through a culture of social work, that revolved around a series of both class and professional values. There were some gendered differences in practice[17], although these seemed to focus on practical issues in terms of worker/client interaction rather than on distinctly different gendered approaches to the work.

The culture of social work *per se* was most obvious in the collegial atmosphere of the area offices and the use of supervision and peer support systems. The interpretation of data through the mediation of various cultural factors was most clearly apparent in the ways in which referrals were dealt with.

The Referral Process

Referrals in respect of all forms of child abuse are made to social services from a variety of sources, and in these two authorities there was little evidence to suggest that any referrals were not acted upon in terms of triggering an initial investigation. As Wattam (1992) makes clear, a referral amounts to more than an individual informing social services of their suspicions of abuse. It is a process comprising the transmission of information; a process with particular outcomes.

The cases that the social workers were dealing with had been referred to social services from five sources:

- Hearsay referrals from neighbours,
- Referrals from the girl's mother,
- Referrals from teachers,
- Self-referrals,
- Referral from social services in Northern Ireland.

Although the sample was too small to allow any evaluation of the typicality of the sources of referral, they did not seem unusual. Research (Farmer and Owen, 1995; Hallett, 1995; Gibbons *et al*, 1995) points to referrals coming from a variety of sources, the vast majority from children themselves, their mothers or welfare professionals. The social workers and their managers saw referrals as tending to fall into three broad categories:

- Those from professionals or other agencies,
- Self referrals,
- Those from other members of the public.

Referrals from professionals were acted upon quickly and it was difficult to determine any preconceptions on the part of the social workers, although a referral from social services in Northern Ireland was criticised by the social worker as lacking detailed information. She said that greater detail on that referral would have prevented her duplicating much of the initial work already carried out in Northern Ireland.

Social workers appeared more circumspect about referrals from members of the public, often seeming, explicitly or implicitly, to question the motive of the referee. Some referrals from the general public were even seen as 'genuinely malicious' (SW). This reflects the findings of Hallett (1995), who found practitioners often felt referrals from the general public were unclear or possibly malicious. The element of suspicion of referrals from the general public tends to support Wattam's (1991) argument in that although all referrals lead to an initial investigation, the direction of that investigation and the investment of time and energy in it by the social worker may be influenced and shaped by the status of the referee. None of the social workers said that they believed the referrals in the cases under discussion were malicious or that they conducted any initial investigation with less commitment than any other, and no evidence emerged to suggest they consciously approached initial investigations differently on the basis of the status of the referee. However, the typification of a referee as untrustworthy or malicious may well have unconsciously influenced their degree of commitment, and, crucially, the interpretation they placed on the information gathered from that investigation. At a practical level the most difficult referrals to investigate were hearsay referrals, as they involved a process of backtracking in order to see where the referee acquired his/her information. It was felt that the easiest referrals to deal with were self-referrals, as in these cases the girl would already be at the point of disclosure, and an initial interview with her would be less difficult to handle than with a girl who had not yet reached that point.

One social worker strongly criticised the voluntary sector. She received a referral of sexual abuse from a girl's school. Upon investigation it transpired that the girl had disclosed abuse by her adoptive grandfather a year earlier, and her mother had contacted Childline. Childline had taken the name and address and given the mother some advice. However, they had not contacted social services, which the social worker felt was irresponsible in that the girl was left for a year without access to social work support. The social worker's criticism indicates a defence of the boundaries of her profession. Her criticism appeared to stem from a view that child protection ought to be solely 'owned' by the professional network of which she was a part, and she seemed to lack any appreciation of the need for confidentiality at the heart of a telephone helpline such as Childline. In maintaining caller confidentiality Childline is operating in ways exactly similar to other voluntary organisations such as Rape Crisis and the Samaritans, and is granting a degree of control of information to individuals (abused children and non-abusing family members) who may be living in an environment where lack of personal autonomy is a defining feature.

Supervision and Peer Support

Child protection work is principally carried out by social workers on an individual basis, although there is some co-working at times. Alongside this idea of autonomous professional practice there have developed both formal and informal systems of support.

The concept of formal supervision is one element that differentiates social work from older established professions such as medicine or the law, wherein professional practice is monitored in less hierarchically organised systems of peer review. The basic supervision structure meant that all social workers were formally supervised by either their team manager or a senior social worker, and senior social workers were supervised by their team manager. Formal supervision fulfils a variety of roles in professional social work. In a functionalist analysis of the degree to which social work could be considered a profession, Toren (1972) identifies two distinct aspects of supervision. Firstly, formal supervision could be seen as fulfilling an administrative function in that it provides the supervisor, on behalf of the organisation, the opportunity to monitor the work of the supervisee. Secondly, supervision has an educative function; it provides the organisation with a mechanism for imparting knowledge to the supervisee. Westheimer (1977), Payne (1979) and Brown (1984) refine the administrative function of supervision into a managerial function in that not only does the supervisor monitor the work of the supervisee, but (s)he also acts as a guide and source of information for the supervisee. Gadsby Waters (1992) defines the administrative or managerial function of supervision as:

> ...that involved with the checking, monitoring and evaluating of work to ensure that it is quantitatively and qualitatively in accordance with agency procedures (Gadsby Waters, 1992, Pg.6).

The close relationship between the administrative and the educative function of supervision is drawn out by Kadushin (1985), who makes clear that they both have the objective of providing the best possible service to the client; the educative aspect of supervision he equates to training. This aspect of training is taken up by Gadsby Waters (1992) who sees the educative function of supervision as being concerned with the transmission and sharing of the various knowledges and competences that the social worker requires in her/his work.

Gadsby Waters (1992) also identifies two other aspects of formal supervision; the supportive or enabling function, and the professional function. She derives the latter category from the work of Westheimer (1977), who stressed the personal development aspect of professionalism and the role supervision can play in this, and from Kadushin (1977), who distinguished the professional element of supervision as that which was concerned with worker development where the focus was job-related, rather than worker-related. From these two sources she develops the idea of the professional function of supervision as that which contributes to the development of the worker as a professional, a concept which remains woolly, primarily because the 'professional' function of supervision need not be distinguished from the educative and the supportive functions.

More importantly Gadsby Waters (1992) goes on to discuss the supportive or enabling function of supervision. Following Payne and Scott (1982) she defines the supportive or enabling function of supervision as:

> ...a recognition of the inherently stressful nature of social work and the need to reduce the stresses that impair worker's ability to give effective help (Gadsby Waters, 1992, Pg.7).

This aspect of supervision is that which social workers see as the central feature of supervision (Parsloe and Stevenson, 1978; Satyamurti, 1981). The reasons for this are plain. In general terms child abuse work is stressful and inadequate supervision can fail to relieve that stress leading to worker 'burn-out' or 'defensive' social work practice. Gadsby Waters (1992) cites both of these as being debilitating to the worker in both personal and professional terms, and, in the final analysis, problematic for the quality of service provided to clients. In sexual abuse work the gender of the worker has been identified as problematic, in terms of male worker guilt and female worker anti-male hostility (Hallett and Stevenson, 1980), and in terms of the self-perceptions of male workers as replicating the abuse (Vizard and Tranter, 1988a). Without adequate supervision this could diminish the capacity of individual workers to accomplish their child protection tasks.

Formal supervision was in place in all the area teams, and varied from fortnightly to three-weekly dependent upon the experience of the worker. Supervision of social workers was by either the team manager or a senior social worker. The role of formal supervision was basically a mixture of caseload assessment and professional development, and the social workers were satisfied though relatively unenthusiastic about it. As far as acting to amend practice in specific cases the impact of formal supervision was negligible.

As well as formal supervision sessions social workers also had access to their team managers and senior social workers on a day-to-day basis. On this day-to-day basis workers had the opportunity to seek advice and guidance from their supervisor and use her/him as a second opinion on difficult issues. This was highly valued by the social workers in contrast to the findings of Farmer and Owen (1995) that found supervision of social workers in child protection to be poor, with almost a quarter of social workers feeling dissatisfied with their supervision and a further third seeing substantial gaps in their supervision, leaving them unfocussed and unsure of themselves and often having to 'go it alone'. The principal complaints of the workers in Farmer and Owen's (1995) sample was that supervision often failed to provide them with emotional support and little time was given over to the discussion of specific cases. Further there was some criticism of the inexperience of supervisors in child protection work. The importance of this aspect of the social worker/supervisor relationship was recognised in one of the authorities in the current research in that careful consideration was given to the relevant expertises of the worker and the supervisor so that any possible weaknesses in the worker were compensated for by the expertise of the supervisor. In practical terms this advice had some effect even to the point where the supervisor would advise closing a case down.

The other role that team managers and senior social workers had in terms of worker support was that of being available to de-brief workers after they have been out on a difficult visit. This was seen to be at its most valuable if the worker had been out on an after-hours visit and had had serious sexual abuse disclosed to her/him. As more has been learnt in respect of child sexual abuse there has been a growing recognition of the stresses incurred not only on victims and their families, but also on practitioners, and it has long been recognised that social services departments must provide emotional and professional support to the social workers involved (Richardson, 1989). Through their practice social workers become privy to the painful realities of some adolescent's lives (Williamson and Butler, 1995). The alternative of having to keep the information to ones-self was seen as intolerable. One senior social worker who had experience both of receiving and of providing support made the point that whenever a social worker went out on a difficult visit either she or the team manager would be in the office when the worker returned so that the worker would not have to hold on to difficult information. She stressed that if that worker did not need de-briefing then perhaps (s)he was in the wrong profession:

> I think the day that we go out and deal with a very painful case for a child and come back and are not shocked is the day that we need to be thinking about what we are doing. (SW).

She told of a visit she had been out on that left her feeling traumatised, and the benefit she derived from her team manager and her colleagues remaining in the office with her discussing the case well into the evening.

This emphasises something very closely related to informal supervision and support; the mutual support social workers received from their peers. This support took three forms. Firstly, there was the debriefing when colleagues had been out on a difficult case. Secondly, there was a general sharing of ideas. This would generally stem from someone asking for ideas in relation to a specific case they were dealing with, rather than ideas and assistance being gratuitously offered. This reinforces Pithouse's (1987) argument that social work offices can be conceived of as micro-systems, comprising persons of equal status. Thirdly, there was support in the form of friendship and a tight knit micro-community. Again this is in line with Pithouse's (1987) view that the Area office as forms 'a close-knit collegial group' (Pithouse, 1987, Pg.24), offering mutual support and mutually defining appropriate professional practice.

The social workers were of the view that without these forms of support the distressing nature of child abuse in general and sexual abuse in particular, would leave them unable to do the job at all. The sharing of ideas was also seen as a useful informal way of enhancing the skill and knowledge base of individual social workers.

Summary

Several aspects of the organisation of social services child protection work and the operation of child protection procedures impacted upon the practice of social workers dealing with child protection cases involving the familial sexual abuse of adolescent girls. Some of these influences are endemic to child protection work generally, others are more specifically related to this client group.

In general terms the organisational structure of child protection could be seen as relatively open and enabling. The work was accomplished within an organisational and management structure, and that structure placed decision-making about specific issues at specific points in the organisation. Decision-making in respect of policy was located in senior management and to some extent with elected members within parameters set by central government.

Decision-making in respect of individual cases was taken at as a low a level as possible. Within the parameters set by procedural imperatives such as statutory procedures and Conference recommendations, practice decisions were made by social workers. The social workers were supported in their decision-making by what was seen by both themselves and management as a relatively open organisational structure. This was offset, however, by a perception on the part of social workers that senior management was preoccupied with administration and procedures rather than the 'realities' of child protection work.

More directly, the levels of access and the availability of various resources in the statutory and the voluntary sectors heavily influenced the social workers' practice. They made day-to-day decisions on the basis of what was available.

Significant findings emerged regarding the operation of the various systems involved in child protection. Firstly, there was a great deal of concern amongst social workers over the ways in which resources within social services were prioritised. This was particularly apparent in respect of preventative work. Although the concept is relatively vague, social workers had a fairly clear idea of what constitutes prevention as far as adolescent sexual abuse is concerned. Primarily, they saw preventative work as aftermath work that both assisted the girl in a full recovery to prevent her from experiencing other problems later, and in terms of breaking the cycle of maternal non-protection, and so potentially preventing her future daughters from being sexually abused.

This suggests a degree of conflation of concepts of prevention by the social workers, between the prevention of further abuse to those already abused girls in the cases they were dealing with, and the prevention of abuse of further unknown girls of a future generation. As far as enhancing the ongoing protection of already sexually abused girls is concerned a whole range of services can be useful. The issue of prevention in terms of preventing the abuse of future generations from sexual abuse is entirely different, and from the social workers perspective appeared to be intimately configured with the concept of a 'cycle of abuse'. The routine acceptance of the concept of a 'cycle of abuse' as at least a partial explanation for child sexual abuse by the social workers in the study emphasised the power of patriarchal and professional normative perspectives within a predominantly female sample, and succinctly illustrated their tendency towards the use of pathological models of child sexual abuse.

The overwhelming experience of social workers was that aftermath work was afforded a very low priority, and that it was basically the initial stages of child protection where the vast majority of effort was expended. This they saw as a crisis-management approach to child protection, with a mistaken deployment of resources.

Social workers were also very sensitive to the fact that they carried high caseloads. They felt themselves to be overworked to the point that they were not always sure that they are performing their child protection tasks as well as their clients deserved. Added to this was the whole issue of procedures. The child protection procedures clearly pointed to a limitation on the autonomy of social workers even without the various resource constraints that impacted upon their work. The procedures were not, however, written in tablets of stone. There was room for mediation and interpretation and in some areas.

It was clear in an overall sense that certain procedural and organisational aspects were enabling factors as far as the work was concerned. Further, both of the authorities in the sample, seemed to have structures or processes in place for information to be passed upwards from front-line workers to senior management as part of the policy review process. This suggested that policy, at least to some extent, would actually confront the realities of working in child protection. It was also clear, however, that the social services departments were managerially driven, and that organisational requirements in terms of fiscal prudence, filling in the right forms, and arranging meetings such as Conferences within prescribed time limits, were dominant over social worker autonomy (Bamford, 1990; Kelly, 1991).

Social work is primarily a 'discursive' profession. Talk is central to a great deal of the therapeutic work in child protection in terms of disclosure and confronting the realities of abuse. This discursive nature is also reflected in intra-team support systems, both in terms of sharing 'difficult' or painful revelations, and in terms of sharing knowledge. Social work is also a predominantly middle-class profession. The fact that social work is both a middle-class and a discursive profession tends to explain why those referrals from neighbours or other non-professionals were treated with more circumspection than those from professionals such as GPs. Although all referrals tend to be relatively lacking in detail it may well be that the social workers exhibited an overly suspicious view of the motives of lay people in making referrals.

4 Practice and the actions of other agencies

Introduction

The child protection practice of social workers both shapes and is shaped to a degree by the practice of other professionals. This occurs within a complex of relationships at both a formal and a personal level, under a general rubric of interagency coordination. It indicates that both elements of structure (in terms of formal coordination procedures) and individual agency (in terms of personal interprofessional relationships) are crucial to an understanding of the impact of the actions of professionals from other agencies on the child protection work of social workers (Giddens, 1984; Sibeon, 1991).

The key issue to confront is that of how the social workers perceived of the actions of other agencies and other professionals impacting upon their child protection work in respect of familialy sexually abused adolescent girls. This necessitates an examination of the ways in which formal imperatives to coordination were mediated through the actions of specific professionals, and how they were intersected by aspects of the various interpersonal relationships the social workers enjoyed with professionals from other agencies (Challis, 1988). The importance of such an approach is stressed by Gough *et al* (1987) and Tibbitt (1983), who argued that 'interorganisational relationships occur through the interactions of individuals' (Tibbitt, 1983, Pg.166). Birchall with Hallett (1995) make clear the lack of attention paid to the effects of cooperation and coordination in child protection on a range of themes such as the domain of expertise and the status of different professionals within various agencies. Hallett (1995) found that the success of collaborative activity was largely dependent upon the quality of the interpersonal relationships between professionals from different agencies.

The relationship between the practice of other professionals and the practice of social workers can be seen to comprise two distinct elements; those issues surrounding referrals by professionals, and those issues concerning the operation of the child protection network from the initial investigation stage onwards.

Significant proportions of sexual abuse referrals in respect of adolescent girls come from professionals from other agencies (Gibbons *et al*, 1995; Hallett, 1995). Some girls disclose directly to a trusted adult such as a teacher or GP. Others disclose indirectly through alluding to something being wrong at home or by exhibiting signs of abuse, such as self-harming, aggressive behaviour, clinical depression or specific types of physical injury (Oppenheimer *et al*, 1985; Palmer *et al*, 1990; Briere, 1992; Kendall-Tackett *et al*, 1993). Although these signs are not themselves conclusive of sexual abuse having taken place, they should be enough to raise the suspicions of professionals such as teachers and GPs. At this stage the relationship between these other professionals and social workers is a relatively one way process. They either make a referral to social services, triggering social services to initiate the child protection process, or they do not. Research (Peters *et al*, 1986; Siegal *et al*, 1987; Kelly *et al*, 1991) shows that most incidents of sexual abuse never come to the attention of social services. This emphasises the need for teachers, GPs, and other professionals to be made more aware of the signs of sexual abuse, the seriousness of its consequences, and the procedures for reporting their suspicion to social services. The referral process thus needs to be examined in terms of the ways in which other professionals refer suspicions of sexual abuse to social services, the meanings such referrals have for social workers, and how such referrals impact upon social work practice. This clearly involves social worker perspectives on both the credibility of such referrals and social workers' perceptions of the possible shortcomings of other professionals to either recognise the signs of abuse or to report them.

Once the child protection process has been initiated a more dynamic and altogether more complex web of interagency relationships comes into play in the form of the child protection network. The operation of the child protection network is located firmly within the concept of inter-agency coordination, and the operation of mandated interagency procedures. The role of the Area Child Protection Committee in enforcing the mandate is made very clear by one social services manager.

> People in general work to the procedures, because the ACPC try to keep a good overview of what is going on (Manager)

The operation of the network is based upon a perceived need for the sharing of expertise at various stages of the child protection process, in terms of information sharing (at Child Protection Conferences etc.) and in terms of intervention itself (the development of criminal prosecutions by the police, the coordination of educational and psychological services etc.).

The process of mandated coordination in child protection may have some negative effects in terms of practitioner resentment. Weiss (1981) points to the tendency of organisations to pull back from cooperative activity whenever possible, and Blyth and Milner (1990) suggest that professionals would prefer to work alone. Hallett (1993) goes further, arguing that the different protagonists in the child protection network may differ in both their desire to accept elements of cooperation, and in their capacity to resist exhortations to cooperate. Degrees of resistance and resentment may relate to issues of relative status, such as levels of professional autonomy, working conditions and rates of pay, both within and across organisations (Woodhouse and Pengelly, 1991). Although there remain very real difficulties in achieving interagency coordination it does appear that there is a high degree of professional will to make it work (Birchall with Hallett, 1995). One aspect of coordination that emerged was that the social workers routinely complained about the rigidity of the procedures for coordination.[1]

Coordination has become such a central feature of the work that it could be that it has become stressed to the detriment of other aspects of the process. Whatever, the benefits or disbenefits of coordinated or collaborative activity may be, it is clear that they cannot of themselves be a 'solution' to the 'problem' of adolescent sexual abuse. Coordination cannot, of itself, make ineffective methods effective, provide additional resources, or devise new processes or therapeutic methods (Weiss, 1981). It is imperative that coordination is seen simply as a means to an end.

A key issue in sexual abuse cases is that any perpetrator of the abuse is committing a Schedule 1 criminal offence. There is thus the question of the role of the police and the Crown Prosecution Service, and their impact upon the therapeutic efforts of social workers. There are a number of issues relating to the girls' other needs, such as education, and how they can be incorporated into the child protection process. Within the overall scenario of the operation of the child protection process there is not only a direct relationship between the practice of social workers and that of other professionals, but also an indirect relationship, mediated through the impact of the actions of various professionals on the girl and her family.

Therefore this chapter will seek to examine the relationship between the social workers' child protection practice and the practice of other professionals in terms of the social workers' responses to referrals from other professionals, and in terms of the impact on their practice of the various aspects of interagency coordination within the child protection process at those stages after referral.

The Impact of Referrals from Professionals and Other Agencies

The social workers found referrals from other agencies and other professionals relatively unproblematic, reflecting the findings of recent research (Hallett, 1995). This suggests a gradual change in attitude and perception since the 1980s when social workers and their managers identified a series of concerns in respect of referrals from other professionals and other agencies. These concerns ranged from anxiety regarding the overidentification of cases (Besharov, 1987) leading to avoidable intrusions into family life based on unsubstantiated suspicions, to anxiety over the underidentification of cases (O'Toole *et al*, 1983; Mrazek *et al*, 1981) due to a series of factors including ignorance in respect of the signs of abuse and uncertainty over the value of reporting abuse (Finkelhor, 1984), and issues (particularly for teachers and GPs) in respect of breaking confidentiality (Wattam 1992). For some professionals disclosure to a wider network was also seen to reduce one's capacity to act independently (James *et al*, 1978). Although they remained slightly concerned that there may be a degree of under- or over-reporting of sexual abuse by professionals from other agencies, the most significant problem the social workers experienced, which also reflects Hallett's (1995) findings, was that they sometimes felt other agencies were not making referrals quickly enough.

Government guidance (DHSS, 1988; DoH, 1991c) and local child protection procedures require all cases of child abuse to be reported either to social services or the police, but, as there are no foolproof 'signs' of child sexual abuse beyond the child's disclosure, that guidance stops short of identifying what the various signs of abuse might be and does not exactly clarify what constitutes actual or potential abuse. The residual concerns of social workers in terms of under- and over-reporting and a possible lack of urgency on the part of other agencies may stem from some professionals and personnel from other agencies exhibiting a degree of ignorance in respect of various aspects of child abuse. Governmental guidance (DoH, 1991c, para. 5.11.2) states clearly that teachers and other professionals who work with children must be alert to the signs of child abuse, and each agency is charged with the responsibility to provide both training and guidance to its personnel in terms of recognition of abuse and an understanding of the child protection procedures. Birchall and Hallett

(1995) showed that health visitors and social workers were acutely aware of the child protection procedures, but other professionals less sure. Teachers, for example, were found by Birchall and Hallett (1995) to show a particular degree of ignorance in this area. One needs to note, however, that, as a professional concern for teachers, child protection is secondary to education. Some of the social workers' concerns reside in the sometimes cumbersome processes of referral developed by other agencies, notably some schools (Hallett, 1995). The current research, however, does not suggest such cumbersome processes. The social workers encountered no specific problems in terms of referrals from schools, or indeed from any other agencies.

Farmer and Owen (1995) identified cases where the victim disclosed to a professional (teacher etc.) rather than to the mother. These disclosures routinely led to an initial investigation prior to the mother becoming aware of the allegations, predisposing the mothers and other non-abusing family members in such cases to become alienated from any process of cooperation within the child protection process. Farmer and Owen (1995) report mothers expressing concern that various professionals were conspiring behind their backs. The social workers in the current research suggested this was not the case in their practice, and stressed that efforts were routinely made to involve the mother and other members of the family in the child protection process from the moment of referral.

The Actions of Other Agencies after the Referral

The local child protection process can best be visualised as a series of stages through which cases pass, each one a potential point for filtering out the case. Gibbons *et al* (1995) liken the system to a fishing net.

> The child protection system might be considered as a small-meshed net, in which are caught a large number of minnows as well as a smaller number of marketable fish. The minnows have to be discarded but no rules exist about the correct size of the mesh. Each fishing fleet may therefore set its own. The 'meshes' are the organisational filters operated by the local child protection systems Gibbons *et al*, 1995, Pg.51).

The organisational filters that Gibbons *et al*, (1995) refer to are a variety of stages within the child protection process that are initially triggered by the referral process. From the initial referral onwards cases can be filtered out and removed from the system. The basic chronology of the process following the initial referral can be summarised as investigation, conference, registration, intervention, review and deregistration. At all points within this chronology there are varying levels of complexity of cases, and differing degrees of coordination between the various agencies concerned.

The form, volume and timing of referrals from other agencies impacted upon the social workers' practice at the post-referral stages, not least in terms of the amount of social worker time they took up, but after the referral process it was governmental injunctions to inter-agency coordination made the strongest impact. Informed by the same ethos that calls for partnership with parents and other family members (DoH, 1991c), the coordination of services between agencies is a prime example of mandated coordination in a public policy sector, albeit with a degree of flexibility that allows the child protection network to develop somewhat differently in different localities. The child protection process operates in terms of a complex series of inter-agency relationships derived from legislation and governmental policy. The most important issues were those of interpretation of the mandate, especially in terms of the differential perceptions of their role in child protection of social workers and the police, and to a lesser extent, other agencies.

Although there were clearly a broad range of issues, they were subsumed within two broad categories. The impact on social workers' child protection practice in respect of familially sexually abused adolescent girls across the various stages of the child protection process fell into two general areas; the direct impact upon practice of the actions of other agencies and professionals (and the ways in which coordination was made manifest), and the indirect impact of the actions of other agencies and professionals (consequent upon the interactions between those other agencies and professionals and the girl and her family).

The Direct Impact of the Actions of Other Agencies and Professionals

The social workers' practice was influenced by the actions of a number of different professionals within the child protection network. Coordination revolved around a process of the various professions to avoid the problems of duplication and unnecessary intervention in the lives of abused children and their families. However, one particular element within the network, the police and the criminal justice system, had a more immediate impact upon social worker practice.

In the early post-referral stages, there were many points of contact between social workers and the police; initial investigation, strategy meetings, joint video interviews and ongoing discussions in respect of what actions the social worker could take in the course of a criminal case. The managers felt that joint working with the police was very successful. The accounts of the social workers, however, suggest that coordination and collaboration with the police was a problematic area with serious implications for social worker practice and a relatively high degree of conflict driven by what the social workers perceived as an endemic clash of organisational interests between social services and the police.

The first area of conflict surrounded issues to do with the initial investigation stage after referral. Hallett (1995) found that in respect of allegations of sexual abuse it was the norm for joint social services/police investigations to take place. Although in some cases this still occurred, it appeared as less of a norm. The police only became involved if, at a strategy meeting, subsequent to the initial investigation, they felt from the social worker's assessment of the situation, there might be sufficient evidence for a criminal prosecution.

> The social worker goes out initially by themselves these days and if the likelihood is there [that a criminal offence has been committed] the police might tag along and we'll have a strategy meeting (SW).

The social workers reported that in the recent past in similar cases the police had involved themselves in joint investigations. The police level of involvement varied by area; some police child protection units routinely became involved, others did not. The attitude of the police to initial visits involving allegations of sexual abuse tended to vary. Farmer and Owen (1995) found that sexual abuse investigations tended to be joint investigations between police and social services, but not always. A similar scenario appeared to be the case in the current research, although the emphasis was somewhat different in that the police tended not to go out on initial investigations, but were more likely to do so if it involved an allegation of sexual abuse. Given Hallett's (1995) findings this may suggest a trend within the police to withdraw from this stage of the process. It could however simply be an indication that these areas are not typical. In those areas within which the police did not involve themselves in initial investigations, the social workers identified a number of practical problems. It often meant that the duty social worker went on the investigation alone. The social workers saw this as bad practice in two ways. They perceived the very real problem of their own personal safety[2], as the situation could be a potentially threatening one, and they felt that without a second pair of eyes and ears during the investigation a great deal of potentially valuable information could be missed.

> You might be talking to a parent, and the child's doing something else or whispering, and you can miss that if you are doing a lone interview (SW).

They also felt that two people on an initial investigation would lead to two opinions, which could in itself be useful. This bears some resonance with some of the issues highlighted by Farmer (1993). Although principally arguing that there is too great an emphasis placed on the criminal justice element of child protection, she does point to the initial investigation as a 'delicate task' (Pg.43) of assessing the benefits and disbenefits for the young person of developing a child protection case, and that task is clearly made more difficult if it is carried out by a lone individual.

In many cases, the duty social worker had no choice but to go alone despite the anxieties and limitations of doing so. However, if the referral suggested to the duty social worker that a child had been physically or sexually assaulted (s)he would try to ensure that (s)he was accompanied by a colleague, if the police were unwilling to involve themselves. Even in cases where the police were willing to cooperate, initial investigations could be difficult, such as one case where the site of the alleged abuse was the family's holiday home. This required the social worker to go on a joint initial investigation with a police officer to the family home and then to liase with a police officer from another constabulary. As resources would not always allow for a second person to go out on initial investigations different teams adopted different approaches to minimise the personal risk attendant upon lone investigations[3].

In general terms social workers felt that this stage of the process had become increasingly difficult in that they would either go out alone on initial investigations and gather information less thoroughly than they would wish, or they would go out with a colleague, with detrimental consequences for the amount of time left in the day for that colleague to do her/his own work. They also saw the police absence from initial investigations placing them in the invidious position of having 'no choice but to inform the police' (SW) if they felt a criminal offence had taken place, implying that they had to pay as much attention to aspects of forensic evidence as they would to initial child protection assessment. The social workers saw the problem as deriving from the police interpretation of what constitutes a joint investigation.

> Our interpretation of a joint investigation is that any investigation in the child protection system is looking at the possibility of an offence having taken place, therefore it should be a joint investigation, but the police interpretation is that unless you as a department find something of evidence that suggests an offence has taken place then we are not going (SW).

Although the police did not always involve themselves in the initial investigation, they became involved immediately afterwards. The findings of the initial investigation provided the basis for a strategy meeting between the duty social worker and the police. The government mandate makes clear the necessity for joint strategic planning at an early stage in the development of child abuse cases.

> It is essential that there is an early strategy discussion,...to plan the investigation, and in particular the role of each agency and the extent of joint investigation...(DoH, 1991c, para.5.13.1).

The strategy meetings concerned themselves with looking at the possibilities of building a criminal case against the perpetrator and associated issues such as the timing of joint video interviews. Other issues, such as the removal of the alleged perpetrator and/or the girl from the family home remained solely within the decision-making realm of the social workers. The social workers' experience of these meetings varied. Many social workers found the police both helpful in organising ongoing investigative work and felt that many police officers understood those issues surrounding disclosure that made planning joint video interviews a delicate task.

The joint video interviews themselves were often difficult. The point of the video interview is to give children and young people the opportunity to give evidence of sexual or physical abuse onto videotape, rather than give it personally in court. Its use, therefore, is only in those cases that the CPS wish to bring to court in order to prosecute the perpetrator. Although the purpose of the joint video interview is to gain statements that will stand up in court, many of the social workers found that the police officers did not prioritise the criminal prosecution over the welfare needs of the girls.

> I don't think the evidence is the be all and end all for the police. They do tend to put the welfare of the young person first. If it is causing them a lot of problems to give the evidence, the police don't push it, and it's always the young person's choice that they can withdraw at any time (SW).

This reflects research findings (Farmer and Owen, 1995) that point to social workers being relatively satisfied with joint investigative work and the timing and handling of joint video interviews, especially when the police officer concerned was a dedicated child protection officer with the appropriate training.

Despite what they saw as the best efforts of the police, some social workers saw serious problems in respect of the process itself. They saw the police as having their hands tied to some extent by the Crown Prosecution Service. This was seen primarily to derive from aspects of the criminal justice system and the exact nature of the rules of evidence.

> The CPS tend to have a very high threshold of what they would regard as a suitable witness (SW).

This led to cases where perpetrators were charged with lesser offences such as assault, even when the police officers involved in the joint interviews were convinced that more serious offences such as rape had occurred, primarily because without corroborating forensic evidence there was often some doubt over the capacity of the girls' evidence to prove the case beyond 'reasonable doubt'. Social workers also cited the rules of evidence as factors that deemed some video evidence as inadmissible, if the least error had been made in taking that evidence. They saw some of these 'errors' as stemming from the relationship between the social worker and the girl. If the girl was asked leading questions the videotape became inadmissible as evidence, yet asking neutral questions often caused the girl to become angry as she was aware that the social worker knew she had been sexually abused. The video evidence could also be tainted if the girl was seen to touch or be touched by a parent, the police officer or the social worker, yet the nature of what she had to commit to videotape was stressful in the extreme. Girls were expected to give details of what they would probably construe as very personal and sordid events, although some social workers felt that the video interview provided a forum for girls to tell their stories and get them out in the open.

The social workers reported that some girls became anxious that although the purpose of the videotape was to present the police with evidence for a prosecution, it would also be seen by other people. One social worker pointed out that perpetrators have access to the tapes through their solicitors, so such worries are justified. The girls were expected to do the interviews without being able to hold on to their mothers, and they were supposed to tell everything in a single hour long attempt. The official (Home Office and DoH, 1992) recommendation of a single video interview caused social workers great problems. They had to try and decide at what point in the disclosure process to go ahead with a video interview. That decision, however, was often mediated through the needs of the police and other exogenous circumstances. The timing of video interviews sometimes had more to do with the availability of the girl's parents and the police's schedule for arresting the perpetrator, than with the social workers' assessments of whether a disclosure was complete or not. Other, practical problems were also highlighted, primarily the lack of video suites in some areas, necessitating relatively long-distance travel that could enhance the level of stress for the girls and draw upon social services scarce resources in terms of the social workers' time.

The attitudes of social workers to doing video interviews varied considerably. Some, for example, found that they worked well and that they struck a useful balance in that they provided the police and through them the CPS with criminal evidence, but they avoided the potentially damaging experience for the girl of giving that evidence direct in court. They felt that the police tended to accept the official (Home Office and DoH, 1992) recommendation of a single interview, even if the interview didn't result in securing the evidence they required for a successful prosecution. Although the social workers saw the emphasis on a single video interview as problematic in terms of dealing with a process as complex and difficult as disclosing sexual abuse, they saw the acceptance by the police of the single video interview without recourse to further interviews, as reflecting a police attitude that placed the welfare of the child above any other considerations.

> The idea of the social worker interviewing in terms of protection and the police officer interviewing for evidential reasons has ended. We do both. It has a lot to do with the personal relationships we have developed with the police officer (SW).

Some social workers, however, were very dissatisfied with the conduct of the police in strategy meetings and joint interviews. They were concerned that the police tended to want to hurry the process along with little regard to the issues involving the emotional and psychological state of the girl and members of her family. This concern manifested itself most strongly in respect of the timing of joint interviews and the attitude of the police within such interviews. They felt the police were pressing to go to video interview too soon, and were far too demanding of the girl in the interview itself, being too preoccupied with gaining exact statements, even if at some cost to the girl herself. This articulates with recent research findings that suggest social workers are concerned that a police imperative to gain detailed forensic evidence dominates the video interview process to the detriment of any social work input (Hallett, 1995), and that if the evidence gathered from the video interview is seen by the police as inadequate, further interviews taking place (Farmer and Owen, 1995), contravening Inquiry recommendations (Secretary of State, 1988) and official guidance (Home Office and DoH, 1992). These concerns were most apparent when the social workers had experienced involvement in joint video interviews with police officers who were not experienced members of police child protection units. They saw them as tending to interview in traditional police ways[4].

The social workers' concerns in respect of the criminal justice system as it impacts on child protection were reinforced in several ways. Firstly, very few cases ever get to court, and of those that do very few secure convictions. They pointed to the problems girls then suffered. The most notable of these was a sense of injustice or of being cheated by the system. Even when prosecution resulted in a conviction girls were often left with a sense of the punishment not fitting the crime, especially if the sentence was a short term of imprisonment or a fine, and when criminal compensation was awarded girls tended to see it as insulting and not reflecting the trauma of the abuse. Perhaps of greatest significance was the anxiety that many girls felt when the perpetrator was found not guilty and thus not punished, yet he had put them through such a high degree of trauma. From the social workers' perspective this often compounded the difficulties of their child protection task, in that the girl's concerned became angry and disillusioned with the process, to the extent that therapeutic work was made more difficult and the time-scale of 'recovery' lengthened. Secondly, although the girls' evidence was on videotape, this did not preclude the possibility of the ordeal of cross-examination, and thirdly if the police were not satisfied with the video evidence they could ask the girl for a statement in the conventional way. Questions such as these have led social workers, with the support of their managers, no longer to routinely go through the video interview process in all cases of sexual abuse. As one of them pointed out,

> ...we have never been criticised for not doing one even if it has gone to court, and there hasn't been a case prevented from going to court through lack of video evidence (SW).

Their principal concern over joint video interviews was that they felt them to be located firmly within a discourse of criminal justice, rather than therapeutic intervention. Parton (1991) points to the development of legalistic systems of child protection, and a preoccupation with the prosecution of the offender articulates closely with such a conceptualisation. Many social workers seemed to perceive of child protection as being either in terms of criminal justice or in terms of therapeutic intervention, and were convinced that joint police-social services work at all levels was doomed to failure.

What clearly emerges here is a (somewhat variable) perception, amongst social workers of two separate agendas operating within the child protection process, their own agenda revolving around what they see as the core issue of protecting the child, and a police/CPS agenda of invoking the criminal justice system. In essence this can be distilled into a conflict of focus; social workers focus being principally on the girl herself and to some extent her family, the police focus being primarily on the perpetrator and a 'just deserts' model criminal justice. This perception is, however, over simplistic. Hallett (1995) in her research into interagency coordination found that the police rarely pressed for prosecution against the advice of others in the child protection network. The current research tends to suggest a greater degree of ambivalence, in that in different cases in different areas, different situations emerge. In several cases social workers made the point that the police tend to seek prosecution far less frequently than in the recent past. This was seen as being in part a consequence of joint training that enabled both agencies to appreciate the needs of the other. This is a very persuasive view in that of the two authorities in the sample, the one with the lesser degree of joint training was also the one in which the social workers reported prosecution as more common. One particular case that occurred in an area where joint training had not taken place illustrates the negative impact the police/CPS insistence on prosecution can have on social workers' practice. The investigation process revealed that the girl been sexually abused by her mother's boyfriend and that her mother had colluded in the abuse. The social worker in the case felt strongly that the man concerned had influenced the mother and it would be in the girl's best interests for the mother not to be prosecuted and the girl and mother remain together. The CPS, however insisted on prosecuting both, and both were convicted. In order for the girl to stay with the mother, who was now a Schedule 1 offender, the social worker had to apply for a Supervision Order. He saw the whole process causing unnecessary stress to the mother and the girl, whilst also incurring an administrative cost in terms of social services finance and in terms of his time.

This strongly suggests the police and social workers following different agendas. However, the police did not routinely seek prosecution and the social workers did not always advise against it. The social worker attitude to prosecution would seem to be that it can be a useful part of the therapeutic process, if a conviction is gained, in that it gives the girl a clear message that she has been believed, and that the perpetrator has done her a wrong, but in general they tended towards the view that the limited value a conviction would have was offset by the problems that would be encountered in trying to obtain a conviction. The police attitude towards conviction would seem to rest on very different grounds. They would tend to seek a prosecution if they were more or less certain that the evidence was strong enough to gain a conviction. Otherwise they tend towards not prosecuting the perpetrator. The social workers and the police can be seen to be on either side of a conflict between the interests of children and the interests of justice, but, as Wattam (1991) concludes, these interests are not necessarily mutually exclusive.

Many commentators (Parton, 1991; Wattam, 1992; Parton *et al*, 1997, for example) point to ways in which child protection has become securely lodged within a legal discourse, characterised by the rules of evidence and formalised techniques of investigation, and clearly the formal systematic nature of this part of the child protection process would tend to bear this out. However, to conceive of the child protection process as inhabiting a legal discourse would also be to imply that the apportioning of blame and the conviction of the guilty as its paramount concern. One then needs to bear in mind the complex nature of disclosure of sexual abuse and remain aware that child and adolescent sexual abuse is often ongoing, routinised and rarely amenable to detailed forensic examination. This places the child protection process in a difficult position *vis a vis* the conviction of the perpetrator. The insistence upon detailed forensic evidence for a successful conviction would tend to mediate against prosecution. This leads one to suggest that however systemised the child protection process might be, the processes of the criminal justice system would seem to act in some ways to prevent the conviction of the perpetrator.

Wattam (1997b), points to inherent problems in the role of the criminal justice system in child protection. The interface between the criminal justice process and other aspects of child protection is not acknowledged by the criminal justice system. There is an assumption that the interests of justice and the interests of children are the same. She points out, however, that in many cases a not guilty verdict is arrived at, yet the courtroom process can be traumatic for the girl.

> There are strong parallels to rape cases, where the victim's character is laid open to dispute and where their culpability, in terms of encouraging the assault, becomes a factor in the decision making. Thus if more children are subjected to the prosecution process, but the only evidence is that of their

own testimony, the likely effect is one of increased trauma for the child (Wattam, 1997b, Pg.104).

She further argues that the result of any prosecution is unlikely to produce adequate compensation or retribution. Some of Wattam's (1997b) arguments are supported by Prior *et al* (1997). In a sample of ten to sixteen year olds who had been sexually abused they found that their experience of the courts ranged from 'very unpleasant' to 'traumatic'. However, they found the children were 'positive' in their evaluation of the police, particularly in respect of the level of understanding they received from police officers. This suggests that although there are serious tensions between the interests of the child and the interests of justice, the agenda being followed by the police is not solely that of justice at the cost of that of the child's best interests.

In those cases where the police and the CPS felt that a prosecution was viable and the criminal justice pathway was followed, the social workers expressed a great deal of frustration in that the criminal justice process tended to have a seriously detrimental impact upon their capacity to carry out what they saw as their primary child protection tasks. The basic problem that they pointed to was that counselling of the girls and other associated types of therapeutic work were severely constrained by the police, who feared that the direct discussion of the abuse between the girl and the social worker may act to 'sully the evidence' (SW). This is not to say that the police attempted to operate any kind of blanket ban on 'victim'/social worker interaction. Rather, those interactions were severely circumscribed, and in practice reduced to sessions wherein the social worker spent time assuring the girl that she was believed, and in explaining how the process of prosecuting the perpetrator would operate. At best the limitations on counselling could mean that the social worker involved was not allowed to counsel the girl as (s)he was also a witness at the trial. This was seen as leading to discontinuities of care. Concerns from social workers and others over the lack of counselling if the criminal justice element of the child protection procedures are enforced have been noted elsewhere (Sharland *et al*, 1995). The lack of opportunity to counsel the girl and develop an appropriate therapeutic regime was seen by the social workers as the most detrimental aspect of the criminal justice aspect of child protection.

You can't just put people on hold, because it affects all parts of their lives (SW).

The social workers also expressed concern over the cross-examination process, often in terms that mirrored feminist concerns in respect of the conduct of rape trials (Lees, 1997; Wattam, 1997b).

> My experience of the criminal justice system for victims is that they are abused far more by a barrister than perhaps they ever were by the parents, unless its a particularly gross assault (SW).

In sum the social workers concerns in respect of the operation of the courts would tend to echo some of the concerns expressed by Wattam (1992). Whilst recognising changes in the operation of the legal system to accommodate the feelings and wishes of the child or young person, Wattam (1992) sees the legal processes in child protection as affording the child the status of 'object of evidence'; a status that potentially reduces the importance of the young person's 'other more individual and social needs' (Pg.30).

Some social workers saw the legal process as too great an invasion of the autonomy of the girls, an attempt to take control of information that the girls may have wished to keep private. Not only can this be seen as a criticism of the notion that the professional should take ownership of the problem leaving the client simply as the object of intervention in ways that mirror some of the criticisms of the medical profession (Illich, 1976; Oakley, 1980) in respect of subjects as diverse as disease, disability and childbirth, but also in terms of the practical problems in respect of the emotions of girls who are subject to persistent inquiry. The social workers pointed to instances where they were left to pick up the pieces and rebuild relationships with girls whose self-esteem had been damaged by the procedures of the criminal justice system to almost as great an extent as by the original abuse.

Some of these problems were exacerbated by what the social workers saw as the unreasonable timescale within which the criminal justice system operated. It was not unusual for a case to take six months to get to court, and one social worker had a case that took over a year. The anxiety clearly felt by social workers in terms of the criminal justice system preventing, or at least delaying, the types of therapeutic intervention they felt appropriate goes some way towards explaining social workers' relatively extreme views *vis a vis* the interface between child protection and criminal justice. Sharland *et al* (1995) report growing doubts amongst social workers as to whether the child protection procedures with their criminal justice element are actually the best way to deal with something as complex as child sexual abuse. Social workers in the current study concur:

> I think the system gets in the way of social work. I think the pressure we are under about not working with people until it has been to court is just ridiculous (SW). [5]

The strength of feeling that social workers exhibited in terms of the actions of the police and the CPS can be seen not only in terms of their anxieties on behalf of their clients in terms of being able to offer them the appropriate therapies at the appropriate time, but also in terms of their anxieties in respect of themselves as welfare professionals. The social workers repeatedly referred to the criminal justice process as impinging on social work. This view was shared to some extent by their managers who saw the criminal justice element of the child protection process as a compulsory aspect of the process that restricted their departmental autonomy in delivering child protection services. This suggests something of the embattled self perception of social workers as described by Pithouse (1987) with their routinised deprecation of other agencies and groups. It also highlighting one of the themes illuminated by Woodhouse and Pengelly (1991); the 'defensive use of discipline boundaries' (Pg.8), which they saw as acting as a limiting factor in collaborative action. Although many of the social workers in the sample saw a great deal of value in the criminal justice element of child protection, at least in principle, others could see nothing to commend it, and expressed the view that it should simply be removed from the child protection equation altogether.

> I think I'd like to see it [child sexual abuse] decriminalised, not because I don't think it should be regarded as a criminal offence, but the legal system in Britain is a load of rubbish for children who have been sexually abused. So I think it would be better to do it completely differently and do it properly, because when it goes to trial and there's a not guilty plea or the verdict is not guilty, it just does so much damage (SW).

The degree to which social workers felt that the criminal justice system constrained their work appeared to bear a direct relationship to the quality of interpersonal relationship they enjoyed with officers from the police child protection unit. In areas with little contact outside that formally mandated by the procedures, social workers felt that their experience pointed to the concept of coordination being little more than political and administrative rhetoric, whereas those areas where joint training took place and social workers and police officers enjoyed closer personal relationships, social workers perceived a higher degree of 'give and take' in terms of a whole range of issues, from whether or not to prosecute the perpetrator through to the amount and form of counselling that could be allowed while a court case was pending. In other words, they saw the police as interpreting the policy of the CPS in ways that were as favourable as possible to social work. The importance social workers place on interpersonal relationships is revealed by Pithouse (1987), who sees it in terms of an,

> Entrepreneurial activity of getting the best out of related occupations through personal contacts... (Pithouse, 1987, Pg.22).

Social work is a complex enterprise engaged in and through a whole series of legal and welfare institutions (Hardiker *et al*, 1991), and central to its practice is the concept of negotiation and communication with clients and other professionals. Pithouse's (1987) analysis, in framing the development and use of communicative skills in such an instrumental framework, is perhaps indicative of its time, the high water mark of Thatcherism. The importance of skills of negotiation and communication are clearly vital to social workers in what is essentially a discursive profession. It is this point that illuminates the misgivings they have in terms of the lack of space for negotiation in those areas where social worker/police relationships are poorest.

It is not only the actions of the police and the criminal justice system that have a direct impact upon social worker practice. The forum that makes the biggest impact upon social worker practice is the Initial Child Protection Conference. Gibbons *et al* (1995) found that there were distinct variations across authorities of which professionals would attend these conferences, drawing the clear inference that both local policies and professional interpersonal relationships could have a real effect upon the decisions conferences made. Further evidence of the importance of the makeup of the conference comes from Birchall with Hallett (1995). They found that although there was a great deal of agreement at conferences across and within the different agencies within the interdisciplinary network in terms of adopting a confrontational approach to sexual abuse, there were considerable variations in decisions and recommendations deriving in part from individual perspectives and values. Farmer and Owen (1995) found obvious benefits in the conference for social workers and other professionals.

> The initial case conference was overtly about the management of risk, but also contributed to the management of professional anxiety. The conference

itself could be regarded as a mechanism for defusing anxiety since it spread the risks and helped to reduce uncertainty (Farmer and Owen, 1995, Pg.85).

They found the real value of the conference was that of information sharing, with the conference acting to spread responsibility. Farmer and Owen (1995) found that the conference was not the place for new information, rather they found that information was made available by the various agencies prior to the conference. This reflects earlier findings (Hallett and Birchall, 1992) that one agency having greater information at the time of convening the conference could place them in a privileged position of power (Foucault, 1978; 1980) and threaten the social network upon which interagency cooperation is founded. This was not entirely reflected in the current study, wherein social workers saw the conference itself as being the forum for the exchange of information. Indeed, one of the rationalisations they gave for their recommendations not being adopted was that new information from other agencies could change the overall picture of a case. However, in most cases the social workers attested that their recommendations were followed. This powerfully reinforces the findings of earlier research (Corby, 1987; Farmer and Owen, 1995; Birchall with Hallett, 1995) that conferences tend towards a consensus approach with little interagency criticism. The clear benefits of this approach are that conferences tend to run smoothly, and little time is wasted in arguing out conflictual positions. It does however suggest that important views may be suppressed (Farmer and Owen, 1995). In general the social workers in the current study tended to express the view that conferences worked well and the various agencies cooperated closely. This reflected the views of their managers who felt that the process worked well up to and including the conference stage, but saw the interest of other agencies waning after that point, especially with long running cases that exhibited little change.

A great deal has been made in the literature (Packman and Randall, 1987; Parton, 1991) in terms of the tendency of child protection to 'overwhelm other child care services' (Hallett, 1995, Pg.89), leaving both children and families with a host of unmet needs, '...which the understandable preoccupation with ...sexual abuse...'(Hallett, 1995, Pg.90) tended to push aside. The current research shows a more ambivalent picture. Although the emphasis of the interagency network was almost principally concerned with meeting the protection needs of the girls concerned, other issues were not ignored. In one particularly messy case, which failed to fully ensure the ongoing protection of the girl, the social worker felt that her protection needs had been swamped by other issues in that other agencies had 'hijacked' (SW) her child protection review with a multiplicity of educational and care needs leaving her ongoing protection needs unaddressed. In terms of previous research (Farmer and Owen, 1995) this seems a little unusual. Farmer and Owen (1995) found that one of the problems inherent in the child protection process was the concentration on the immediate protection needs of the abused child, that failed to take into account both her ongoing needs for other aspects of her welfare and psychological well-being and the needs of other family members, such as non-abusing mothers and siblings. The social worker in the case referred to above saw the problem arising as a consequence of the child protection review being jointly convened with a child care review, a practice since abandoned in that area. That case, however, was exceptional. The more usual response was that throughout the child protection process there was a great deal of interagency cooperation that highlighted the girls' protection needs, but within a context of an overall strategy that incorporated other care needs.

As the ages of the girls in the cases ranged from eleven to fifteen, they were at an important stage of their school careers. This was recognised by the social workers and their educational needs were not overlooked. Indeed, the level of cooperation the social workers reported between themselves on the one hand and the schools and the education service on the other hand was very high, and appeared to involve a recognition of both protection and educational needs. The social workers had direct contact with the schools, usually through a designated member of staff with pastoral responsibility for pupils, and contact with educational social workers in the education department. The social workers felt that schools generally adopted a very helpful approach in terms of child protection, such as allowing the social worker access to the girl in school, and by allowing time off school for the girl to attend therapy sessions and other aspects of the child protection process. They were particularly impressed by the mechanisms schools set up to ensure that confidentiality was maintained at as high a level as possible. The social workers saw the schools as being very positive indeed in negotiating such things as part-time schooling and help back to school for girls who had lost their self-esteem, and in finding appropriate school places for girls who had been removed from the family home. In one particular case the social worker concerned found the education service very helpful indeed in funding the girl to study in her chosen field at age sixteen in a college away from home. This appeared to meet both her educational needs and her protection needs simultaneously.

The high degree of satisfaction social workers expressed with the education service could well relate to the fact that their first point of interagency contact was often an educational social worker. It may be that the social services social workers tended to feel at ease in a professional sense when dealing with social workers from the education department, in that in many ways they shared a professional culture and ethos. The organisation of educational social work, however, also caused them extra work. Whereas in child protection, except in exceptional circumstances, a case remained with a specific social worker after the Initial Child Protection Conference, in the education department cases tended to move from one worker to another. This was seen as frustrating by social services social workers as it meant having to explain and re-explain the important aspects of particular cases time and again. The overall level of satisfaction the social workers felt in their interactions with the education service was largely because they found schools cooperative and helpful in the child protection process at a number of levels. Teachers were seen in many cases to fulfil the role of 'trusted person' (Furniss, 1991) sensitively and responsibly, referring girls to social services appropriately and giving relatively detailed referrals. Schools were also seen as helpful and cooperative at later stages within the process, making girls available for interview with social workers, whilst successfully protecting their confidentiality within the school. This became apparent in that those girls who had been sexually abused often expressed surprise that other girls in their school had also suffered abuse on previous occasions. The social workers recognised that confidentiality in terms of other pupils in schools was strictly observed, and teachers other than the person the girl had confided in and/or the teacher with pastoral responsibility would only find out about the abuse on a need to know basis. The social workers were confident that individual cases of sexual abuse never became the subject of teachers staff room conversation.

If social workers were relatively satisfied with their interprofessional interface with the education service, the same could not be said of their relationship with elements of the health service. Although some social workers made clear that in some cases there was well developed coordinated practice with the psychological service, others found the health service in general a very unwilling partner, with often bitter disputes over who should pay for particular treatments. Some of the problems that came about with the health service may have stemmed from the fact that government guidance and administrative procedures make clear the lead role of social services in child protection, and the social workers were very aware of themselves as the lead professionals in specific cases [6]. Problems could then arise in terms of the psychological and physical health of the girls concerned, in that their ill-health may or may not have been directly related to the sexual abuse. In other words there were occasions when the health service appeared to question the lead role of social services in some aspects of the overall package of client care and protection. The social workers expressed annoyance and frustration with various elements of the health service both in general terms and in respect of specific cases. Although in many cases the general health services and mental health services fully accepted the lead role of social services in child protection, in some cases individual doctors in Child Protection Conferences were loathe to see sexual abuse outside some form of medical model and displayed a tendency to press for registration and removal of the child when this was not always seen as the best option by other members of the Conference. Social workers also saw the health services as too defensive in respect of their budgets. Disagreements in terms of the mental health needs of several girls between different elements of the health service were viewed somewhat cynically by social workers. They saw fierce debates in terms of the appropriateness of psychiatric or psychological treatment regimes as having more to do with protecting departmental budgets than any genuine concern for the girls. They also found themselves frustrated in terms of waiting lists, finding that in some cases that they simply could not refer a girl for psychological therapy or counselling in the immediate aftermath, but had to wait until she reached the top of the waiting list. They saw this diminishing the efficacy of any counselling or other treatment. The general view to emerge was that social workers felt that if they were the lead agency in the coordination of services it should be they who organised how and when those services should be initiated, although they recognised that budgetary constraints within the health service rather than a deliberate lack of will by health professionals was one cause of the problems.

In terms of interagency coordination the girl herself and her family do not remain as just recipients of services or as passive bystanders. Various services were offered and various agencies made specific efforts towards the meeting the complexity of needs of the girls concerned. However, some girls simply refused the help that was offered. 'Coordination depends upon the girl herself being prepared to accept various services' (SW).

The Indirect Impact of the Actions of Other Agencies and Professionals

The research literature in respect of the participation of other agencies within the child protection network tends to concentrate either upon the interface between social services and the police/CPS, or upon the role of other agencies in the referral process. What research literature there is in respect of the ongoing interactions between professionals within the network and the victims of sexual abuse and their families tends to focus on the various professional attitudes towards parental and child participation in child protection conferences, showing social workers either in favour of such participation (Lonsdale, 1990; Merchant and Luckham, 1991; North Yorkshire ACPC, 1991) or opposed to it (Taylor and Godfrey, 1991). Research also points to both professional and gender divisions in attitudes towards child and parental participation (Birchall and Hallett, 1995) and a greater support for parental participation than for child participation (Hallett, 1995).

There is also some research that offers variable findings in terms of how children's and parental participation impacts upon the conduct of child protection conferences. Driscoll and Evans (1992) found members of the conference prepared in greater detail when family members were to participate. Merchant and Luckham (1991) found parental participation led to a greater level of professional disagreement within the conference, whereas Thorburn *et al* (1995) found parental participation had little impact on discussion, as parents tended not to understand what was going on (Woodhill and Ashworth, 1989).

One of the most significant findings from research in this area is that social workers and children and their families experienced the child protection process in terms of an inexorable process leaving them with little sense of control of events (Farmer and Owen, 1995). It also suggests that in many cases parents experience a sense of anger and betrayal (Farmer and Owen, 1995) when other professionals in whom they had confided then report their statements to social services.

Despite the significance of these issues, it remains that there is a paucity of literature dealing with the impact on social workers of the interactions between sexually abused adolescent girls and their families on the one hand and professionals other than social workers on the other. Yet, within a process of mandated interagency coordination, the complex network of consequences of such interactions must assume some significance.

The concept of the 'best interests of the child' is purported to be at the heart of the child protection process, implying that an holistic approach to child protection as an integral part of child welfare is an important feature of the process. This is alluded to by Sharland *et al* (1995), who propose that the development of a working relationship between the primary carer (usually, but not always, the mother) and different professionals in the network, can be taken as a sign that a child protection intervention has served its purpose. Woodhouse and Pengelly (1991) make the significance of the complex of interactions between the various protagonists comprising the child protection process clearer still.

> ...behind the specifics of any given case or circumstances calling for collaboration there is inevitably a general anxiety arising from the stress of triangular relationships – a dynamic field of unconscious forces liable to inhibit collaborative behaviour (Woodhouse and Pengelly, 1991, Pg.221).

Although Woodhouse and Pengelly (1991) distil the barriers to collaborative working down to an internalised conflict within the social worker between meeting the needs of her client and those of her organisation, an extension of their logic points towards a complex of triangular situations, wherein social workers, other professionals and the client and her family, engage in a series of interactions that each have consequences for the other. One particular aspect of this is that the interactions the client and her family have with other professionals within the child protection network will impact upon the interactions between the client and her family and the social worker. The social workers practice must thus be indirectly impacted upon by the actions of other professionals within the child protection network.

In the current research, the social workers saw some interactions between clients and their families and professionals from other agencies as having a detrimental affect on their practice. Apart from those issues to do with the criminal justice system, which have already been discussed, social workers talked of the police losing interest in specific cases after giving the girls assurances they would be there for them, leading to a loss of trust that had to be slowly rebuilt. They also pointed in a more general sense to problems associated with other professionals giving the girls assurances of confidentiality that could not be maintained, but had to be shared with other members of the child protection network. Again the social workers saw the girls experiencing this as a loss of trust that had to be regained if therapeutic progress was to be made.

The social workers also pointed to some of the beneficial effects of the interactions of other agencies with the girls and their families. In most of the cases, the social workers concerned saw the efforts of the education service in a positive light. They saw schools and educational social workers as recognising the difficulties for the girls concerned, and being sensitive to their needs. Indeed, the school was seen by many of the social workers as a stabilising feature that helped to rebuild the girls' fractured sense of trust in adults and authority. Those schools that seemed to the social workers to deal best with the situation were those in which similar cases had previously occurred.

The social workers did not see all the efforts of the education service as beneficial, however. They pointed to cases where the efforts of the education service made little impact. In doing so they tended to reaffirm a key motif running throughout this study. The efforts of all professionals in the child protection network were severely circumscribed by the choices of the client. In terms of education, this meant that whatever arrangements the schools or educational social workers put to the girls, they were only successful if the girls decided to accept them, and in some cases the girls were simply unwilling to cooperate. A similar story was told in respect of psychological services.

One needs at this point to consider why a significant proportion of girls appear to refuse services that are offered. The social workers, although they clearly made every effort to persuade girls who refused various services to think again, tended to be very aware of the 'nearly adult' [7] status of the girls and remained fixed on their right to refuse various form of help. This seemed to override any consideration as to why the girls refused specific services. The social workers speculated that in various cases the girls perhaps felt that they had nothing to gain from going back to school or from counselling, or that they were frightened of any psychological intervention. Beyond that level they said little in their accounts that would suggest why some girls appeared to simply refuse the help that was offered. The psychological literature on child sexual abuse and the recovery from it (Finkelhor, 1984; Finkelhor, 1996; Herman, 1994, for example) offers some clues. Amongst the emotional/psychological effects of child and adolescent sexual abuse are the development of low self-esteem, dissociation, and extreme anxiety. These are not psychological states conducive to even understanding the implications of different forms of help that may be offered. It may well be that girls refused help simply because they were at a stage in the aftermath process that left them too confused and disturbed to appreciate the value of the help offered.

Transfers from Other Jurisdictions

There was one further aspect of coordination that impinged on social worker practice. This emerged in one of the area offices in the research sample that was located close to a military base. Social workers in that office found some problems in respect of cases being transferred from other jurisdictions. They all had some cases that had been transferred from Northern Ireland, Scotland, or the military overseas. As far as cases coming from Northern Ireland or Scotland was concerned, minor differences in the system sometimes led to confusion, often to the point of having to commence the initial investigation all over again. As far as the military was concerned, they spoke of the culture of welfare in the military and the lack of confidentiality involved as leading to problems being 'hidden', only to emerge when the family were posted back to England. In other words, they felt that perpetrators made even more strenuous efforts at concealment through fear of the consequences of their colleagues finding out. The problems would only emerge when the family returned to England. In respect of such cases this was seen to mean that the situation was often worse than if the case had been a civilian one. In those cases that had developed in the military, social workers endured similar but more difficult problems to those coming from Northern Ireland or Scotland. Principally, the social work system within the forces is run by SAAFA, and the legislation and procedures are very different to those operating in England and Wales. The major problem of coordinating activity in respect of transfers from other jurisdictions was that it tended to create a great deal of additional administrative work.

Summary

The actions of professionals from other agency within the child protection process can be seen to have a crucial impact on social workers' child protection practice. Firstly, the child protection process can clearly be seen as a complex network of interagency coordination at both a formal and an informal level. An integral part of the formal level is that of mandated coordination in respect of a governmental evocation of coordination within a specific policy sector; child protection. This policy sector can be seen to have a number of external relationships with other policy sectors, such as community care and the welfare state in general. More importantly, it comprises a whole series of internal relationships. These internal relationships are both those relationships within social work and the various interfaces of local authority social work and other agencies covered by the government child protection mandate. These formal relationships are mirrored by a whole series of informal relationships between individual social workers and police officers and GPs etc. Both previous research and the current research point to wide variations in exactly how interagency coordination takes place, variations that are influenced by a range of factors such as the quality and type of informal relationships that exist, the levels of joint training in specific areas and the geographical proximity of one agency office to that of another agency.

Coordination itself is difficult to define, and seems to take two forms. The general rubric of interagency coordination appears to have developed to mean the removal of duplication and the clear ordering of the demarcation of responsibility for specific aspects of particular cases. However, in respect of the relationship between social workers and the police, a closer form of coordination has developed that involves a degree of collaborative activity.

Interagency coordination clearly takes place at two distinct phases within the process. Firstly, there is the referral stage, wherein professionals from other agencies refer cases to social services. With some reservations the social workers in the sample were satisfied both with the timing and the quality of these referrals. They were certainly more satisfied with them than with referrals from lay people. This was borne out in that there appeared to be some kind of assumption that such referrals were serious to an extent that was not apparent with referrals from the general public. The social workers also appeared keen to involve the non-abusing parent at the earliest stages of an investigation to avoid any accusation of professional conspiracy.

At the post referral stage, the social workers were relatively satisfied with the outcomes of conferences and did not feel that they unduly added to their work burden. They expressed far more ambivalent feelings, however, in respect of coordination with the police in investigations and joint video interviews. The ambivalence in attitude towards police involvement in initial investigations seemed to stem from varying police interpretations of what was meant by an initial investigation, an interpretation that seemed to be differentiated by area. Similarly, they also expressed some reservations in respect of themselves and the police operating to different agendas in terms of prosecuting perpetrators, the social work view being prosecution if it benefits the client, the police view being prosecution if there is a reasonable likelihood of a conviction. These reservations were less in those areas where joint social services/police training was established, and/or the individual social worker and police child protection officer had a good personal working relationship. Some of the social workers made clear that in some cases the interaction between the police/CPS and the girl and her family, and the choices that emerged from that, could be advantageous to the girl. Firstly, as already discussed, they saw distinct benefits in terms of affirmation of blamelessness on the part of the girl in successful convictions of perpetrators. They also, however, pointed to cases wherein the police advised the CPS against prosecution, based upon their interpretation in consultation with the social worker, of the needs and circumstances of the girl and her family. This could indicate a more sensitive approach by the police, or could be seen as further evidence that in some areas a more collaborative approach to child protection between police and social services is leading to a more holistic approach, a pragmatic approach that attempts to do what is for the best in each specific case. Even in such cases, the police were still seen to be tied by the CPS and the rules of evidence, This was clearly an area of serious professional tension.

The CPS were seen as a block to good social work in a number of ways. The social workers were particularly concerned over restrictions on counselling when court cases were pending, were concerned over the time cases took to reach court, and many had serious reservations over the benefits of prosecution, any benefits for the girl to be derived from conviction being outweighed by the fact that few prosecutions resulted in conviction without a perpetrator confession.

The real problem as far as social work practice was concerned was that if a criminal prosecution was being sought the social workers felt they had lost autonomy to act in ways that they deemed in the best interests of their client, in an environment within which the influence of the courts and the criminal justice system was becoming dominant (Parton, 1991; Parton *et al*, 1997). There was a feeling amongst some social workers that the criminal justice element of the process and its associated procedures failed to take into account the needs and requirements of the girl.

> I mean it's interview, statement, here we go, no thought about how the girl feels (SW).

These feelings were echoed by one of the managers who saw the official guidance (Home Office and DoH, 1992) as being in the best interests of the CPS rather than those of the victim of abuse.

Towards the other services in the interagency network, there was a mixed response, except in respect of education. In almost all cases the social workers felt that their tasks were eased by the efforts of the schools and the educational social workers, and they also felt that the schools in particular helped them indirectly through helping to rebuild the confidence of the girls involved and by acting as stabilising features at a time of great emotional stress. They expressed a great deal of confidence in the pastoral arrangements schools made for those girls that had been subject to sexual abuse, and the efforts they made to ensure the girls were able to continue their education. This suggest that something of an holistic approach to the welfare of sexually abused adolescent girls that places child protection within an overall welfare framework was in operation at least in terms of their educational needs.

The social workers were far less positive in respect of meeting the health needs of the girls. They found it difficult to develop a coordinated approach with many elements of the health services, to the point that they were concerned that many of the psychological and psychiatric needs of the girls were not met. This was seen in part to do with problems in respect of psychologists and psychiatrists waiting lists, and in part due to issues of disagreement between different areas of the mental health services. These problems were clearly overlaid by the issues referred to above in terms of the CPS constraining therapeutic inputs such as counselling. The social workers also felt that many mental health professionals were less committed to coordination than other members of the child protection network. The consequence of these issues, as far as social workers were concerned, was that they felt they were not meeting the mental health needs of the girls to the extent that they wished, and thus not helping the girls recover as quickly or as thoroughly as they might. Even from a narrow child protection perspective, they were concerned that this left many girls inhabiting the status of victim, leaving them vulnerable to further abuse. The only other area that seemed to cause them extra work involved the cultural and administrative problem of cases transferred from other jurisdictions.

In sum, the direct and indirect impact upon the social workers' practice of the actions of other agencies and professionals was complex. The impact varied considerably. Different cases required different inputs from different professionals.

The influence the actions of these different professionals on the social workers' practice depended upon the quality of the interagency relationship between social services and the agency concerned. It also depended upon the particular interpretations made by the different agencies and the professionals within them of the child protection 'mandate', and the quality of the triangular interpersonal relationships comprising the specific clients, social workers and other professionals involved in any particular case.

Areas of tension between social workers and the courts and the police, and between social workers and some health professionals were clearly evident, but these tensions were not of a uniform nature. Some cases indicated a great deal of mutual interagency understanding and coordinated practice, whilst others highlighted serious differences between professionals within the child protection network. It was also apparent that interacting with these various issues of interagency coordination and tension were profound issues relating to social workers' normative assessments of both clients and degrees of risk that were often at odds with aspects of client choice and a service ethos of client autonomy. The degree of importance placed on the age of the girls in these cases meant that client autonomy tended to prevail over normative assessments of risk, giving rise to a degree of anxiety in child protection practice.

5 The girl and practice

Introduction

Factors associated with the girl herself also have a significant impact on social workers' practice. These factors are of two types; those relating to the personality and attitude of the girl herself, and those relating to her abuse. The ways in which these factors are configured have implications for the short-term and long-term psychological well being of the girl (Stein *et al*, 1988; Palmer *et al*, 1990; Wyatt and Newcombe, 1990), and her physical health.

Further, abused children and adolescents have needs of two distinct types; protection needs and other, broader, welfare needs (Farmer and Owen, 1995). Meeting these needs can be complementary, but can equally be the focus of conflict. There is, therefore, an inherent tension within social work practice in terms of meeting these differing needs. Issues emanating from the age of the girls concerned exacerbate this potential conflict, which themselves highlight a further tension in child protection that derives from differing formulations of children's rights. This effectively means a tension between ideas of protection and issues of client autonomy. For Freeman (1983) child abuse can only be understood in terms of children's rights, as:

> Children without defined rights are by that very fact vulnerable (Freeman, 1983, Pg.105)

Children's rights are conceived of in three basic forms. Firstly, there are manifesto-type goals, which form much of the political rhetoric of children's rights (Freeman, 1983; King, 1996), develop no definitive claims making procedures, but tend to elicit much support as a general common good (King, 1996). Secondly, there are protection rights. These stress the vulnerability and incompetence of children, who thus need to be cared for and protected by adults. This formulation is criticised as being paternalistic (Freeman, 1983) as it tends to focus on normative definitions of the child's best interests rather than her expressed wishes, and rests upon the 'perceived incompetence' of children generally rather than the 'displayed incompetence' of individual children (Archard, 1993). Archard (1993) is also critical in that some formulations of this type imply that the primary caretaker (usually parent) of a child should take decisions for that child on the basis of the decisions that child would take if (s) he were a competent adult, implying retrospective consent. In essence, criticism of protection rights is that they deny autonomy to the child. Thirdly, there are child liberationist formulations of children's rights (Holt, 1975; Farson, 1978; for example). These tend to stress the child's autonomy in making choices and taking decisions. Although such formulations vary a great deal they basically argue that the ascription of rights on the basis of age is unjust. Such formulations have great difficulty explaining by what process an infant can act autonomously, although more moderate formulations accept certain age related aspects of incompetence. A particular liberationist position is that children should have rights against parents, and that older children in particular ought to have the right to challenge parent's decisions over important aspects of their lives. [1] The general thrust of the liberationist argument is that rights should be acquired solely on the basis of competence, regardless of age. This is criticised (Archard, 1993) on the basis that it derives from the false premise that society makes distinctions on the basis of age alone. Archard (1993) accepts that there is a tendency to underestimate the capacities of children, but argues that rights are granted through a perceived correlation between age and the development of specific capacities. He argues that the ages at which specific rights accrue ought to be lower. Freeman (1983) adopts a similar stance through reference to the lived reality of adolescents, who in theory have no right to autonomy in respect of issues such as alcohol use and sexual activity, but in practice exercise a great deal of freedom.

Social workers working with sexually abused adolescent girls thus occupy a position where there are tensions between protecting vulnerable children from abuse and granting autonomy to young women as a countervailing psychological influence to the restrictions on their autonomy inherent in their abuse. This reflects a tension inherent in social work generally between the need to protect the vulnerable and core social work values of empowerment and client choice, which is further complicated by the consequences of the sexual abuse in inhibiting the girls' capacity for autonomous action, both due to the lack of opportunity for autonomous action to refer back to and through the interruption of cognitive and emotional aspects of the development of adult identity (Herman, 1994). [2]

The issues are compounded by external influences on the direct social worker-client relationship, in that the social workers' preferred intervention strategies might be circumscribed by the courts' ascription of 'nearly adult' status to the older girls. This effectively leaves social workers with little choice but to accept a high degree of autonomous decision-making by the girls, regardless of any protectionist concerns the social worker may have.

In this chapter I intend to examine the particular way these themes influence the social workers' perceptions and understanding of specific cases, and thus their child protection practices. I shall examine the ways in which social workers perceive the disclosure process, the girls' attitude to and expectations of the child protection process, and the emotional and psychological state of the girls. I also intend to look at the ways in which the social workers make their assessments of the seriousness of the abuse and the ways in which they see forms of abusive practice relating to the duration of the abuse and the girl-perpetrator relationship. Crosscutting all these themes is the central issue of the age of the girls concerned and the impact that has on the social workers perceptions and practice.

The Safety of the Girl

Central to the child protection task is the termination of the abuse and the minimisation of the risk of future abuse. The social workers' concerns in this area were clearly of two distinct types; the cessation of the abuse, and the creation of conditions to minimise future risk. As identifying exactly which children are at risk is an almost impossible, social workers employ a series of risk criteria that suggest the probability of risk, engaging in 'risk insurance' (Parton *et al* (1997). In the early stages of the process, the immediate safety of the girl was accorded great significance.

> I had to ensure that she was safe, while I slowed down the process and then we got into the child protection procedures (SW).

The social workers actions at this point varied a great deal along two distinct pathways. The first of these was the age of the girl. In cases involving older girls there was a tendency to accept any arrangements the girls had made for themselves in terms of safe accommodation. Some social workers referred to older girls as young women with rights to make their own decisions, others referred to their hands being tied by the courts. With the younger girls the social workers tended to seek Care Orders or Emergency Protection Orders. The critical age appeared to be around twelve or thirteen.

The second pathway involved their assessment of the degree of risk the girl was in. The social workers were less likely to accept the girls' own arrangements if they thought the degree of risk remained high, regardless of the age of the girls. A degree of cultural collision became apparent here deriving from the relative class and educational backgrounds of the social workers and the girls. The social workers tended to underestimate the effectiveness of familial and other support networks in what appeared to remain an abusive environment. One can also see that there may have been a tendency for some girls, in a disturbed psychological state as a consequence of their abuse, to minimise the abuse, alter their own conscious perceptions of it, and thus underestimate the degree of risk they remained in (Herman, 1994).

More girls exercised a higher degree of autonomy at this stage than the social workers would have wished, with the consequence that many of them remained at home at least until the Initial Child Protection Conference. Some girls insisted on remaining at home even though they knew they remained at risk. One girl insisted on remaining in the family home to protect her younger sister. This was a clear example of an individual placing her perceived responsibility to others above and beyond her own best interests. This is a well documented theme within feminist analysis of child and woman abuse in particular and female oppression generally that shows contemporary constructions of femininity as involving a high degree of responsibility for others to the detriment of self. However, most of the girls either was taken into care or found themselves other accommodation. The social workers saw this as very important as it ensured the physical separation of the girl and the perpetrator[3] in terms of co-residence, and to some extent in terms of day-to-day contact. Research suggests such separation is 'the most important element in protection' (Farmer and Owen, 1995, Pg.311). In those cases involving older girls who remained at home the social workers remained anxious that the balance between client self-determination and child protection had left the girls at some degree of risk.

The concept of physical separation remained central to the social workers' thinking in terms of long-term 'risk insurance'. The criminal justice system was seen by some as assisting in that task if bail conditions involved provisions that the perpetrator moves out of the family home, or conviction resulted in imprisonment. [4] As few perpetrators were prosecuted the social workers made strenuous efforts to persuade perpetrators to leave the family home and to convince other family members of the risks of the perpetrator returning. If such efforts failed they considered care proceedings, although there were considerable practical and therapeutic problems associated with this strategy, particularly in rural areas. Placements some distance from home can be counterproductive (Farmer and Owen, 1995), as the girl may decide to return home. This increases her own degree of risk, whilst simultaneously making apparent the social worker's inability to influence events. The social workers' reluctance to initiate care proceedings also reflects their concerns over the problems associated with returning young people to their families (Farmer and Parker, 1991) and their worries that removing the girl from the family home may 'send out the wrong messages' (SW) in that she might see herself as being punished and thus be reinforced in any guilt she may feel for her own abuse.

This highlights a further tension for social workers. Physical separation between the girl and the perpetrator can be achieved through care proceedings and placements a considerable distance from home can diminish the opportunities even for chance meetings. However, such placements can also significantly reduce levels of family and peer support, by making contact between the girl and her non-abusing family and friends more difficult.

Social workers' decisions over taking girls into care were also subject to other influences, such as the often changing attitudes of the perpetrator and the mother (Parton *et al*, 1997) and the decisions taken by the criminal justice system. This resulted in some girls oscillating between home and care, in effect experiencing a 'protection career'. [5]

The social workers anxieties about the mother-perpetrator relationship revolved around two related themes. They were anxious that if the relationship persisted the mother might invite the perpetrator back into the family home, recreating the original abusive environment, and they were concerned that the continuance of the relationship could engender fear in the girl that he might return. They referred to girls seeing the continuance of these relationships as minimising what the perpetrator had done, or mothers even doubting that the abuse had ever occurred. The continuance of a close mother-perpetrator relationship was seen by the social workers as a significant risk factor, leading them to persuade reviews that the girl remain on the Child Protection Register and be subject to close monitoring.

The tension between protection and physical separation and client choice and autonomy was also apparent in that some girls' desire for the termination of the abuse did not automatically translate into a desire to sever all relations with the perpetrator. Then social workers confronted this tension in terms of risk management. They sought compromises that would grant a relative degree of safety without breaking the familial link. One method was that of supervised contact. This was seen to leave the door open to future reconciliation, although few of the social workers felt the perpetrators would amend their behaviour.

The Process of Disclosure

The social workers stressed that disclosure needs to be seen as an often slow interactive process involving the girl taking a series of decisions to gradually divulge things that had happened to her which were highly personal and difficult to speak of.

> I had a case where it took a year to get a full picture of what had actually gone on (SW).

Research (Vizard and Tranter, 1988a) suggests that the quality and depth of disclosure bears a direct relationship to the degree of trust the girl can build up with a significant adult within the disclosure process, the child or young person choosing originally to disclose to an adult she trusts (Furniss, 1991). This 'trusted person' then becomes the key adult for the child during the initial stages of disclosure and any disclosure interviews ought to take place in front of this 'trusted person', who could be the child's mother, teacher or any other adult. The 'trusted person' does not have to be an expert in the child protection process; rather her/his presence is primarily as an attachment figure for the child, who provides her with emotional backup and explicit licence to disclose the abuse, and gradually gives the child 'permission' to disclose the abuse to the child protection professionals through a process of handing over this private knowledge. As the 'trusted person' is often a teacher, youth worker or other professional that inhabits a social space between home and the child protection network, Furniss (1991) is clear of the need for those who work with children and adolescents to be aware of the indirect hints and signals that abused children will give out.

> Usually children do not dare to disclose when these indirect hints as cry for help have been dismissed or disregarded. Not taking up a secret communication about sexual abuse can therefore be very damaging (Furniss, 1991, Pg. 43).

The disclosure process is also bounded by the 'social organisation of 'telling" (Wattam, 1992, Pg.46), and there is 'a moral obligation' (Wattam, 1992, Pg.46) attached to what we tell to whom and in what order. Issues involving sexual activity simply cannot be spoken of to just anyone, despite the apparent contemporary insatiability for discussing and debating sexual matters. Although sex is constantly spoken of in the abstract, it remains a 'dark secret' at a personal level (Foucault, 1990). Specific sexual experiences, whether pleasurable or painful, are culturally defined as personal and not amenable to general discursive examination. The social organisation of 'telling' indicates that before a sexually abused girl tells the social worker anything she will probably have told her mother or other close confidant (Herman, 1981; Waldby, 1981; Wattam, 1992) and in most cases in this sample it was the mother who was first disclosed to. Few girls disclosed to the social workers prior to telling their mothers, and the mothers' responses profoundly influenced subsequent aspects of the disclosure. Maternal belief and support is the single most important factor in ensuring the abuse comes to the attention of social services (Wattam, 1992), and is crucial in the recovery process (Conte and Schuerman, 1987; Wyatt and Mickey, 1988; Berliner, 1991).

Although girls clearly disclose in order to terminate the abuse or prevent its recurrence, abused children and young people disclose at a specific time for a number of additional reasons (Wattam, 1992; Farmer and Owen, 1995), including a desire to prevent a younger sibling suffering similar abuse, an increased sense of victimisation as the seriousness of the abuse escalates, or simply through a growing realisation as they get older of the inappropriateness of their experiences. These subsidiary reasons are best thought of as triggers to disclosure.

The social workers found these triggers relatively unproblematic. They were less comfortable, however, when some girls appeared to disclose with the specific desire to see the perpetrator punished. Their concern clearly emanated from their knowledge and experience of the criminal justice system, and the relatively slim chances of a perpetrator being successfully convicted. They spent a great deal of time at an early stage explaining that conviction was unlikely, in order to minimise any negative impact (Dingwall *et al*, 1983; Corby, 1987) a not guilty verdict or a decision not to prosecute might have for the girl, whilst simultaneously trying to explain to the girl the short term and long term benefits she could gain from disclosure. One particular benefit the social workers stressed was that it gave them the opportunity to begin to instigate therapeutic interventions that would help to assure the girls that they were not to blame for their abuse.

Aside from the procedural implications about when to time joint video interviews, [6] social workers found significant difficulties in judging whether or not a disclosure was complete. Summit (1983) and Bentovim and Boston (1988) developed a model of child sexual abuse accommodation syndrome comprising five stages of secrecy, helplessness, entrapment and accommodation, partial or conflicting disclosure, and retraction. Although very different in many ways, the stages of 'helplessness' and 'entrapment and accommodation' bear some resonance with aspects of despair and resignation in bereavement or upon receipt of a diagnosis of a terminal illness (Kubler-Ross, 1970). Clearly, there are major differences, but this does emphasise the ways in which abuse can be experienced as loss and it lends support to Herman's (1994) view that child or adolescent sexual abuse is closely related to other forms of traumatic experience. The social workers found the process of partial disclosure, retraction and further disclosure relatively common. Similarly some girls would disclose in great detail and insist that the disclosure represented the sum total of the abuse, leaving the social worker to wonder if this was true or whether there was continuing abuse that the girl was not prepared to talk about.

> She would only tell you what she wanted you to know. She would only tell you so much (SW).

Familial sexual abuse is rarely a one-off (Vizard and Tranter, 1988a), and it is very difficult to disclose sexual abuse (Bowlby, 1988; Roberts and Taylor, 1993; Farmer and Owen, 1995), indeed most incidents of child and adolescent sexual abuse are never disclosed to anyone (Nasjletu, 1980; Waterhouse, 1993). In a detailed prevalence study (Kelly *et al*, 1991) found that around half of all incidents of sexual abuse were not disclosed at the time. However, one can see the level of disclosure as being higher if one takes a longer view, as some adult women disclose abuse at a later date, triggered by traumatic events such as the discovery of the sexual abuse of their own children (Hooper, 1992). The social workers recognised that disclosure can be far from straightforward, often girls will only give hints that something is wrong without even referring to any sexual abuse.

The social workers experienced some difficulties in that several girls seemed unable to find the language to explain what had happened to them. This tended to be less of a problem with older girls, although the degree of traumatisation of the girls also had an effect on this. The social workers recognised the psychological pain that some girls endured in disclosing the abuse, especially in the artificial and structured environment of the joint video interview, describing it variously as 'very difficult' (SW) and 'agony for her' (SW). The problems the social workers found at this stage of the process also tended to reflect the circumstances of the original referral. Those girls who had self-referred were 'clearly motivated' (SW) and tended to disclose more freely than those who had been referred by a third party.

In terms of disclosure there was a degree of conflict between the social workers and their managers. The managers felt there was a significant risk of girls making false allegations, although the research (Jones and McGraw, 1987; Gibbons *et al*, 1995) refutes this. The social workers, however, tended to make the basic assumption that all allegations were true. In many cases they found it easy to believe the girls, as they found girls lacking the sexual knowledge to make it up, or found cases fitting closely to patterns they had experienced in previous cases. In other cases they found it more difficult to believe the girls, especially if the story changed over time. Some girls (Finkelhor, 1979; Bentovim and Boston, 1988) can feel some aspects of the sexual practices that comprise the abuse as pleasurable. In such cases it can often be more difficult for mothers and other non-abusing family members to come to terms with a complex of conflicting emotions and express their belief and support to the girl. In such cases, the social workers appeared to feel that their belief was even more important, as the girl's sense of guilt may be greater and support from the family less.

Their belief of all allegations seemed to reflect issues of 'risk insurance'. They feared the physical and psychological consequences for the girl if their disbelief proved to be wrong. Disbelief by social workers of sexual abuse allegations can lead to depression and despair, and is a significant factor in young female homelessness (Hendessi, 1992), whilst belief is a significant factor in validating the experiences of sexually abused young women and can have a positive effect on self-esteem (Women's Resource Centre, 1989). The social workers also saw believing the girl as a way of gaining the girl's confidence, itself a major step towards a successful child protection intervention.

> She had faith in our involvement because we believed her, and I have no doubt that she told the truth (SW).

In contrast to the managers fears over false allegations one social worker expressed her concerns over the vast numbers of girls who never disclose sexual abuse, and one of the reasons why they do not disclose. She suggested that girls are less likely to disclose than in the past, as adolescent girls are now more aware of the consequences of disclosure in terms of family breakdown. This resonates with research findings (Waldby, 1985;

Wattam, 1992; Monck *et al*, 1995) that show self-blame and fear of family breakdown as significant reasons for non-disclosure, but begs the question why girls are more knowledgeable than they used to be. Clearly the past ten years has seen a vast increase of academic and professional knowledge of child sexual abuse, and it may be that the social worker was imputing her own increased sensitivity to the subject to others. Her views may also reflect, however, a changing public awareness of child sexual abuse. My own daughters (aged sixteen and fourteen) have told me that child abuse and child protection are rarely discussed among their peer group, but the media coverage of sexual abuse has moved a long way from issues of stranger danger, and telephone helplines such as ChildLine are widely advertised. Thus it may well be the case that adolescent girls are a little more aware than they used to be. Other reasons given in the literature for non-disclosure, such as the fear of not being believed (Finkelhor, 1979; Waldby, 1995; Nash and West, 1986: Wattam, 1992), injunctions to secrecy brought to bear by the perpetrator (Waldby, 1985; Women's Resource Centre, 1989) and an ambivalence in the girls' feelings about others knowing of the abuse (Hooper, 1992), remain, however, more convincing reasons for non-disclosure.

One of the serious problems that the social workers encountered was an injunction to confidentiality by the girls. This was a problem that went beyond the disclosure process in that at all stages of the child protection process the girls were anxious about who would know what details of their abuse. Sexual abuse is too complex a topic for one individual to deal with (Vizard and Tranter, 1988b). The social worker must therefore make efforts to find ways acceptable to the girl concerned to inform others within the child protection network of the abuse (Wattam, 1992). The social workers found this task difficult and a source of potential conflict. They found persuading the girl took up a significant amount of their time and effort and was not always successful. In two cases it led to retraction as the girls could not overcome their fears of others knowing.

The disclosure process also illustrates two of the tensions inherent in the child protection process. The social workers were unhappy at the lack of time and space allowed for work after the initial disclosure. The sociological and social policy/social work body of research has gradually established a whole series of complexities involved in revealing sexual abuse, and the long term nature of such revelations fits uneasily within a child protection process that prioritises cases within a crisis management perspective, but affords less priority to ongoing work. This shows a serious conflict between certain core social work values of empowerment and assistance on the one hand and the constraints of administrative priorities when resources are limited. The disclosure process also indicated the tension between therapeutic concerns and the criminal justice system. Some social workers were critical of the need to gain detailed knowledge of the abuse for criminal justice purposes, as they felt this could be invasive with little therapeutic value. The social workers felt strongly that a full disclosure could have therapeutic value for the girl (Finkelhor, 1979). They further felt that as only the perpetrator and the girl would know the reality and duration of the abuse (Berliner, 1991), and the operation of the criminal justice system made it unlikely that there would be a spontaneous confession from the perpetrator: [7]

> ...the child's own confirmation was the most important factor substantiating allegations of abuse (Farmer and Owen, 1995, Pg.49).

The Girls' Expectations of the Child Protection Process

One aspect of working with sexually abused adolescent girls that the social workers routinely had to confront was the girls' understanding of the child protection process and their expectations of it, including a general reluctance from the point of disclosure onwards to talk about the abuse (Roberts and Taylor, 1993), disillusion with the child protection process (Wattam, 1992; Farmer and Owen, 1995), and regrets over ever disclosing.

> If I'd known what I was letting myself in for, I'd never have done it, Girl aged 16, during research interview for the child protection study (Wattam, 1992, Pg.ix).

Many of the girls had expectations of retribution and social workers made great efforts to attempt to move the girls' focus away from this. Although they saw that some therapeutic benefits could be gained from giving evidence in court (Runyan *et al*, 1988) and in gaining a conviction (Berliner, 1991), as validation of the girls' abusive experiences, the social workers' antipathy to retribution seemed to go beyond the inherent tension between therapeutic and criminal justice elements within the child protection process. They tended to routinely redefine the girls' desire for justice as a very desire for revenge, thus reinterpreting of the client's perspective as constituting part of the problem (Pithouse, 1987). For the social workers revenge was loaded with pejorative overtones. Revenge, however, can be seen in a positive light.

> Revenge is the great mobiliser. It inverts the humiliation caused by an
> undefended attack. By visiting hurt on the perpetrator, you try to transfer the
> pain of being unable to protect or defend what you feel is rightfully yours.
> Revenge expunges the stain caused by the humiliation (Orbach, 1997).

Orbach (1997) notes aspects of revenge as the antithesis of appreciating the
perspective of the other, and this appears to be what the social workers saw
as unwelcome in the abused girls. What social workers saw as revenge,
however, could also be viewed as a desire for justice and the public
acknowledgement of the perpetration of a wrong. To conceive of such a
desire as a negative concept of revenge implies an all-consuming passion to
get one's own back that dominates one's thinking, displacing all other
motives for action. At one level this suggests that the social workers
operated within a frame of reference that places individual issues such as
recovery in complete opposition to social issues such as justice. However,
despite their concerns that retribution could be an overwhelming motive in
some girls' disclosures, the social workers also recognised other motives in
the same girls. Their concern over retribution may owe less to their
conceptualisations of the role of retribution in the recovery process and
more to do with a fear of loss of ownership of child protection to the police
and the courts. A central role for justice and retribution in child protection
would transfer expertise away from social workers to the police and other
professionals in the criminal justice system.

Although not all the social workers saw the girls' desire for
retribution in a negative light, and although they all saw the benefits of
conviction in terms of validating the girls' experiences, the overarching
theme to emerge was that they made strenuous efforts to talk girls out of a
desire for retribution and to persuade them to see that any disclosure must
first and foremost be 'for her own peace of mind' (SW).

A second theme to emerge in girls' expectations of the process was
that they had varying degrees of knowledge of the realities of the process.
The social workers found some girls with a clear understanding of what
would happen, either through their own past experience or that of people
known to them. They saw many of these girls as fully prepared for the
consequences of any decisions they might make within the process, as long
as it terminated the abuse. Other girls they found had a much poorer
understanding of the process and often-unreasonable expectations of it. The
social workers attempted to explain how each stage of the process would
work and the implications of various decisions. This was not always
successful. One girl, for example, wanted her mother's boyfriend to stop

abusing her, but to continue living with them and taking her out in the car. The social worker failed to make her understand this could not happen. The social workers found the process itself left several girls confused and feeling 'very helpless' (SW). They saw the criminal justice system in particular as implicated in this. The *Memorandum of Good Practice* (Home Office and DoH, 1992) rules for video interviews left many girls bemused and angry at being asked non-leading questions about abuse they had already reported to the social worker. They found girls feeling they were not listened to at Child Protection Conferences, 'lost' within the process and simply being 'shoved around' (SW). The general impression to emerge was that of a significant number of girls being swept along with little or no control of their circumstances, reflecting earlier research findings (Farmer and Owen, 1995). The social workers' concern for these girls draws attention back to a central theme in child protection. A sense of helplessness or disempowerment is relatively frequent consequence of adolescent sexual abuse (Herman, 1994), yet the operation of the child protection process can work to reinforce those feelings. Clearly the triggers for disclosure for particular girls cannot be divorced entirely from the girls expectations of the process, and there was some evidence to suggest that those who self-referred or were referred by their mothers tended to have more realistic expectations then those referred by other professionals.

The social workers found some girls extremely difficult to work with, as at various points in the process they saw them as attempting to meet 'normal' expectations. There is a corpus of literature in sociology and social psychology (see Mills, 1940; Goffman, 1971; Foucault, 1977; for example) that show the powerful forces one is subject to in meeting 'normal' expectations in social interaction, both for psychologically healthy and mentally ill people. This suggests that the trauma of sexual abuse would not prevent individuals from being subject to those same 'normalising' forces. Thus the girls' efforts to meet the social workers' expectations of a 'normal' client does not suggest that their responses to specific situations within the process were not sincere. Some social workers also spoke of girls trying to 'play the system' (SW), or, in one case, ensure she gave the social worker enough work. This implies that in some cases the girls were making the best efforts they could to retain a sense of control in situations of relative powerlessness. The apparently cynical tone with which some social workers spoke of these difficult cases is perhaps best interpreted not as cynicism *per se*, but as exasperation in terms of the time consuming nature of trying to work with them in an environment of scarce resources and strict time management. It also suggests a sense of 'occupational impotence' (Pithouse, 1987) and a fear of loss of control of elements of the process to the girls that reinforces the specificity of this client group and their 'near adult' status.

The social workers saw the girls' levels of satisfaction with the process as varying a great deal (see also Farmer and Owen, 1995) on a continuum relating to the seriousness of the original abuse. In those cases where the abuse had been relatively minor the tangible benefits of terminating the abuse were outweighed by the girls experiences of the process itself.

> Most of her personal experiences of the child protection system were pretty negative (SW).

This variability of benefit also draws attention to government guidance (DoH, 1991b) and the non-intervention principle, suggesting that the need for intervention needs to be considered very carefully on a case by case basis. [8] There were cases where girls remained at risk, despite the best efforts of social workers, and the hopes and expectations the girls had of the capacity of services to protect them. Some cases are clearly intractable (DoH, 1995).

> ...poor outcome should not be taken as evidence of professional failure. Important as it is, a skilled intervention can be outweighed by the nature and severity of the case: even the best practice may be unable to alter the course of events (DoH, 1995, Pp.45/46).

The protection and recovery of sexually abused adolescent girls is strongly influenced by the attitudes and actions of family and friends. [9] This influence can be beneficial or detrimental and may well be at least as important as any action taken by social workers.

Some girls were unhappy not with outcomes but with elements of the process itself. Thorburn *et al* (1995) found children objected to being interviewed on school premises or taken out of school for interview. The social workers found dissatisfaction with elements of the process most likely once the abuse had terminated several girls finding aftermath work 'a bit of an intrusion' (SW).

The girls' expectations appeared to be best met in those cases where the social worker expended significant time and effort in explaining what was happening and listened to the girls' expressions of their needs. Similar kinds of satisfaction from the process were found in other recent research

(DoH, 1995). The whole area of client expectation was one that the social workers found it difficult to deal with.

> Sometimes we met up to what she expected and sometimes it was different (SW).

The Attitude of the Girls to the Child Protection Process

The social workers had to confront the girls' (often-changing) attitudes towards elements of the child protection process. They had to deal with issues such as the girls' willingness to actively participate in plans for their own protection and varying degrees of cooperation and conflict between themselves and the girls. Before these issues could be confronted social workers needed to gain access to the girls.

Access only emerged as an issue in those cases where attempts were made to deny or limit it, the social workers in such cases expressing concern over not being able to become or remain aware of what was going on. They found that girls rarely attempted to avoid contact. Rather, it was members of the girls' families who attempted to make access to the girls more difficult. The social workers saw these attempts at minimising contact as tending to coincide with times when girls were beginning to retract their allegations or minimise the degree of risk they were subject to. They saw these two factors as related, families bringing pressure to bear on girls to retract as part of an overall familial effort to minimise what had happened (or was happening) and thus remove themselves from the scrutiny of the child protection process. There is a well established motif in the research literature (Waldby, 1985; Vizard and Tranter, 1988a; for example) that shows families adopting strategies to minimise or rationalise girls' allegations of sexual abuse, and persuading or coercing girls to retract those allegations. Survivors' accounts (Bass and Thornton, 1983; Women's Resource Centre, 1989) suggest these strategies are largely perpetrator driven, both directly through coercion of the girl, and indirectly through bringing pressure to bear on the girl's mother.

When access was made difficult the social workers were concerned about the familial pressure they believed the girl was probably under, and about the reduction in their own capacity to observe the eruption of any emotional problems or any increase of risk for the girl. The social workers saw familial influences on girl's change over time and exert a substantial influence on the degree of cooperation between the girls and themselves. Often girls would appear fully cooperative in their interactions with the social workers, but would fail to cooperate in their behaviour outside those interactions, by, say, maintaining contact with the perpetrator. Dingwall *et al* (1983) point to parental non-compliance and/or refusal of access as a critical point in the transformation of a child abuse concern into a fully fledged child protection case. The social workers took any parental refusal of access as an indicator that something was amiss. Once they gained access the social workers tended to informally assess the girls' attitude to the child protection process.

One way in which they understood the girls' attitude was through their willingness to participate in various procedural aspects of the process, such as the Initial Child Protection Conference. [10] Several girls attended Initial Child Protection Conferences, and the social workers took this as a sign that they were prepared to cooperate in the child protection process in general. Non-attendance, however, was not taken as a sign of non-cooperation. However, the social workers saw none of the girls as actively participating in Child Protection Conferences. There was a clear feeling that the process itself also inhibited the girls' participation. They saw difficulties for the girls in participating in a forum where they were the objects of discussion in relation to something as invasive as sexual abuse, and found perpetrator attendance at Conferences adding to the trauma to the point those girls might not even attend. Some social workers proffered a solution that echoes the views of Morrison *et al* (1990) and Fisher (1990), that the child's view needed to remain at the centre of any Conference deliberations, but that the child should not have to face her parents within that forum. Whereas the research suggests the use of an advocate, the social workers suggested that the girl and the perpetrator attend only to give their accounts, avoiding contact with each other and obviating the need for the girl to sit through the discussions. Other social workers suggested the outright exclusion of the perpetrator from the conference, thus removing many of the constraints on the girl's attendance. These various views reflect a concern that a holistic view of the girl as an individual is lost in the prioritisation of procedures.

> I wonder if she shouldn't be there and not him. It's her life, and anyway it's not about blame, it's about sorting things out (SW).

If a criminal prosecution was being sought, the social workers saw the joint video interview as a further critical factor in the girls' willingness to participate. The crucial issue at this stage appeared to be the degree of empathy or sympathy between the girls and the police officers concerned, something, which appeared to relate directly to the levels of joint social services/police training. The social workers' perceptions seemed to revolve around a notion of an 'ideal' video interview, with both the girls and the other participants behaving in appropriate ways: an ideal that was constantly being violated by the realities of video interviews in concrete situations. This reflects Pithouse's (1987) argument that social workers tend to perceive real clients in concrete situations in relatively pejorative terms by contrast with the 'ideal' client who is central to the rationale for the work. It also further indicates the grave misgivings most of the social workers had about of he criminal justice system.

Beyond any particulars of participation, the social workers believed the key aspect of the girls' attitudes was the degree of cooperation or conflict that developed between girls and social workers as the child protection process ran its course. As one manager spelt out.

> So much depends whether they want to be involved or whether they want to shut it [the abuse] off (Manager).

The social workers concurred. The central issue revolved around the capacity or desire of the girls to confront their abuse. The social workers saw gaining the girls' confidence and developing trusting relationships as a crucial task in the earliest stages of the process. This reflects research findings that social workers found their relationships with abused adolescents critical (Farmer and Owen, 1995), and that a good working relationship is crucial to a successful outcome (Sharland *et al*, 1995). In some cases the social workers developed good working relationships with the girls within a few days through simply visiting them, explaining the procedures, generally chatting to them and 'sitting having a cup of tea' (SW). In other cases they found the process more difficult.

> She didn't particularly want to talk and have her feelings clarified. That was quite difficult to do. We did get a sort of reasonable relationship but it took ages and ages. She was very quiet and it was often difficult to draw her out to say what she did (SW).

The social workers realised that developing a rapport with the girl depended on a variety of factors, not least the compatibility of their personalities.

> She didn't see my colleague as offering her anything at all and she wasn't prepared to tell her [of the abuse] (SW).

This problem of matching the worker to the girl was a significant one and in reality a relatively complex issue to deal with, involving the interplay of client choice, caseload management and worker competences. [11] Farmer and Owen, 1995, Pg.252) point to the statistical probability of the benefits of the Conference appointing someone other than the original duty worker as key worker. Clearly in some cases the original worker-client match may be more beneficial than a change of worker, as some combinations will 'hit it off' whereas others will not. The girls' choice of worker in terms of age and gender, for instance, may well be compromised by who is available in terms of workload, something which may well be exacerbated if the girl has a disability or any other special need that requires the worker to have a specific competence over and above child protection skills.

The social workers found the girls' degree of cooperation often changed over time. Specific episodes tended to push the relationship towards conflict. One of the most critical of these episodes derived from the age boundary of the child protection process and involved social workers introducing the topic of independent living programmes to girls around the age of sixteen or seventeen. They found many girls in that situation withdrew into themselves in response to a fear of being left without support.

The social workers also had to confront the girls' attitudes to their abuse, the perpetrators and the child protection process in general, attitudes that varied a great deal, and were derived from behaviours that were interpreted differently by different social workers. Many girls would oscillate between a high degree of cooperation and being deliberately awkward. Some social workers saw this as manipulative behaviour, yet others saw it as girls attempting to exhibit autonomy and trying to make choices within the confines of the child protection process. Although for several of the social workers the girls' exercise of a degree of autonomy within the process posed few difficulties and was often positively welcomed, for others it proved problematic. The older the girls were the more likely the social workers appeared to accept the girls' decisions.

Some social workers also felt concern when girls refused counselling or decided to retain some form of familial relationship with the perpetrator. However, for many social workers the notion of client choice remained a dominant theme in their accounts. They saw the girls' choices as paramount, arguing that it had been her choice to disclose and involve them in the first place, and that as 'near adults' they must retain the right to make their own choices in the light of the best advice the social workers could provide. The concept of client choice is a key theme in governmental policy (Children Act, 1989, s.1 (3)(a); DoH, 1991a; DoH, 1991b) which stresses concepts of partnership, child and family participation, and the paramountcy of the child's wishes.

The importance attributed by most of the social workers to client choice in child protection decision-making can be seen in terms of three distinct discourses. Firstly, it equates to a discourse of empowerment that encompasses the rights of young people to a degree of self-determination. Secondly, it equates to a high degree of managerialism in the delivery of social services (Howe, 1986) in that legislative and procedural injunctions to partnership are invoked at the expense of normatively derived professional social work decisions (Parton, 1991). Thirdly, the placing of responsibility back on to the client implies a degree of autonomy that comes very close to 'blaming the victim' for her abuse. This articulates closely with some of the findings of Howe (1990) and Thorpe (1994) in that 'client' is a status conferred on an individual by an agency, a status that can be 'coated in moral rectitude' (Pithouse, 1987, Pg.81). Although all the social workers in the sample embraced the concept of client choice they did so with varying degrees of enthusiasm and for differing reasons. Some simply took a lead from the courts and the ascription of 'nearly adult' status to adolescent girls and appeared to retain a sense of threat to their professional expertise by client decision-making, for example, whilst others felt strongly that the client had some personal responsibility for her own welfare.

The social workers felt a key factor in lack of cooperation was that many girls feared they would lose their place in the family, and on balance returned to the family home against the wishes of the social worker. There were also examples of girls refusing educational and psychological help, something social workers took as evidence of uncertainty. One social worker spoke of a girl who was very keen on a variety of inputs in respect of her psychological and educational needs yet who would always back down at the last minute. The social worker was unable to understand why the girl adopted such an attitude, although one could suggest that she had an inherent fear of intimacy or dependency and perhaps a fear of failure in anything she might try because of low self-esteem as a consequence of her abuse.

The girls' attitudes had some influence on the ways in which workers saw the cases. Some saw their clients as difficult or contrary in that they would change their minds a great deal, often refusing the help that was offered. Others saw the girls as working with them because social services intervention represented the least poor scenario for them.

> I think she agreed to go with us because she wanted to be away from the village, where she feared her father. So in effect our offer wasn't very attractive, but it was more attractive than having her father on her doorstep (SW).

The principal attitude of the girls to the child protection process was that they wanted it to ensure that the abuse stopped and didn't recommence. The social workers shared that view. However, beyond that primary objective there existed a continuum of cooperation and conflict that varied both from case to case and from time to time within cases. That continuum was influenced both by the quality of the relationship between the girl and the social worker, and by the actions of external factors, such as the attitude of members of the girls' families. A model of cooperation/conflict can thus be clearly developed. The influence upon the social worker's practice in terms of cooperation or conflict between her/himself and the girl can be seen to circulate around twin axes; the quality of the relationship between the social worker and the girl, and the variability of those exogenous influences on the girl. The difficulties social workers experienced in their relationships with the girls reinforced the need for supervision and peer support in order to give them the space to talk through their difficulties.

The Age of the Girls and 'Nearly Adult' Status

The central issues that the social workers faced that were specific to their work with sexually abused adolescent girls were those issues relating to the age of the girls.

These issues fell into four areas; issues of autonomy for clients of 'near adult' status, issues deriving from the tendency of the courts to prioritise the wishes of teenagers in any issues relating to their own welfare and protection, the upper age limit of the child protection process, and the specificity of adolescent cognitive, sexual and emotional development. Although there is a clear analytical division between these different sets of issues, in practice the configuration between them meant that the social workers felt their actions to be circumscribed by the wishes of the girl, even when this compromised what they saw as meeting the protection needs of the girl.

> Had she been something like ten then we could have done something about it, but at fifteen she's old enough to make her own decisions (SW).

The older the girls were, the greater weight the social workers afforded to the girls' own perceptions of their best interests, to the point that girls of fourteen or fifteen tended to exercise simple choice over issues such as whether to be looked after by the local authority. Although the social worker-client relationship is balanced in favour of the worker in terms of her/his professional status (Pithouse, 1987), her/his superior knowledge and control (Foucault, 1980) within the child protection process, and in terms of the patriarchal power located in the adult-child relationship (Veerman, 1992), the 'near adult' status of girls over the age of twelve or thirteen rendered their wishes viable and legitimate. This degree of autonomy derives both from social work values in terms of client's rights, and from the growing dominance of juridical power within the child protection process (Parton, 1991; Parton *et al*, 1997), mediated through the social workers' awareness of the operation of the courts.

> As soon as a girl of that age says I don't want to go to a foster home, ...that would be taken into account (SW).

The social workers found courts tended to see girls in terms of chronological age with little regard to maturity. The routine use of age as a proxy for maturity reflects a modality of thought in western societies generally that perceives of childhood development as a finite process leading to adulthood (Archard, 1993). [12] The social workers saw the courts failing to recognise that sexually abused adolescent girls were often developmentally damaged as a consequence of the abuse (Finkelhor, 1984; Herman, 1994) and in a sense less mature than their non-abused peers, leaving some girls to make decisions that the social workers saw as not in their best interests. The social workers clearly experienced a degree of professional anxiety, being charged with the protection of individual fourteen or fifteen-year-old immature or psychologically disturbed adolescent girls making judgements and decisions that left them at risk. It may be, however, that the decisions taken by any particular girl may have appeared immature because the social worker simply did not agree with them.

In terms of client choice and children's rights the child protection process displays both protectionist and liberationist tendencies, although the age criteria adopted by the courts and many of the social workers imply that within the operation of the process itself older adolescents are seen in terms similar to adults. The social workers felt the courts failed to abide by the 'maturity' principle in the Children Act (s.(1)(3)(a)), and the courts have adopted a chronological principle that sees age as a proxy for maturity. One aspect of this that added a dimension to the social workers' task with girls in this age group was that it led to a tendency for the CPS to treat the girls as 'nearly adult'. The CPS were thus more likely to seek prosecution in these cases than in cases involving younger girls, as older girls were seen as more reliable witnesses. This reinforces the view held by many social workers that the agendas followed by themselves and the criminal justice system are very different. [13] The social workers, however, although they differed widely in the levels of autonomy they saw as appropriate for the girls, tended towards a less rigid perspective, similar to Freeman's (1983) suggestion, of judging each case on the basis of the sexual, emotional and cognitive development the girl concerned.

The importance the social workers attached to the concept of maturity and their perception of the arbitrariness of the courts' attitude to the girls' age suggests social worker concerns in terms of losing ownership or control of aspects of child protection to both the criminal justice system and the clients. One social worker made clear her anxieties in working with this age group. She found it very difficult watching a girl make decisions that were clearly not in her best interests, without being able to intercede and alter those decisions,

> Whereas with a more naive, more manipulable child of a younger ages you can twist and do it your way (SW).

This perception of work with older girls was not shared by all the social workers. Some felt that if the criminal justice pathway was followed then procedures such as the joint video interview were much easier with adolescent rather than younger girls. They saw issues such as the type of referral and the individual level of development of the girl as significant, but in general felt older girls more capable of expressing what had happened to them and what help they needed.

> Adolescents...can articulate themselves better about what they feel their needs are, whereas younger children...find it a lot harder (SW).

The social workers pointed to a variety of experiences working with adolescent girls. In some case they felt that the girls 'have the language' (SW) to enable them to express their feelings and needs. In others they were less sure and were aware that it was too easy to assume levels of sexual understanding and information that some girls simply did not have. They also spoke about being careful not to assume too much sexual knowledge from the forms of talk employed by girls when interacting with their peer group or in survivors groups, as the terminology used by girls in group situations was often very different from that employed in individual sessions. One social worker suggested that although many girls used relatively graphic language in girls' groups this did not necessarily indicate that the 'meanings' that language held for them was the same as it would hold for adults. [14]

A specific age related issue in respect of adolescent sexual abuse is that it is not unusual for girls of fourteen or fifteen to be sexually active. A particular view of child protection deriving from a criminal justice perspective that prioritises issues such as the age of consent may well define such activities as constituting child sexual abuse. The key issues from a social services point of view, however, appeared to be those of consent or coercion [15] and the relative ages of the girl and the 'perpetrator'. Non-coercive sexual activity with an age appropriate partner, who may be related to the girl, as long as that relationship was not one of authority or caretaking was not seen by either the managers or the social workers as necessarily constituting abuse. If, however, there was coercion involved they were clear that social services would classify the relationship in terms of abuse and intervene accordingly, including using the criminal law if that was seen as the most appropriate method of intervening. This indicates the central role social services play not only in delivering child protection but also in defining what constitutes child abuse (Thorpe, 1994).

The greatest impact the girls' age appeared to have on social worker practice stems from the structure of the child protection procedures themselves. There are clear indications that the way in which the Children Act and its associated procedures are implemented on a daily basis is primarily based on a model of child protection to deal with immediate risk in terms of neglect and physical injury, that pays little attention to issues concerning children in need, including meeting the long-term psychological needs of sexually abused young women.

By the time a girl reaches eighteen the child protection procedures will have terminated. A significant number of young people are routinely removed from the child protection register for no other reason than they have reached the upper age limit of the child protection process. One manager said, without a great deal of conviction:

I hope no social worker would dump a kid at seventeen (Manager).

Social workers spoke of girls of seventeen and eighteen who had left the system but still had serious problems deriving from the aftermath of their abuse. The structure of the system left social workers feeling that they were giving out mixed messages to older teenage girls.

> Although you've got the support systems there for them you are also winding the support systems down because they're slowly leaving Children and Families and going into Adults (SW).

They saw this problem being compounded, as access to adult services was not guaranteed. One manager felt the best hope for many girls was that their ongoing needs had been recognised by the health services or various therapeutic groups in the voluntary sector during the course of the child protection process, and they would continue to work with them into adulthood. The intersection of the upper age limit of the process and underresourcing within it did not allow social workers to remain involved in ongoing aftermath work.

> You've got to cut your caseload, you've got too much on, what can you get rid of (Manager).

However, child protection social work is more than 'just a job'. The social workers pointed to instances where they or their colleagues continued to work with girls who had officially been removed from their caseloads upon reaching the upper age limit of the process. This work was unpaid and unofficial, yet illustrates the social workers' concerns over the complexity of aftermath work and the need for continuity of care. It also demonstrates a degree of personal commitment on the part of some social workers, whilst indicating one of the causes of social worker stress. To do the job to there own satisfaction may well mean having to do unpaid work outside their official role. The social workers saw the upper age limit as the most serious difficulty they encountered in working with adolescent girls.

> I don't think the system is particularly well geared up for dealing with women of that age coming into the system. I think it is comfier with thirteen or twenty year olds than it is with fifteen to eighteen year olds (SW).

The problem is further complicated by significant differences in the support systems in place for older girls dependent upon the status they acquired whilst in the child protection process. The support systems in place for moving girls of sixteen and seventeen into adult services were far better if those girls were in care. This leads one to question whether to some extent the non-intervention principle represents an attempt to save on resources. Whatever the benefits to abused girls in remaining in the family home, it may be that the routine non-use of Care Orders offers a short and long term financial saving to local authorities.

Although transitional support services were better for those in care, the social workers stressed that they were fairly poor for all girls. This problem is integral to a wider range of issues that tend to mean that the older a child gets the less sympathetic the public and professional agencies are to his/her needs, part of the dichotomy between 'children in trouble' and 'troublesome children' (Scraton, 1997). What is also apparent is that the age at which children are thought to be 'troublesome' rather than 'in trouble' is falling. A constantly perceived problem of delinquent youth has led to more and more draconian measures to deal with children. [16] Both the major political parties emphasise to an ever increasing level the need to control children, whilst simultaneously claiming the same measures are for the benefit of children at risk. This lack of public sympathy for teenagers with problems was recognised by social services managers in that they found it more difficult to persuade councillors to provide services for older children than for younger ones.

Some of the social workers saw the abuse occurring at a stage in the girls' development when they were becoming aware of their own sexual identity and beginning to form sexual relationships with boys (and/or girls). They felt that sexual abuse at this stage could have an adverse effect on future sexual development (Bentovim and Vizard, 1988), and those effects would be greater than for younger children as older girls would be more aware of being the victims of abusive power relationships.

Any sense of pleasure the girls may have gained from elements of the abuse were seen by the social workers as interacting with feelings of powerlessness to exaggerate their feelings of repulsion, betrayal and guilt. Elton (1988) emphasises that some sexually victimised adolescents will begin to believe that they will only be liked through being sexually available, leading them into serious problems within their own peer group. They may well become recognised as an 'easy lay' and fall prey to being routinely abused by boys of their own age, or conversely avoid the sexual role altogether. This cuts across the day to day problems girls encounter in adolescence (Hudson, 1984), wherein they are subject to the contradictory expectations of adolescence including being sexually active, and the expectations of femininity with its implications of chastity. These issues are particularly intensified where the original sexual abuse is from a father figure and they are caught in the 'double-bind' of the contradictory patriarchal imperatives of 'good' chaste behaviour and obedience to the father figure (Vizard and Tranter, 1988a; Gordon, 1988).

Social workers found that a large part of their work revolved around reassuring the girls that the information would remain confidential within the child protection network. They tended to find this difficult. Some of the girls feared for their sexual reputations. The sexual reputation of a teenage girl can be very much a defining feature of her identity (Lees, 1986; Lees, 1997), a derogatory sexual reputation being very damaging to her. This illustrates two important socio-political points. Firstly, there exists in contemporary society a very powerful discourse centred around concepts of autonomy and success, a discourse that has been given significant reinforcement in recent years through the development of an 'enterprise culture' and the growth of 'privatisation' in its many political, economic and social forms. The degree of personal and professional success, and levels of autonomy individuals enjoy in part explains the status we accord them. To be a victim is a complete negation of this sense of success; victims have little autonomy. Secondly, however much social workers attempt to demonstrate to sexually abused adolescent girls that it is the perpetrator who is to blame for the abuse, the widespread circulation of patriarchal discourses deriving from the Judeo-Christian tradition that envision women either as angels or temptresses (Rich, 1977; Daly, 1978), as in the 'Lolita' myth (Gordon, 1988), ensure that sexually abused girls will fear for their reputations if knowledge of their abuse becomes public. The social workers could not be sure that confidentiality would not be breached. Although in the cases they discussed the actions of the schools, for example, were sensitive and ensured confidentiality only on a need to know basis, they also told of occasions where teachers had not respected the confidential nature of the information they were given. The social workers also pointed out that any video interview, which would be used in court, could not be considered confidential.

Although many of the emotional and psychological problems that adolescent girls suffered as a result of sexual abuse were similar to those suffered by younger children, the social workers saw the immediate effects as being potentially more serious. For example, the loss of self-esteem was seen to affect girls of all ages and often led to them becoming withdrawn, unable to concentrate at school (Farmer and Owen, 1995) or even refusing to go to school. For a girl of fourteen or fifteen this was seen as particularly serious in that the loss of education at this point could have a detrimental long term effect for the girl that would only add to her problems in later life. They also spoke of encountering anxiety problems with this age group that they did not encounter in younger girls. The greater level of understanding of adolescent girls in terms of sexual issues led them to fear pregnancy or infection from sexually transmitted diseases.

These various issues led several social workers to suggest that child protection work with this group was much more difficult than with younger children.

> It is easier to work with a younger child, because there is more time to work with them, but I also think that if it happens at an older age the level of understanding is so much greater and the abuse has more impact (SW).

Other social workers did not agree. They saw older girls as more likely to disclose at an earlier stage than younger ones, because of their greater understanding of the abusive nature of their experiences. Taking the view that the length of time for recovery mirrors to some extent the duration of the abuse, they felt this made aftermath work with older girls easier. The most problematic scenario was seen as being those girls who had been 'normalised' into abuse at a relatively early age who then disclosed in their teenage years after they had become aware of the inappropriateness of what was happening to them. To a great extent whether any individual social worker found working with adolescent girls easier or more difficult than working with younger girls depended upon her/his personality, skills and preferences.

The Health and Emotional State of the Girls

A principal set of issues the social workers saw in terms of working with sexually abused adolescent girls was the complex and often very serious consequences of the abuse on the girls' physical and mental health (Women's Resource Centre, 1989). Although physical abuse can often be present in conjunction with sexual abuse, the girls in the cases concerned had few symptoms of physical ill health. Where physical symptoms did exist, they tended to be anxiety-related symptoms.

> The girl recently had a series of blackouts, and she's been to see a paediatrician and the paediatrician thinks it was due to stuff that was repressed (SW).

They found the girls' anxieties tended to focus on fears of infection, concerns over their future capacity to have children and general fears that they had been sexually damaged. Research showing difficulties in adult sexual relations as a consequence of child or adolescent sexual abuse (Meiselman, 1978; Courtois, 1979; Langmade, 1983; Finkelhor, 1984; Browne and Finkelhor, 1986; Briere and Runtz, 1987; Women's Resource Centre, 1989) suggests that the anxieties themselves can be more damaging than the specifics of physical injury or damage. The major health issues the social workers had to confront were those of the girls' emotional and psychological condition. They saw such problems as extremely serious, one manager even questioning whether one can ever recover.

Early in the process the social workers found many girls exhibiting understandable responses of grief or anger over their abuse. In other cases the level of trauma the girls had endured meant individuals confronted the social workers with serious psychological problems. These problems ranged from surliness and loss of interest in their appearance through to self-mutilation, attempted arson, various eating disorders, and attempted suicide. The common thread running through these manifestations of psychological disturbance was a sense of low self-esteem or worthlessness at best, and at worst a loathing for self and others. The social workers did not find these problems unusual. They are well documented in the literature (Meiselman, 1978; Adams-Tucker, 1982; Browne and Finkelhor, 1986; Women's Resource Centre, 1989) and the social workers had confronted similar problems in past cases. Many of them, nevertheless, found it difficult to empathise.

> It's difficult when you've got an angry young woman telling you don't know how she feels, because you don't (SW).

The difficulties the social workers experienced in coming to terms with the intense emotional states of some of the girls seemed to derive from three sources. Firstly, they may have lacked knowledge as a consequence of the pressures of overburdened caseloads that left little time for reading research and professional literature (Fisher, 1995). Secondly, their difficulties could also derive from issues of transference and countertransference (Herman, 1994; Hooper *et al*, 1997), that led them to associate with the perpetrator or the helplessness of the girl. Although none of the social workers in the sample talked in terms of transference or countertransference, one male social worker stressed that it was important for men working with sexually abused girls to confront their own feelings of sadism and sexual cruelty.

Thirdly, their difficulties may have stemmed from their own experiences of abuse. Wattam (1992), in a brief review of the literature, suggests that the prevalence of child sexual abuse may be up to two thousand times higher than the numbers officially reported. Therefore, it is not unreasonable to expect some social workers to have they been abused when younger. Dependent upon the degree, to which they had come to terms with their own abuse, this may enhance their capacity to empathise with the girls. One needs also to hold in mind the disturbing thought that some of the social workers might themselves be abusers. The capacity to empathise and the ways in which any social worker would be able to interact with the girl were clearly influenced by the whole panoply of experiences of both interactants. However, due to the gendered structuring of sexual abuse it may well be that female social workers find it easier to empathise with sexually abused girls than do male workers.

The social workers found the girls experiencing the abuse as a loss of control over their lives, whether accompanied by serious psychological disturbance or not. Much of their work at this stage was to help the girl regain control of her situation and understand that she was not to blame for her abuse, and so begin the process of recovery.

A striking feature to emerge from the research was the wide variety of responses to having been sexually abused and how difficult the social workers found it to predict the ways in which the girls' emotional and psychological state would change as the process developed. The consequences of similar practices can differ significantly for different individuals (Corby, 1993). The social workers saw the differing emotional and psychological responses of the girls as stemming as much from their differing personalities as from the nature or severity of the abuse.

The social workers and their managers saw the emotional and psychological reactions by adolescent girls to sexual abuse as similar to those exhibited by adult women who had been subject to sexual assault or domestic violence, with the added components of adolescence and inappropriate familial relationships. The managers saw familial abuse as involving a betrayal of trust, with consequences such as a confused response to authority (Women's Resource Centre, 1989), absconding and problems at school (Browne and Finkelhor, 1986) that could be difficult to deal with. They felt that for some social workers there could be a struggle to come to terms with the fact that many of these girls wanted the abuse to stop but still loved their abusive fathers, although the social workers appeared not to find it as problematic as their managers assumed.

Many of the social workers concerns derived from their worries over the long-term consequences the abuse might hold for the girls. They saw the long-term effects as very serious, occurring at a stage in life before adult sexuality identity is fully realised. Survivors accounts point to the long-term difficulties experienced in future intimate relationships.

Sometimes,
When my lover breathes a certain
　　　way
In his passion,
My heart goes cold,
My mind goes dark,
I wait silently.
　　　(Kelly, L. AFTERMATH, in Bass and Thornton, 1983)

The social workers found the girls' emotional state often fluctuated over time. They observed certain critical points of change. Some of these were the result of the direct impact of the criminal justice system. Girls grew angry at the slowness of the criminal justice system, and disillusioned and depressed whilst waiting to go to court. Other changes related to familial pressures to retract their allegations or minimise their abuse. Many of these emotional changes were the backdrops to the girl's changes in attitude discussed above.

Although different girls exhibited different emotions at different stages within the process, the social workers found that they tended to often express conflicting feelings for various members of their families. One social worker characterised this as 'turmoil' (SW). In attempting to deal with this complex of emotions the social workers tried to arrange counselling sessions for the girls with themselves or with psychologists. Some of these sessions took place; others did not. There were a variety of reasons why counselling did not always take place. The courts on occasions 'banned' counselling sessions whilst a criminal prosecution was pending[17], psychologists waiting lists meant that the girls simply had to wait[18] often until a point when counselling was no longer appropriate, and some girls simply refused to be counselled. The social workers tried to persuade those girls who refused counselling to think again.

The girls' emotional turmoil often made the social workers' child protection task very difficult. The girls tended to be unpredictable in their behaviour and often changed their minds in terms of how they wished the process to develop. The social workers felt that many girls were confused and did not know what they wanted, and felt that even those girls who were consistent and made their wishes plain were not always acting in their own best interests. This does not preclude a number of cases where the social workers felt their intervention strategies led to a marked improvement in the emotional and psychological condition of the girls concerned. The reasons the social workers cited for these improvements included accessing specific resources such as survivors groups, the efforts of psychologists and other mental health workers, intensive counselling from the social workers themselves and changes in family structures (notably the rejection of the perpetrator from the family circle). They saw much of the success as accruing from the provision of the appropriate counselling services at the right time. Farmer and Owen (1995), drawing on the work of Faller (1989) and the American Academy of Pediatrics (1991), (that showed that many sexually abused children would benefit from counselling), and the findings of Frothingham *et al* (1993) and Sharland *et al* (1993, 1995), point out that the lack of provision of such services leaves a significant number of sexually abused children with 'continuing high levels of disturbance' (Pg.313). They then draw attention to the loss of many of these services due to the 'diminishing number of child and family guidance clinics' (Pg.314). Several social workers emphasised that the paucity of resourcing for appropriate counselling services left the child protection process meeting the immediate protection needs of most girls and preventing further abuse, but many girls left the process with psychological problems remaining. Some of the social workers saw the child protection process itself as constituting part of the problem. They felt themselves to be working within a crisis management system that sidelined therapeutic intentions in favour of other more pressing concerns of immediate protection, yet research (Gomes-Schwartz *et al*, 1990) has shown that relatively long-term support is needed by both the girl and her family in the aftermath of sexual abuse.

The social workers main concerns revolved around the interplay of the girls' emotional and psychological state and the workings of the criminal justice system and other procedure led processes within child protection. They saw administrative procedures and aspects of the criminal justice process as often being prioritised over the consideration of the girls' psychological and emotional needs.

This clearly indicates that there are serious therapeutic consequences deriving from the increasing detachment of a legalistically informed child protection process (Wattam, 1992) from other elements of childcare (Parton, 1991, Parton *et al*, 1997). It also suggests that many of the procedures, such as Child Protection Conferences are more concerned with 'risk management' (Gibbons *et al*, 1995) from standpoint of protecting the professionals within the interagency network, than they are with the protection of children.

The social workers were well aware of the complex needs of adolescent girls who had been sexually abused, and understood the benefits in psychological terms of a variety of diverse services.

> For a full recovery you need to have a whole range of services (SW).

They saw this as important as different girls responded differently to different forms of therapy. The social workers saw the recognition of the girls' specific emotional and psychological needs and the consequent provision of or accessing of the appropriate therapeutic services as one of their key tasks. Social workers reported significant improvements in the emotional well being and psychological health of girls in cases they were dealing with that seemed to stem directly from the provision of a diverse series of strategies and services. These ranged from referring the girl to psychological or psychiatric services for counselling and other individual work, through to short term foster care to enable the girl and her mother to reassess their relationship and their priorities in the aftermath of the disclosure of the abuse, and included such initiatives as encouraging the girl to join a survivors group. The social workers encountered some problems, however, in that the psychological condition of the girl in some cases proved to be the focus of disagreement between the psychiatric and psychological services, leaving the social worker in the untenable position of trying to maintain a service for the girl whilst the psychologists and psychiatrists failed to agree an appropriate therapy. This highlighted a problem that social services managers were well aware of in that the coordination and provision of psychiatric and psychological services to sexually abused adolescent girls was seen as an endemic problem in some areas. The managers felt this reflected a general rule in the health services that adolescent girls were more capable than younger children of overcoming the trauma of abuse without health service intervention, unless they exhibited profound psychiatric disturbance.

> My suspicion is that you are more likely to get health services involved the younger the child is and the more disturbed the child is (Manager).

The social workers' concerns over the girls' emotional and psychological states were constantly interpenetrated by other concerns such as client choice, safety and the degree of risk. For a variety of reasons particular strategies were adopted that on balance were seen as the best way to proceed, but they had a negative effect upon the emotional/psychological state of the girl. The example to emerge most often was the added trauma to sexually abused girls of being placed in foster care or in the care of the local authority, meeting the girls' safety needs whilst cutting them off from their major sources of emotional support. Very few placements were as insensitive as one that one social worker reported, where the girl was removed from the family home and placed in a children's home where all the other residents were boys. Inappropriate as such a placement might be, and the girl in the case was indeed very angry at being placed in an all-male environment, the choice of placements can be very limited. The Utting Report (DoH, 1997) shows that there has been a considerable contraction in residential care to the point that there simply are not enough places, and social workers are accessing whatever they can get. The social workers saw other placements as exacerbating problems that were already beginning to emerge. The difficulty seemed to be a problem of what was in the girl's best interests on balance, and questions of safety, in terms of reducing the chances of continuing or future abuse tended to predominate. In some cases the consequences of a placement proved to be very dangerous.

> She was with emergency foster carers for two weeks before she took a massive overdose and was then placed on an adolescent psychiatric unit (SW).

The problem appears to be that until a crisis point was reached there was little opportunity for social workers to access any form of psychiatric hospitalisation for the girls. Their managers bore out this complaint, making the point that unless a girl was exhibiting life-threatening behaviour it was unlikely that psychological or psychiatric services would involve themselves.

The social workers were alert to the difficulties girls could have in foster placements, and were equally aware of the problems this might pose for foster carers, but in many cases they were left with little alternative.

> We were anxious about placing her in foster care, because that's too much of a burden to place with foster carers. So it was with some risk that we placed her back in the community with foster carers (SW).

Those cases where girls exhibited serious and ongoing life-threatening behaviour were the source of a great deal of professional anxiety, not only to the social workers themselves, but also to social services departments as a whole. Social workers spoke of cases where senior managers, even up the level of Assistant Director of Social Services, became actively involved in cases. This suggests not only the anxiety of a profession with a relatively poor public profile attempting to minimise any risk to its reputation, but also that of specific local authorities not be left with a suicide on their hands. One of the most difficult tasks that individual social workers were faced with was that of assessing quickly enough the degree of risk any girl posed in terms of harming herself. In cases where girls attempted suicide, even though the risk factors were perhaps evident, the attempts always came as something of a surprise.

Closely associated with the ways in which social workers perceived the emotional and psychological condition of the girls were ways in which they perceived of girls being of particular types. In other words a process of routine typification could be seen to be in operation[19]. The social workers appeared to be making judgements as to the type of girl they were dealing with through an extrapolation of her reactions in what needs to be seen as unusual circumstances. Some girls were seen as unable to speak in detail of their abuse, not because of the inherent repugnance or horror they may have felt, but because they were uncommunicative.

> She found it difficult to talk about a lot of subjects so something as painful as that would have been very difficult for her to talk about (SW).

Some social workers saw girls as having difficulties building or maintaining relationships based upon the fact that the girls seemed quiet and withdrawn, yet withdrawing in on oneself can be a particular psychological response to sexual abuse. Perhaps the most striking typifying comment came from a social worker that referred to a girl with a learning disability as:

> ...that kind of girl...the type of girl who was happy with the simple pleasures in life (SW).

Clearly such typifications are a part of attempts by social workers to create a 'social map' of their work environment (Pithouse, 1987) and are a routine part of social work in particular and life in general. Nevertheless, there is a danger inherent in such typifications in that they can lead to a rather one-dimensional view of the client, losing sight of the holistic nature of her complex of protection and other welfare needs, although this is qualified to some degree by the interdisciplinary nature of the child protection process.

The Form and Seriousness of the Abuse

The social workers' practice was routinely influenced by issues concerning the form and seriousness of the abuse, located within conceptualisations of actual and potential 'significant harm'. The concept of 'seriousness' is inextricably linked to forms of material practice in official definitions and criteria in respect of child abuse, organised around the principle of 'significant harm' (Children Act, 1989, s.31(2(a)); DoH, 1991a, para.3.2), and local authority criteria for placing children on the Child Protection Register. Although they regarded all forms of adult sexual behaviour towards adolescents as inappropriate, the social workers' assessment of the actual harm experienced by the girls bore a close correlation to what they saw as the degree of seriousness of the sexual abuse itself, with the form of sexual practice being a key indicator of the level of seriousness.

> It was quite a serious assault really. It was fondling and digital penetration of her vagina. So it was a pretty serious assault by her father on her (SW).

The social workers' perception of the seriousness of adolescent sexual abuse is best seen in terms of a continuum ranging from moderately serious inappropriate behaviours, such as touching through the clothes, to gross acts of indecency and serious sexual assaults, such as actual or attempted rape. Whilst all sexual abuse is clearly serious, within a context of heavy caseloads, social workers recognise that those young people with the most pressing protection needs will tend to be those with the greatest degree of suffering, thus, the social workers saw cases involving more serious sexual acts as more urgent then those involving more moderate acts[20]. This makes clear that even though only a small proportion of incidents of sexual abuse come to the attention of social services, processes of filtering at the practitioner level, deriving solely from resource constraints, are a routine aspect of the process.

Not all-local authorities prioritise the nature of the sexual activity as the key indicator of seriousness in sexual abuse cases (O'Hagan, 1989). O'Hagan (1989) argues that such prioritisation can be problematic. O'Hagan (1989) further argues that the concept of child sexual abuse itself has only limited value as it covers too wide a range of activities, and calls for its replacement by reference to specific sexual practices. Hooper (1992), however, argues that the broader definition is useful, as it allows one to recognise both the similarities and differences of experience of various forms of abuse. Other issues, such as early attachment experiences that can be a factor in the individual's response to the abuse (Hooper *et al*, 1997), and the quality of the mother-daughter relationship at the time of the abuse (Hooper and Humphreys, 1998) also informs some feminist perceptions of 'seriousness'.

There are significant practical problems for the police and social services in respect of the legal implications of sexual abuse cases. Inappropriate touching can sometimes be explained away by perpetrators in terms of the girls' misinterpretation of events, and, without vaginal or anal penetration, forensic evidence of an incident may be entirely absent.

The social workers saw a close configuration between duration and seriousness; the abuse considered more serious the longer it persisted. Research (Waterhouse and Pitcairn, 1991) shows child sexual abuse tending to be an enduring pattern of behaviours, often becoming 'normalised' within specific interpersonal relationships. The social workers appeared to internalise this view as an element of their professional 'common-sense', seeing the disclosure of a single incident as being only a partial disclosure. The literature (Giller *et al*, 1992; Wattam, 1992) strongly suggests that social workers' understanding in this respect is principally derived from their own professional experience rather than from reference to the academic literature. [21] The literature suggests only around five per cent of incidents of sexual abuse come to the attention of any agency (Kelly *et al*, 1991), the majority being dealt with by family and friends. It also suggests stranger abuse is relatively uncommon (Finkelhor, 1984) and that the majority of incidents are perpetrated not by family members but by known adults or peers (Kelly *et al* (1991). One social worker's account of a case that included a successful conviction of a man for sexually assaulting his daughter and her friend illustrates how in some respects experiential knowledge articulates with academic research findings.

> The only time when you find one-offs it's usually a stranger, which is not usual (SW).

The social workers saw the issue of duration and its configuration with seriousness as implicated in the process of 'recovery', the more embedded the abusive behaviour had become the longer the journey from 'victim' to 'survivor'.

> It's almost as if the length of time of the abuse is mirrored by the length of time of the recovery (SW).

They also saw the duration of the abuse as linked to the degree of seriousness in another way. They saw child and adolescent sexual abuse in terms of an emergent, or developing, set of material practices, that would begin at a relatively moderate level of seriousness and develop over time into something more serious, a feature of child sexual abuse also referred to in the research literature (Boon, 1984). In some cases this view was supported by the girls' disclosures which indicated increasing levels of abuse both in terms of rates of incidence and forms of practice, yet in other cases it remained in the realms of supposition.

> It was just the beginning really. It was touching through clothes etc. It had never gone to sort of penetration or anything like that (SW).

The social workers' perceptions of the level of seriousness were located within a discourse of appropriate relationships. Sexual abuse by fathers and other relatives was seen as more serious than that perpetrated by strangers, indicating a normative perspective of appropriate familial behaviour patterns. The social workers did not see acts of abuse by strangers as intrinsically less serious, rather they were acutely aware of the issues in respect of relationships driving from abuse by a family member. Although the social workers clearly saw a familial relationship as adding to the seriousness of the abuse, they appeared to see issues of age appropriateness even more significant. Non-coercive sexual activity between an adolescent girl and a young adult man was seen as less serious than similar activities involving an older man. This clearly suggests that child protection practice goes beyond legally defined issues of child sexual abuse into a concern that adolescent girls are at a greater risk of sexual exploitation by older men than they are by young men at similar stage of emotional and cognitive development to themselves.

The 'seriousness' attributed to any specific case of adolescent sexual abuse was also influenced by the presence of other forms of abuse. The literature points to sexual abuse often being accompanied by other forms of abuse (Gil, 1970; Briere, 1992) and the social workers made clear that different form child abuse 'often go together in a variety of ways' (SW). In cases that had originally come to their attention for sexual abuse, the presence of other forms of abuse was seen as a simple factor that added to the seriousness of the abuse. However, many sexual abuse cases came to their attention in the first instance as referrals for physical abuse or suspicions raised by other professionals such as teachers when a girl had attended school with a physical injury. Some of the social workers took disclosures of physical abuse as triggers to attempt to discover if sexual abuse had taken place.

> I think when you are dealing with a case where there is other abuse, other concerns, it can become apparent that sexual abuse is a factor (SW).

Amongst the signs of sexual abuse that they would pick up on when working with girls who had come to their attention for other reasons were unusual behaviour patterns, sexualised knowledge beyond what would be expected of girls of their age, and other behavioural manifestations of emotional disturbance. The research (Madge, 1983; Smith and Grocke, 1995) suggests that in isolation these signs can be far from reliable indicators of sexual abuse. Further, girls over the age of twelve may have a relatively sophisticated knowledge of sexual matters without having been involved in any inappropriate sexual activities (Vizard and Tranter, 1988a). This indicates some of the difficulties social workers faced when they suspected sexual abuse in girls that had presented for other reasons. Some social workers reported that the presence of physical abuse or neglect was routinely seen as a risk factor for sexual abuse, along with a whole series of other factors relating to the family, such as drug and alcohol misuse.

Social workers saw the degree of seriousness of the abuse being exacerbated by the development or continuation of other forms of abuse after disclosure, once a case had become 'live'. This ongoing abuse often seemed to manifest itself in terms of a lack of family (especially maternal) support that was seen by many social workers to constitute emotional abuse, although very few girls were placed on the register under that category. Instances of this form of abuse ranged from a mother refusing even telephone contact with her daughter in a foster placement to several examples of mothers appearing to make a simple choice of believing their partners rather than their daughters. In other cases the emotional abuse was seen in more generalised terms,

> We also heard about some emotional punishment in the house, and that house had a very frozen nature to it (SW).

Some social workers suggested that the co-presence of physical abuse with sexual abuse make their task easier in terms of effecting the removal of the perpetrator from the family home, as it enhanced the chances of gaining a criminal conviction, and gave a number of examples of cases where the principal abuse was sexual but the perpetrator had been convicted of offences of cruelty and assault.

The final factor that influenced the social workers perception of the seriousness of the abuse was the presence of a physical or learning disability in the girl. This seemed to indicate a concern in terms of the increased vulnerability to physical and/or mental coercion that such disabilities could present. It could also suggest a paternalistic conjunction of discourses of sexuality and disability that routinely portray disability and a sexual life as mutually exclusive. The evidence from the data in the two cases concerned suggests a clear professional concern for vulnerable adolescents. However, the language with which the social workers described the particular girls was infantilising and implied a degree of desexualising of them due to their disabilities.

The social workers experienced specific practical problems working with girls with disabilities, particularly in terms of communication skills and the level at which to interact with the girls. Several social workers spoke of past cases where the presence of a learning disability in the girl had required intensive intervention techniques.

> We had a special person for the girl who spoke to her on a very simplistic level about growing up, using material that we found effective (SW).

The whole area of special needs was seen by social workers as one which required a different approach to other cases, and one in which several felt themselves ill-equipped to work effectively in. Through a process of infantalising, the social workers perceived girls with learning disabilities as incapable of lying.

> I wouldn't have said she had developed the skills to tell lies, and I think that also goes with the fact that she has a learning disability and they don't seem to develop the skills as early (SW).

There is, however, no evidence to suggest that young people with a learning disability are less likely to fabricate stories than any other young person, and to conceive of learning disabilities in terms of chronological sequences of intellectual development is an oversimplification of complex processes of development. It may well be that the girls were not lying as without the experience of the abuse they would lack the specific knowledge of sexual matters to make the allegation, in exactly similar ways to those in which young children exhibiting sexual knowledge above and beyond what is appropriate and to be expected for their age can be taken as an indicator of child sexual abuse. The obverse side of dealing with cases involving a girl with a learning disability was demonstrated by a case in which the abused girl was particularly intelligent. The focus of the social worker's practice in this case was to place far more responsibility onto the girl for her own passage through the child protection process than was usually the case.

> I mean she's not anybody's fool, so we put a lot of responsibility on her, giving her the options (SW).

It is clear that in terms of learning disabilities in particular and disabilities in general the seriousness of the abuse can clearly be seen to be located in terms of the degree of vulnerability of the girl on some form of continuum from relatively capable of self-protection to extremely vulnerable. This appears to be reflected in practice in that the less vulnerable the girl the greater the degree of autonomy allowed her, the more vulnerable she is the more protectionist the workers response.

The social workers made a number of judgements in specific cases as to the seriousness of the abuse. These judgements centred on themes of the form of sexual practice, the vulnerability of the girl and the duration of the abuse. It becomes clear that the sexual abuse of adolescent girls and its degree of seriousness is dependent upon 'complex processes of identification, confirmation and disposal' (Dingwall *et al*, 1983, Pg.31), with certain behaviours being deemed inappropriate within a normative framework of appropriate behaviours (Wattam, 1992), suggesting that it is important that official definitions of child sexual abuse (DoH, 1991b, para.6.40) must necessarily remain vague. The social workers' practice in terms of the age of the perpetrator, her/his relationship to the girl and in terms of the girl's level of intelligence and physical capacities ranged from taking a particularly paternalistic stance of protecting vulnerable children to a liberationist stance of enabling young women to protect themselves. It also varied along a continuum of urgency in terms of the type of material practice involved the presence of other forms of abuse, and the duration of the abuse. In other words, the influence of the various factors that the social workers saw as constituting the degree of seriousness of the abuse can be seen to manifest itself along two separate, yet intimately configured axes; factors of vulnerability being related to the individuals involved (the girl and the perpetrator), factors of urgency being related to the activities themselves. Clearly both of these axes relate to actual and potential 'significant harm'. In terms of potential significant harm they can be used to form distinct bases for risk assessment. The axis of urgency can be seen in terms of risk of recurrence of specific types of incident, and the axis of vulnerability can be seen in terms of risk of replication of the abusive environment or relationship.

Summary

The social workers' practice was influenced by a number of issues relating specifically to the girl herself. These issues fell broadly into three areas, the girl's safety, her attitude towards the child protection process and her expectations of it, and the various emotional and psychological consequences of adolescent sexual abuse.

As far as issues to do with impact upon the social workers' practice of issues to do with the safety of the girl were concerned, this could be seen to fall into two distinct but overlapping themes. They were concerned at as early a stage as possible to ensure the short-term safety of the girl. The long-term objective was the cessation of the abuse and the reduction of the risk of its recurrence. In both of these areas the most important point was seen as ensuring the physical separation of the girl and the perpetrator, which suggests that a 'rule of pessimism' in terms of the role of the family exists within child protection practice with sexually abuse adolescent girls.

The girl's attitude to the process and her expectations of it were seen to begin at the point of referral and first develop within the disclosure process. The social workers saw the disclosure process as long-term and often comprising a whole series of allegations, retractions and further disclosures. The social workers also found that there were a wide variety of expectations of the process amongst the girls, some having accurate expectations based upon knowledge they had gained in a variety of ways. Other girls they saw as being manipulative and trying to 'work the system', whilst others they saw as completely lost with no idea of what was going to happen to them, and no sense of control over their own destinies. They also found that some girls came out of the process with very positive feelings, usually when the outcomes had been beneficial, whilst others felt that the whole process, including the outcome, had been a disbenefit to them. The levels of participation by the girl in the process of her own protection were seen by social workers to vary according to the willingness of individual girls to act cooperatively, and it was felt that the stronger the social worker/client relationship the more cooperative the girls became and the more actively they participated.

Four key themes also emerged that related specifically to the age of the age of the girls. Firstly, their 'nearly adult' status and the degree of autonomy that they were afforded by the courts meant in practice the social workers were in a relatively weak position in terms of any conflict that might arise between themselves and the girls over what was in the girls best interests. Deriving to some extent from this, and partly from a concern with client choice interpenetrated by perceptions of childhood development that saw girls approaching adulthood as cognitively similar to adults, older girls were granted a far greater degree of autonomy within the process than were younger girls. Secondly, adolescent girls were more likely to have their cases taken up by the criminal justice element of child protection. This was seen as an added dimension by social workers, qualified by the view that older girls were much easier to deal with in video interviews than younger girls, and in general terms were easier to talk to in terms both of their abuse and the child protection process and that in cases that went to court they tended to be treated as adult witnesses. The third age related theme is that of the age boundary of the child protection process. Social workers found that they did not have enough time for adequate aftermath work before the girl became too old for the process, and they expressed anxiety that there were no clear pathways into adult support services for girls leaving the child protection process. The final age related theme is best seen in terms of the interpenetration of sexual abuse with the normative expectations of adolescence. There was a real concern over girls' fear for their reputations in the aftermath of the abuse, although the major concern for the social workers was the impact the abuse may have at a significant stage in their emotional, sexual and cognitive development.

Social workers also found they had to confront a host of issues surrounding the emotional disturbance and psychological ill-health consequent upon the abuse. The girls expressed some degree of anxiety in respect of sexual damage and sexually transmitted diseases. They also to varying degrees exhibited psychological consequences of sexual abuse that ranged from minor disruptive behaviour through to behaviours that were damaging to self and others. Many social workers, although sympathetic, found it difficult to empathise. They also commonly found the girls to be suffering from a sense of guilt and self-blame both for the abuse and for the family breakdown that on occasions followed disclosure.

Finally the social workers had to confront the degree of seriousness of the abuse, This was seen to be rooted in the concept of 'significant harm' and was closely related to the form of sexual practice that constituted the abuse. The degree of seriousness was also intimately configured with the duration of the abuse and the presence of other forms of abuse. The social workers also held to an idea that sexual abuse tended to escalate over time.

They seemed to have some evidence of this, but it was far from conclusive. Rather, it appeared simply to hold as a 'common-sense' view. The social workers, in determining the seriousness of the abuse; also drew upon concepts of the degree of vulnerability of the girl. This tended to be seen in terms of the presence/absence of a physical or learning disability. The ways in which issues of seriousness impacted on the social workers' practice can be seen in terms of a continuum ranging from moderately serious to extremely serious, that revolves around two distinct but intimately configured axes; an axis of vulnerability involving issues of intelligence, disability, and the appropriateness of relationships, and an axis of material practices, involving the form, duration and frequency of sexually abusive practices.

The influence on the social workers' practice of those issues arising from the situation of the girls' themselves were complex and often contradictory. The social workers practice was often impelled along contradictory pathways. On the one hand there was a primary concern to terminate the abuse and prevent its recurrence, influenced to some extent by normative perceptions of what was in the girls' best interests. On the other hand there was a concern with client autonomy that appeared to correlate closely with the girls' age. Crosscutting these basic themes were procedural issues to do with the upper age boundary of the child protection process and its implications for aftermath work, and the greater involvement of the criminal justice system in child abuse issues with older children.

At various points within the process it became apparent that there were significant tensions between issues of therapy and empowerment on the one hand, and procedural injunctions and aspects of the criminal justice system on the other. Some of the ways in which these tensions played out, such as the difficulties inherent in accessing appropriate counselling and providing aftermath care of the right type and duration were clearly detrimental to the girls. The ways in which other tensions played themselves out saw high levels of autonomy to the girls within the process at the expense of social workers' normative decision-making. A clear theme to emerge was that, for a complex of reasons, the girls, particularly the older ones exercised a considerable degree of client choice within the process. Yet, a significant proportion of those girls remained at risk and unprotected when leaving the child protection process at the upper age limit. This suggests that the balance in terms of children's rights for this particular client group may need to be examined more closely in future. Clearly, in an area such as sexual abuse recovery, rights of autonomy can themselves have significant therapeutic value. Nevertheless, to great a stress on autonomy and client choice implies too much client responsibility for her own welfare, when clearly the girls in this sample were in need of protection. Although adolescent girls tend to have a greater degree of cognitive development and are more articulate than younger children, the overall impression was that these various factors made child protection work with this particular client group different from that with younger children and in many ways more difficult.

6 The girls' families and practice

Introduction

The delivery of child protection services in respect of familially sexually abused adolescent girls involved social workers in a complex series of tasks. These tasks were accomplished within a framework in part delineated by the contours of legislation and the workers' personal and professional judgements of issues surrounding the girl herself and the nature and seriousness of the abuse, involving to some extent a degree of uncertainty of outcome (Hallett and Stevenson, 1980). However, in all cases, the girl's environment was a critical factor both in terms of assessing the levels of support available to the child and/or the levels of risk that (s)he remained exposed to. Issues relating to the family of the child were thus at the centre of any child protection intervention. In cases of adolescent sexual abuse, the psychiatric/psychological research (Finkelhor and Browne, 1988), research into child protection practice (Farmer and Owen, 1995), and survivors accounts (Women's Resource Centre, 1989) all point to serious psychological and social consequences for the abused. If that abuse has been perpetrated by a member of the family, aspects of betrayal and personal violation that attach to the young person's environment, render issues relating to the family of even greater importance.

In practical terms these issues were of two distinct kinds. Firstly, the family was seen as the locus of a series of 'risk' factors that could contribute to the continuation or recommencement of the abuse.

> Child Protection programmes do not restrict themselves solely to the condition and experiences of children, but exhibit a concern with the totality of the physical and social circumstances of particular childrearing settings, especially the moral character of parents (Parton *et al* 1997, Pg.154).

Lasch (1977) speaks of the family as a 'haven in a heartless world', but it can equally be a site of violence, conflict and abuse. Secondly, individuals within the family were seen as potential partners in the child protection process. In effect, the social workers saw the family, in all its complexity, as containing both the cause and the remedy of the abuse.

Some of the questions pertaining to risk and the stress placed on family participation and partnership in the child protection process raise a particularly pertinent question that of exactly who constitutes the client in child protection cases. Working from the premise that the client is a professional construction (Howe, 1990), a status or description conferred upon specified individuals by a particular agency (Thorpe 1994), there appeared to be some contradictions in determining exactly who was seen as the client in such cases. Clearly the girls themselves were the clients, the central actors within the 'child protection cases', and, in other aspects of social work the development of partnerships and client participation has rested upon some form of recognition of client's rights. However, in these child protection cases, much of the stress was placed on working together with parents and other family members, and Conference recommendations tended to include aspects of therapeutic work with a variety of members of the girls' families. This mirrors some of the issues raised by Fox-Harding (1991a, 1991b) in respect of the complex of the competing rights of 'children', parents and the state in child care and protection both historically and within the present legislative and procedural framework.

Although there are serious questions as to the ways in which various family members were implicated in the abuse, there were clearly a variety of elements that were taken into account as far as the assessment of risk was concerned. The intervention strategies adopted by the social workers were also influenced to some extent by the levels of participation and partnership developed by certain family members. The purpose of this chapter is to examine the ways in which specific aspects of the girls' families impacted on the social workers' practice, both in terms of the assessment of risk to the girl, and in terms of cooperation, partnership and family participation.

There are also issues involving meeting the needs of parents and other family members that may have had direct therapeutic value for the girls themselves. For example, assessing and dealing with the protection needs of a mother whose child is being abused, who is herself the victim of an abusive domestic relationship may have the effect of enhancing her capacities to protect her child. Some analogies can be drawn with Julia Twigg's theoretical models of the relationship between social services and carers in respect of the care of elderly, mentally ill and disabled people (Twigg, ed., 1992; Twigg and Atkin, 1994). Twigg develops four models of carers in the service system, each deriving from a different series of assumptions and perspectives among social services professionals. Carers are variously seen as resources, co-workers, and co-clients and as in need of being superseded.

- Resources model - carers are taken for granted in terms of the care they will give to a relative, usually in their own household, thus representing a cost-effective option for social services.
- Co-worker model - the agencies attempt to work alongside the informal carer providing an integrated package of support for the cared for person.

Both these models pay little attention to the needs of carers, although the co-worker model does take into account their physical needs inasmuch as they impact upon the level of care that can be provided for the elderly or disabled person.

- Co-client model - the carer is also perceived to have needs of her/his own and services are aimed at relief and support for the carer even if this may on occasions not be in the short-term interest of the cared-for person.
- Superseded carer model - the whole process of the care package is to attempt to enhance the cared-for person's capacity for independent living. This derives both from a concern to reduce the burden of care on the carer and in terms of a concern to maximise the independence of the cared-for person *per se.*

Twigg (1992) makes clear that these models are ideal types and in real cases social services do not necessarily hold fast to one model in particular.

> Agencies do not hold to any one exclusively, but shift between the different frames of reference according to the particular circumstances that present themselves. Sometimes one will be more appropriate than another (Twigg, 1992, Pg.63/64).

There is a clear analogy with the perspectives the social workers adopted towards parents and other family members in child protection cases. The governmental guidance points towards a both the co-worker model and the superseded carer model. However, there are clear assumptions that mothers in particular will care for their children (a free resource) and in many cases the social workers felt it important to deal with the emotional and psychological needs of mothers in order to secure the long-term benefits for the abused girls, even if such interventions were not necessarily to the short term benefit of the girls. This bears a close resemblance to the co-client model.

Within this context, it is important to examine the impact upon the social workers' practice of the constitution of the families and the relationships within them, the mental health of family members and their emotional state, specific issues relating to mothers and non-abusing family members, patterns of abuse within the families, the levels of participation of various family members in the child protection process, wider familial and neighbourhood support networks, and the issues that need to be confronted in terms of perpetrators. The complexity of the work and the difficulties for social workers were admirably summed up by one of their managers:

> It's such a complex area. You've got to be thinking about all the family and not just focussing on the girl (Manager).

The Assessment of Risk

The literature (Giller *et al*, 1992; Wattam, 1992) points to social workers making risk assessments on a relatively ad *hoc* basis. Research (Farmer and Owen, 1995) found that social workers and other members of the child protection network tended to use little theoretical reasoning in their assessments of risk, and tended neither to analyse the dynamics between various risk factors, nor to negotiate with the parents of abused children to give them the opportunity to refute, amend or accept their perceptions of risk.

The assessment of risk tended to be based on a relatively uncritical use of models relating to certain parental and familial characteristics (Brearly, 1982; Madge, 1983; Greenland, 1987). These models principally focus on the parents, referring to factors such as their age and maturity, their own previous experiences of childhood abuse, their past record in respect of violent or sexual crime, their intellectual capacity, and their state of physical and mental health. These models also take account, to a greater or lesser degree, of the formulation of the family, its degree of isolation or support, the material conditions the family is living in, and the relationships between individuals within the family. Parton *et al* (1997) in their analysis of thirty child protection investigations in Western Australia in 1987 found that in sexual abuse cases the assessment of risk tended to focus almost entirely on issues concerning the mother-child relationship, her responses to the child and her psychiatric history, at the expense of issues relating to the material conditions of the family.

Feminists have criticised the use of these models of risk assessment in that they overemphasise the responsibility of mothers in terms of protecting their children, whilst to some degree underemphasising the individual responsibility of the perpetrator. Hooper and Humphreys (1998) make point to the fact that feminists have also noted that many of the problems referred to in family systems literature that are seen as risk factors in child sexual abuse cannot be shown to have a causal link. They suggest that some of these 'risk factors' may actually be dysfunctional family dynamics that are a consequence of the abuse rather than a cause.

Finkelhor's (1984) four precondition model [1] is far more sophisticated, as it leaves responsibility firmly with the perpetrator, but allows for aspects of the family in the form of the mother-child relationship to have some bearing on the possibilities of abuse for any individual child. Although the mother-child relationship is not a causal factor in terms of the abuse, it can contribute to the degree of risk, and allow identification of certain children as being at greater risk than others are (Finkelhor and Baron, 1986). [2]

One of the major problems of risk assessment models generally is that the various factors that have been developed both in terms of predicting abuse prior to any occurrence and in assessing the risk of a recommencement or continuation of abuse are relatively unreliable. The use of various predictive factors across all areas of child abuse has resulted in a significant proportion of 'false positives' (Lealman *et al*, 1983) and 'false negatives' (Wakefield and Underwager, 1988).

Madge (1983), although primarily referring to physical abuse, warns against simplistic cause and effect models, that fail to take into account the consequences that may pertain from the complex interaction between a variety of factors that may originate both within the dynamics of the family and in the wider society. In their discussion of risk assessment in Initial Child Protection Conferences, Farmer and Owen (1995) found this advice had not been heeded. They point to social workers and other professionals involved in conferences adopting a simple arithmetical model of risk factors, that failed to take into account the interrelationship between various factors, and also tended to discount issues such as the presence of family support networks, which could act to diminish the level of risk for the young person. They saw serious deficits in Conference risk assessments in terms of a tendency towards an over simplistic comparison between the context of the family's circumstances at the time of the assessment and at the time of the abuse and in terms of a failure to conduct any analysis of the dynamics between various risk factors, the personality of family members and the quality of intra-familial interactions. As far as social workers are concerned, this reflects earlier findings (Corby, 1987; Dingwall, 1989) that found the assessment of risk in child abuse cases very basic and theoretically ill-informed, with social workers rarely referring to the research literature on risk analysis (Giller *et al*, 1992).

> In short, the diversity of human behaviour requires, as it were, theoretical subplots which can reside within more generalised theories of family functioning. Without such theory being available, the social worker, or indeed any other professional, is left floundering (Stevenson, 1989, Pg.162).

This can be seen, at least in part, to be an organisational issue, as the dissemination of research is not prioritised within social services area offices (Fisher, 1995). The research literature suggests that the social workers' risk assessment in child protection cases tends to rely upon judgements of probability that can be seen to take the form of value judgements (Higginson, 1990) and moral judgements (Thorpe, 1991) in respect of both the girls and their families. Parton and Parton (1989) contend that the whole concept of risk assessment is wrongly focussed, in that it tends to concentrate on the assessment of dangerousness of individuals, rather than the dangerousness of situations. It is not entirely clear, however, whether this is another formulation of the criticism of social work practice being relatively atheoretical or if it is a critique of the theoretical models of risk assessment, which tend to be grounded in concepts of family dynamics. If it is the latter, it is not entirely well founded as the various risk assessment models take account of both individual and situational factors to a greater or lesser extent.

The social workers clearly saw the assessment of risk to the girl as a central part of their role. This was an ongoing process, and revolved around the assessment of risk at the initial stages from investigation to the initial child protection conference, followed by the monitoring and evaluating of changes in that level of risk. They saw certain features of the family as particularly significant. These features were principally those relating to individuals such as the perpetrator and the mother, and those relating to the structure and situation of the family such as the quality of support networks and whether the family was an original or reconstituted family.

Family Structure and Familial Relationships

The managers believed that an understanding of the aetiology of sexual abuse was far from simple, but were convinced that it articulated closely with the structure and dynamics of the families within which it occurred. They offered various tentative explanations relating to critical shifts in relationships both within and without the family, although the bottom line was that 'we don't really know what triggers it off' (Manager). They were convinced, nevertheless, of the need for practice to constantly take account of the constitution and dynamics of the families concerned and to be alert to any changes in them.

> ...there has to be sensitivity to the individual's own experience, the families that they've come from and the patterns of behaviour and relationships. You'd have to set up something that took account of that, and looked at the family system and how the young person is perceived in that, how the rest of the family functions and all sorts of things (Manager).

The familial arrangements that the girl was living within were a major organising feature of the social workers' practice. These arrangements comprised two analytically distinct, yet intimately configured elements; the structure or constitution of the family unit, and the interpersonal relationships within the family unit. These formed the focus of much of the their risk assessment and conform closely to elements within the risk assessment model developed by Vizard and Tranter (1988b). This form of assessment also articulates closely with a professional objective of child protection work; that of effecting change in order to terminate the abuse. At an abstract level the social workers saw their role as attempting to change either the structure of the family unit, ideally through the removal of the perpetrator (or failing this through the removal of the girl), or through changing the focus of intra-familial relationships.

The social workers saw two elements of family structure being of primary importance. Reflecting elements of risk assessment models that point to stepfathers as a risk factor (Finkelhor and Baron, 1986; Greenland, 1987), there was a tendency at the point of referral to be more concerned if the girl lived within a reconstituted family, especially if the allegations were made against a stepfather. Recent research shows allegations of sexual abuse by natural fathers at a slightly higher rate than allegations against stepfathers (Gibbons *et al*, 1995), although there is some evidence that there is a higher rate of abuse by stepfathers than natural fathers proportional to their prevalence in the population (Russell, 1984). Parker and Parker (1986) point to evidence that men involved in the nurturing of a child in its early years are less likely to abuse that child than those with less early involvement. Hooper (1996) suggests that this could to some extent explain the higher rates of abuse by stepfathers, as they would, as a group, be less likely to be involved in the nurturing of the child in its early years. This issue, however, was overloaded in the social workers accounts to a great extent with an implied meaning that reduced the perpetration of child sexual abuse by stepfathers to something of a norm. Social workers spoke of a case being unusual when both parents were the girl's natural parents, and of an individual being abused by 'the archetypal evil stepfather' (SW). It also seemed to contrast sharply with some of the more generalised comments they made that afforded no exclusive role to stepfathers in sexual abuse. This suggests that on a general level the social workers were loathe to 'scapegoat' a particular group, but, lacking a coherent formulation of risk assessment, displayed a tendency to draw upon elements of long-standing models of risk assessment in an uncritical *ad hoc* way, and upon common-sense views that have their roots in long-standing myths of wicked step-fathers.

The social workers also saw the presence/absence of siblings as significant in assessing the degree of risk. Farmer and Parker (1991) make the importance of sibling relationships in child protection clear in a slightly different context. In their research into the outcomes for abused children in the care of the local authority being placed home on trial, they found an enhanced level of successful outcomes when siblings returned to the family home together. The social workers saw sibling presence as important in two ways. Any sibling present in the household may also be subject to abuse. Alternatively, a brother or sister could either act as a support to the abused girl, or be involved in supporting the perpetrator to the detriment of the girl's welfare.

The degree of risk, and therefore the intervention strategy to be adopted, bore a close relationship to whether or not the alleged perpetrator remained in the family home. Previous research (Barth and Berry, 1987; Farmer and Parker, 1991, Gibbons *et al*, 1993) found the risk of reabuse to be significantly reduced when the total physical separation of the victim and the abuser was assured. Farmer and Owen (1995) found a close correlation between children being placed on the register and situations where the abuser or the child had recently been removed from the home, clearly indicating the separation of the victim and the abuser as a critical point in the protection process. They also found that a principal reason for removing the child from the register was if the abuser had permanently left the family home. As Wattam (1992) points out, registration of a child is a way of officially recognising degrees of risk. Research (Gibbons *et al*, 1995) shows that the level of access of the perpetrator to the child is a key element of risk assessment, and children are more likely to be filtered out of the child protection system if the perpetrator does not remain in the household.

If the perpetrator remained in the family home the social workers were far more likely to remove the girl either voluntarily or through application for a Care Order. The option of removing the girl was seen as a last resort. This suggests both that the principal of minimum intervention (Children Act 1989; DoH, 1991c) informed their practice, and that the social workers were aware of the problems inherent in removing the victim from the home. Farmer and Owen (1995), however, make the point that at the initial stages of many cases children are removed from the home, often because social workers are unsure of the degree of risk the home environment poses for the child. This was reflected in the present study in that in many cases the social worker's concern for the immediate safety of the girl meant that she was initially removed from the family home, albeit on a voluntary basis. The problems associated with this removal, the problems associated with discontinuities in care (Stevenson, 1989), and the 'double pain' (Farmer and Owen, 1995; Pg.77) for the girls of having to come to terms with both telling of the abuse and losing their place in the family, clearly informed the social workers actions, and the early removal of the perpetrator and return of the girl to the family home was attempted wherever this was possible.

The social workers also saw the quality and form of family relationships as extremely important. The principal area of concern to social workers was that of the quality of parenting. This clearly derived from a family dynamics perception of child abuse and protection and reflected many elements of the risk assessment models in that tradition (see Finkelhor and Baron, 1986; Greenland, 1987, for example). The ways in which this was articulated tended to place the primary parental responsibility for child welfare squarely on mothers (Thorpe, 1994). Although it was often formulated in different terms it was clear that a concept of 'poor parenting' permeated the social workers' thinking in the majority of cases. This tended to concentrate on the parenting skills of mothers who failed to protect their children. This reflects an enduring motif in the research literature (Hooper, 1992; Farmer, 1993; Sharland *et al*, 1995), and can be visualised in terms of the social control element of social work, in that it expresses a degree of regulation of family life in accordance with a set of normative gender prescribed roles (Wilson, 1977; Brook and Davis, 1985; Sullivan, 1987).

Other familial relationships were also seen as important, particularly the relationship between the parents. The social workers' perceptions in this area tended to reside within two differing patriarchal discourses.

Firstly, there was a degree of ambivalence in the social workers' thinking. Some of them tended to visualise the breakdown of marital relations as bearing some relationship to a failure of the women involved carrying out their wifely duties. This contrasted sharply with their view that the women's' role as mothers, within which they ought to give total commitment to their child's protection, was their primary role. [3] Women are simultaneously exposed to the pressure to conform as autonomous self-reliant mothers and submissive, dependent wives. In families within which a child had been sexually abused, these tensions could often reached breaking point, placing these women in an invidious situation. Implicit in much of the social workers' discourse was the view that the sexual abuse may have been triggered through the man's lack of opportunity for sexual release in other ways. His wife was not fulfilling her duty in submitting to his sexual requests. More explicitly social workers' spoke of mothers failing to protect their daughters from abusive husbands/partners. Whatever actions these women took they were condemned as either 'bad' wives or 'bad' mothers. There was a clear perception on the part of the social workers that there were ideals of wifeliness and motherhood that these mothers had failed to live up to, despite the impossibility of concurrently fulfilling both roles to the full.

Secondly, there appeared to be an implicit belief in the uncontrollable nature of male desire. The breakdown in marital sexual relations was seen as a clear contributory factor to the commencement of the abuse in a number of cases.

> ...when the relationship with his wife deteriorated, again in a classical sense, he did turn inwards and his daughter's burgeoning sexuality at that time would have been very apparent to him. She's a very mature, advanced, young woman, and I think he would have found it hard to ignore at that time (SW).

The attitude of siblings to the girl and to the perpetrator were also seen as important in terms of the levels of support the girl would receive at home, and thus, to some extent, the degree of support she would need from the social worker. Social workers provided specific examples of all these varying levels of sibling support or lack of support in their accounts. In each case the level of sibling support formed an important part of the social workers assessment of risk and had a significant influence on the way the (s)he proceeded with the case. Social workers spoke of cases in which siblings were very unsupportive and tended to blame the girl either for what they saw as false allegations or as 'asking for it'. The disbelief of the girl by her siblings is to some extent understandable. Not only will they feel shock and bewilderment in much the same way as the mothers of sexually abused girls (Hooper, 1992; Farmer and Owen, 1995), but they are also subject to a pervasive discourse in the public arena that stresses the 'dangers' of false allegations out of all proportion to their prevalence (*Independent*, 11th May, 1994). Whether the siblings saw the girl as lying or as having 'deserved' the abuse, in either case social workers saw this leaving the girl in a very vulnerable position with an increased level of risk. They felt it emphasised the importance of their own role in terms of therapy and support to the girl. In cases where there was sibling support, social workers saw the siblings as fulfilling a vital role in maintaining the self-esteem of the abused girl. They also saw them as possibly reducing the level of risk and assisting with the girl's future safety, in that they tended to provide a bulwark against future abuse.

The Role of the mother and Non-abusing Family Members

The role played by siblings both in terms of the abuse and in terms of believing and supporting the girl, and the role played by the girl's mother had a profound influence on the way social workers saw cases developing, and the various strategies they adopted. Although it is accepted within the social work profession that sexual abuse is a male 'problem' (Creighton, 1992) and that the vast majority of perpetrators in cases referred to them will be men (Gibbons *et al*, 1995), child protection is seen as a female responsibility (Merrick, 1996). The social workers saw a key role for the mother in any child abuse/child protection case, and they considered maternal capacity to protect as an important factor in assessing the degree of risk to the girl.

Although almost all the cases in this study involved the sexual abuse of adolescent girls by a man occupying what could be seen as a paternal role, the degree to which the girls' mothers were implicated in the abuse, and the forms of their involvement had a critical influence on the ways in which the social workers proceeded. Mothers' involvement in the abuse took two distinct forms. In only one case was the mother directly involved in the sexual abuse of her daughter, and the criminal justice path was followed and both the mother and her boyfriend were convicted.

A more common theme in terms of mother's involvement in the abuse of their daughters revolved around concepts of implicit maternal acceptance of the abuse or collusion, and was perceived by the social workers in terms of emotional abuse. Early research in the field of child sexual abuse (Glick and Kessler 1980) tended to assume a degree of maternal collusion, and went on to suggest that complex mechanisms were at work, wherein the non-abusive spouse was colluding in the abuse as a means of diminishing sexual relations with the abuser. This has been refuted by feminist critiques (McIntyre, 1981; Wattenberg, 1985; Gavey *et al*, 1990). More recent research on the effects of sexual abuse on mothers (Sirles and Franke, 1989; De Jong, 1988a; De Jong, 1988b; Everson *et al*, 1989; Johnston, 1992; De Young, 1994a, 1994b) has pointed to empirical analyses that show the mothers of incest victims tend to support their daughters. The evidence suggests that they do not sanction the sexual abuse, but they are caught up in an appalling situation of having to decide what and who to believe and to choose between their child and their partner. Research suggests that social workers, in their practice, however, retain a view that at least implies collusion. This manifests itself in the ways social workers interpret the signals given out by mothers (Hooper, 1992; Sharland *et al*, 1995) which are taken by social workers to signify acceptance or resignation, when in actuality they are signs of bewilderment and shock (Sharland *et al*, 1995; Farmer and Owen, 1995). In her research into mothers surviving the sexual abuse of their children, Hooper (1992) found that some of the women she interviewed, far from disbelieving their daughters, were actually preoccupied with trying to discover the truth of the abuse to the extent that they were failing to develop effective protection strategies for their children. Following the insights of earlier research (Macleod and Saraga, 1988; Faller, 1989; Gomes-Schwartz *et al*, 1990), Farmer and Owen (1995) are critical of social workers' belief that mothers should sever all connections with the abuser immediately, arguing that mothers in this situation need time to sort out their conflicting feelings.

The social workers saw mothers as perpetrators of emotional abuse when they believed their daughter's allegations of sexual abuse by the father figure, but refused to sever their relationship with him. This was seen as not giving the girl the appropriate level of support, and was seen to add to the girl's level of risk of further abuse. This concurs with the findings of Farmer and Owen (1995). In some cases the Initial Case Conference or a subsequent Review placed the girl on the register under emotional abuse as well as sexual abuse, but in others it did not, often in seemingly similar cases. A great deal depended on the variation of child protection strategies adopted by different local authorities (O'Hagan, 1989) and the different prioritising of cases within different area offices. Within the study sample the label of emotional abuse tended to be applied in those cases where the social worker perceived the girl as being excluded emotionally from the family or psychologically isolated within the family. Social workers spoke of girls being blamed for the stigma brought upon the family by disclosure, others pointed to girls being scapegoated within the family for all its problems. Emotional abuse was also cited by social workers in cases where the mother did not believe the girl, although the key point was that the blame appeared to be attached to the making public of the family's problems rather than being attached to the perpetrator of the sexual abuse.

The other aspect of mothers' involvement in sexual abuse cases was in terms of whether or not they believed their daughters' allegations. When sexually abused girls first disclose the abuse it is most often to their mothers, and there is a lively debate within academia and within the social work profession as to how much and how often the mothers of girls who have been sexually abused within the family believe their daughters allegations (Wattam, 1992). One of the managers pointed to some difficulties stemming from the ways in which girls may attempt to disclose the abuse to their mothers. They may believe they have told their mothers, but they may have told them in such a way that is perhaps ambivalent. Some social workers pointed to cases where mothers found it hard to believe their daughters as the disclosure had lacked specificity in terms of actual incidents and times. This view was not shared entirely by the social workers, several of whom were of the opinion that 'mothers believe far more than is commonly thought' (SW), and that the mother's degree of belief of their daughters' allegations was a crucial factor in the prognosis for the girl's long-term mental health. Whilst fully endorsing the view that the mother's belief and support are crucial elements in the recovery process for sexually abused girls, Hooper (1992), points to the sometimes ambivalent feelings that sexually abused children have in respect of the potential loss to themselves consequent upon disclosure, that leads some of them to 'make great efforts not to let their mothers know' (Hooper, 1992 Pg. 53).

Feminist research (Hooper, 1992; Humphreys, 1992) also points to a great deal of complexity when addressing issues of maternal belief/disbelief of their daughters' allegations of sexual abuse. There is a complex process of discovery deriving from fragmentary and often contradictory information that women need to interpret both cognitively and emotionally that can lead them to almost concurrently believing and disbelieving. Smith (1995), in arguing for professional assessment of women's protectiveness capacities to be more alert to temporal fluctuations, argues that belief and protectiveness can change over time. Given the backdrop of intense and conflicting relationships within families where child sexual abuse has occurred, the holding of contradictory beliefs by mothers in terms of their children's sexual abuse allegations can be seen as inevitable.

In those cases where the mother did believe the girl social workers saw that as being a major benefit to the girl. Firstly, if they believed the girl they were more likely to agree to the perpetrator being removed from the family home, and this obviated the need to think in terms of accommodation for the girl. Secondly, they were more likely to provide the girl with support, and their belief in itself 'sent out the right messages' (SW) to the girl in terms absolving her from blame for the abuse and any subsequent family breakdown. This articulates with the psychological research (Conte and Schuerman, 1987; Wyatt and Mickey, 1988; Berliner, 1991) that stresses the importance of parental belief and support for the recovery process. The social workers also gave accounts of several cases where they saw the mother as not believing the girl. This perception of non-belief by mothers had serious implications for the social workers in the ways in which they progressed the cases. In these cases the mothers were far less likely to agree to the father figure leaving the family home, which had implications in terms of the safety of the girl and thus involved social workers in securing accommodation for the girl. Non-belief by mothers was also seen as detrimental to both the girl and the perpetrator:

> What the mum can't see is that if she actually believed her daughter more openly it might get him [perpetrator] to acknowledge his responsibility in what took place. She is at the moment very much preventing him acknowledging his guilt and also preventing the girl moving on very far (SW).

One of the very real difficulty social workers faced in terms of mothers believing their daughters was that early expressions of belief and support could melt away over time.

> You often get either an element of belief initially which is then questioned later on...(SW).

The social workers tended to ascribe this to pressure being brought to bear by the perpetrator in terms of, for example, saving the marriage. They also conceded that the complexities of family life may lead the mother into, publicly at least, recanting her belief, in that she could be making judgements as to what she saw as the least destructive option for the family. [4] One social worker, for example, spoke of a case in which the mother's initial belief and support for her daughter gradually dissipated, primarily as she was concerned that the fuss was causing serious problems for her son who was in the process of taking his GCSEs. The mother was in this case being placed in the position of either doing what she saw as the best by her daughter or what she saw as the best by her son, and found it impossible to do both.

Not only did social workers come across cases where initial maternal belief and support for the girl dwindled away over time, but they also gave accounts of cases where an initial disbelief by mothers, who could not visualise their partner as an abuser, gradually gave way to a recognition that the abuse had actually happened. [5] Social workers spoke of mothers beginning to recognise the significance of specific events and incidents in the past and question their own construction of the meanings of those events as the realisation gradually dawned upon them that their partner was an abuser. This was often accompanied by a level of self-blame for not recognising the signs of the abuse at the time.

Once sexual abuse has been identified in a family the child protection process seemed to place mothers in a difficult position. At the level of 'everyday theory' the social workers had a tendency to impute some degree of failure on women for the breakdown of marital relations, which they also saw as a critical point in the commencement of sexual abuse. Simultaneously, although they would strenuously deny locating the blame for the abuse anywhere other than with the perpetrator, and although there are legitimate reasons to investigate, question and confront the attitudes and responses of mothers within sexually abusive families (Finkelhor, 1984), the emphasis the social workers placed on the mothers' failure to protect implicitly served to displace a degree of blame away from perpetrators. In some cases the social workers' preoccupation with the mothers' role was transmitted directly to the abused girls:

> We kept saying your mum should be protecting you and she's not (SW).

In effect with very little consideration as to the complexities of the mother's emotional life, some social workers' expectations of maternal support for the girl seemed to mean severing all ties with the perpetrator, who in some instances was a sexual and emotional partner of long standing, yet as one social worker pointed out:

> It's absolutely dreadful for her. She's caught slap-bang in the middle of it all (SW).

To some extent some of the social workers were aware of the difficult position that the mothers were in in these cases.

> We regard the woman as the mother and sometimes forget that she is wife, partner, whatever, and that the implications for her are the fact that her family has collapsed, the business has disintegrated, you know. There's the loss of home and a lot of implications for them, which we don't always take into consideration (SW).

The managers were aware that social workers tended to neglect the difficulties women faced when having to confront the fact that their partner and breadwinner was an abuser, and that the process itself had a tendency to imply criticism of women in their role as mothers and compound any feelings of maternal inadequacy that might stem from the abuse.

Many of the issues that pertain to the mother in adolescent sexual abuse cases also apply to other non-abusing family members. The degree of belief and support given by siblings was a significant influence on the development of specific cases. Farmer and Owen (1995) found that in cases where the father figure was the abuser, the relationship between the father figure and the abused child's sibling was a crucial factor in determining the reaction of that sibling to the abuse. They also found that the nature of the sibling's reaction tended to be relatively intense when the abuse was sexual abuse. In most of the cases in the present study, where there was a sibling present in the family, it seemed that the sibling(s) took a lead from the mother as to whether or not they believed the girl. This was not, however, always straightforward. Social workers gave accounts of cases where, although the mother believed the abused girl, any support for the girl from within the immediate family came from a brother or sister.

In cases where the mother did not believe the girl, the non-belief by siblings served only to exacerbate the degree of exclusion experienced by the girl within the family. The worst example of total exclusion within the family to come from the social workers' accounts concerned a girl of fourteen whom was sexually abused by her mother's boyfriend. One of the results of the abuse was a clear gender split in the immediate and extended family, with the male members of the family subjecting her to a regime of verbal and physical abuse. The extremity of this reaction by her brothers and other male members of the family as given in the social worker's account, however, may need to be treated with some circumspection. Firstly, in comparison to the other cases discussed in the social workers' accounts this reaction seemed very extreme. Secondly the social worker described the family as working class and transient, and was generally disapproving of their living arrangements. The social worker concerned extrapolated from the case in terms of the demographic complexion of the area, making the claim that there were a significant number of working class men in the area who drifted from one vulnerable woman to another using them both sexually and for domestic labour and shelter. The concept of the lone female parent as being vulnerable to the attentions of would be child abusers, and the children of such women being more at risk of sexual abuse is well documented in the literature (Vizard and Tranter, 1988b; Renvoize, 1993). The more usual consequences of belief or non-belief by mothers and close family members were seen by social workers in terms of the psychological well being of the girl. In cases where the girl was not believed it was more likely that she would blame herself for the abuse. This bears close resemblance to some of the risk factors developed in family dynamics models of risk assessment. [6]

Family Patterns of Child Abuse

To some extent the social workers predicated their practice upon perceived patterns of child sexual abuse within families. If initial investigations revealed abusive strands within the family this was seen as having some bearing upon levels of risk and how best to proceed. It also seemed that the discovery of child abuse in previous generations of the family served as a way of explaining the current abuse.

This 'explanation' is clearly located within a form of social learning theory; a discourse relating to cycles of abuse. The basic premise of the cycle of abuse thesis is that individuals who are abused as children or adolescents will in turn abuse their own children. This concept appeared to be deeply embedded within the thinking of the social workers, and previous research shows that it routinely informs the assessment of risk (Waterhouse and Carnie, 1992; Gibbons, *et al*, 1995). This goes a long way towards explaining the importance social workers placed on aftermath work as a form of prevention. [7] As a concept it demonstrates some heuristic force with reference to the generational replication of physical injury within families and does appear to have some common sense appeal. In terms of Sexual abuse the use of cycles of abuse as an explanatory factor is more difficult to sustain (Hooper, 1995), but was nevertheless still maintained by the social workers, albeit with various adaptations and reservations.

Firstly, they clearly held to the belief that certain families contained within them abusive streams. However, those families that come to the attention of social services in terms child sexual abuse tend to be of poorer economic and educational backgrounds, and may already known to the authorities as recipients of welfare benefits (Thorburn *et al*, 1995). For a variety of reasons better off abusive families are more skilled at keeping away from the attention of social services and keeping their problems to themselves (Renvoize, 1993). Thus the existence or otherwise of abusive streams within the families of the girls they are working with is not statistically significant. Secondly, the perpetrators of sexual abuse are almost always men, and the victims of the abuse are usually girls. This seemingly insurmountable difficulty was explained away by the social workers in various ways. Some of them suggested that men who had either been physically or sexually abused as children or adolescents were more likely than other men to become abusers, and the form of that abuse could be either physical or sexual. This is not a particularly unreasonable suggestion in that it links sexual and physical abuse very closely and implies that sexual abuse has as much to do with power and control as it is with sex. The research is inconclusive. Bagley (1995), drawing upon the work of Lane (1991) argues that it is 'well established' (Bagley, 1995, Pg.123) that some sexually abused boys become sexually abusing men, but that the reasons for the development of this abusing cycle are unclear. The evidence that this cycle of sexual abuse is well established is tenuous. Finkelhor (1986), whilst making clear that some sexually abused boys do become sexually abusing men, points out that many others do not, and not all abusing men were themselves abused. Other social workers adopted a more psychoanalytic or symbolic interactionist perspective and suggested that boys who were sexually abused by their fathers or observed their fathers sexually abusing their sisters grew into adult men that perceived the sexual abuse of one's offspring as inherent in the father's role. In other words they took their abusing father as a role model. A further twist on this theme turned the blame for abuse back onto mothers. Many of the social workers held simultaneously to a concept of cycles of abuse and a notion of mothers failing to protect their daughters. Those who held this view seemed to place special emphasis on the discovery of sexual abuse of the mother as a child or adolescent. Research (Macfarlane, 1978; Goodwin *et al*, 1981; Cooper and Cormier, 1982; Sheldon, 1988) shows mothers of incest victims more likely than other women to have been incest victims themselves. In this perspective it is girls growing into a role modelled on that of their own mothers who lacked the skills to protect their children that was given the major emphasis. The social workers also seemed to engage with the multiple victim theses (Lees, 1981; Russell, 1982) that suggests that girls who had been abused gravitated towards abusive men in their adult relationships, i.e. men who resembled their fathers. There was some variation of opinion amongst social workers that tended to suggest that the concept of cycles of abuse is something that is embedded in the professional ideology of social workers. Those who were more recently qualified seemed to question the concept whereas more experienced workers accepted it as 'obvious'.

Other aspects of family patterns of adolescent sexual abuse also emerged from the interviews. Although, as discussed earlier, stepfathers were seen in practical terms as presenting a risk factor per *se*, in general discussion the social workers made it clear that it was men generally that perpetrated sexual abuse. This idea, however, was held in different forms by different workers; some saw sexual abuse as a 'problem' of men as such, others held to some concept of paedeophilia in that only certain men presented a problem, those that were sexually attracted to children and adolescents (see Becker, 1991). Some of the social workers also located the sexual abuse of adolescent girls within a view of certain men that preyed upon vulnerable women. They pointed to cases where men had attached themselves to lone parents as a way of getting a roof over their heads. These same men had then sexually assaulted the adolescent daughters of these women. This clearly indicated another 'risk' factor, in that girls in families headed by a lone woman were at an enhanced level of risk (Greenland, 1987), and it also demonstrated a view of sexual abuse as having something to do with a lack of respect for women, selfishness, and a complete disregard for social mores. [8]

One of the aspects of abusive patterns within the family that was routinely used by the social workers to attempt to ascertain risk was that of the known abuse of a sibling. This corresponds with research findings (Farmer and Owen, 1995) that previous family involvement with child protection agencies is routinely seen as a risk factor by social workers. The social workers believed that if a girl's siblings had also come to the attention of social services for sexual abuse then the likelihood of that girl being sexually abused was significantly increased. This concern seems to be borne out by research. Farmer and Parker (1991) found that of those non-abused children who were in care due to the abuse of a sibling, seventeen per cent suffered abuse upon returning home, although it needs to be borne in mind that Farmer and Parker in this instance were aggregating all forms of child abuse. Closely associated with this were cases reported by the social workers where the investigation of sexual abuse allegations in respect of one child had revealed previous incidents of abuse involving older siblings.

Family Support Networks

The social workers also took into account the attitudes towards the girl and the perpetrator of extended family members such as aunts, uncles and grandparents. The social services managers made clear that in a general sense when social workers confronted the structure and dynamics of the family they needed to include such things as the degree of contact the immediate family had with extended family members and the attitudes such members had to the abuse. Farmer and Owen (1995) found that the availability of family support systems was seen by social workers and other professionals in the child protection network as a mitigating factor to set against any risks when conferences decided whether or not to register a child. The social workers perceived of issues to do with the extended family both in terms of the formulation of networks of support and in terms of the strength of support from specific members of the extended family.

In one of the area teams this often proved problematic. Due to the location of the office a significant number of the cases they dealt with concerned the families of military personnel. These families were less likely than other families to have members of the extended family living within the vicinity. In these cases social workers were less likely to look for support from extended family members, on the premise that already existing interlocking networks of kinship support were less likely to be in place than within extended families whose members remained in closer geographical proximity. Even in those extended families that were geographically dispersed that did retain a large degree of contact with each other, the social workers saw severe limitations in the degree of support that could be mobilised. Support might, for example, entail the provision of a temporary safe haven for the girl, but the use value of this would be offset by issues such as the disruption to the girl's education and the removal of the girl from networks of peer support in ways very similar to the problems attendant upon reception into care. This problem of distance was discounted in one particular case in the social workers accounts, when, with the assistance of social services, the abused girl moved out from the home of her mother and stepfather to go and live with her father and stepmother in another town. This may, however, be seen in terms of the specific complications inherent in child protection cases where reconstituted families are concerned.

The importance the social workers attached to family support networks was highlighted by their concerns when such networks were not in place. In the majority of the cases that the social workers discussed it was the father figure that was the perpetrator. In many of these cases the mother was financially and emotionally dependent upon her partner, and this seriously impacted upon her capacity to support her daughter. If there was no other input from family members this left the girl unsupported within the family and thus in a position of risk, which in turn necessitated a more intrusive intervention from the social worker. The presence of supportive extended family networks was seen by the social workers to have two beneficial effects. Firstly, they could provide direct support to the girl, both in terms of the provision of a safe haven from the abusive situation, and in believing her story and thus potentially enhancing her psychological well being. Survivors of child and adolescent sexual abuse make clear the importance of being believed (Women's Resource Centre, 1989; Hendessi, 1992). Secondly, they could provide the mother with emotional support that could go some way towards enabling her to support her daughter, without recourse to the emotional support of the perpetrator.

More usually the social workers perceptions of family support networks resided in the attitudes struck up by extended family members. Whilst realising the complexity and ambivalence of such attitudes, the social workers saw them as generally falling into two distinct modes that mirrored the attitudes of immediate family members. They either believed the girl or the perpetrator. Social workers felt that in exactly similar ways to immediate family members, there was a greater likelihood to believe the allegations if the alleged abuser was not a family member. Although the sexual abuse of children and adolescents is more likely to occur within the family and their close associates, research (Wattam, 1992) shows that various members of the family are more likely to believe the girl when the allegations are made against an outsider, and in such cases members of the extended family are also very likely to offer support. In cases where the alleged abuser was a family member support was far less likely to be forthcoming. This was not always the case, however. Social workers pointed to cases where the non-abusing members of the immediate family believed the girl and were very supportive, whilst members of the extended family gave no support. If such support was not forthcoming, and the family was close to the extended family, it was more likely that the girl would be seen to remain at risk and as such she would remain on the register.

Issues of support from extended family networks were not confined to whether or not grandparents, uncles and aunts necessarily believed the girl. There were also issues surrounding the support given to other non-abusing family members. One case involved the brother of the abused girl supporting her within the family unit, but he himself was sustained by the support he received from his long-term girlfriend in coming to terms with the actions of his father. The social worker involved in the case was convinced that the young man's own mental health was preserved by this supportive relationship. Other social workers spoke of support to the girl and her mother from other members of the community such as neighbours influencing the ways in which they proceeded in specific cases. This highlights a very important issue. The concept of supportive networks, although seen by most of the social workers primarily in terms of extended family networks and, to some extent, peer support, needs to be seen in terms of the presence or absence of networks of support for the girl, her mother, and non-abusing family members within the local community as a whole.

Health and Disability Issues in Respect of the Family

A key series of factors that social workers utilised in their assessment of cases related to the physical and mental health of family members and the presence of any type of disability. In ways similar to the majority of risk factors that they used this follows the broad path of risk assessment factors that appear in the literature (Madge, 1983; Finkelhor and Baron, 1986; Greenland, 1987; Vizard and Tranter, 1988b). Apart from factors related specifically to the girl herself, the key area of health within the family that social workers granted importance to was the physical and mental health of the mother. They spoke in terms of risk if the mother was suffering from a chronic condition. This begs the question as to who is the client. If risks are being seen as present for the mother then clearly she is seen as a client in the case. Conversely, it may be a particular expression of the specific role the social workers attributed to mothers. In other words the presence of a chronic condition such as epilepsy or diabetes in the mother may be seen as negatively impacting upon her capacity to protect her daughter within an abusive situation.

Similar concerns were expressed in terms of maternal mental health, although these focussed more specifically on the problems associated with the barriers that mental health problems may pose for the relationship between the girl and the mother in the aftermath of the abuse. The social workers tended to see mental health problems for the mother and those for the girl feeding off one another, making necessary the introduction of psychological services to attempt to repair the relationship, although the degree to which this impacted upon the ways in which the social workers acted was severely circumscribed by what they saw as a chronically poor level of access to psychological services. As far as mental health was concerned, it was clear that social workers remained fixed into conceptions of cycles of abuse. In cases where the mother had been sexually abused as an adolescent social workers tended to see any mental health problems suffered by girls as reflecting the mental health career of their mothers.

Issues of disability were also seen as clear risk factors, especially the presence of maternal learning difficulties. In some cases the mother's lack of intellectual capacity was taken by social workers as a way of explaining her failure to protect the child, or her active involvement in the abuse. The key point is that the social workers routinely used factors relating to the presence of learning difficulties as a risk factor in their assessments of cases, although, on occasions maternal learning disabilities were also seen as mitigation for involvement in the abuse.

> We actually felt that it wouldn't be right to split this mother and daughter up, and what we really had to do was to give her a lot of support back at home, and we did (SW).

This contradicts research findings (Farmer and Owen, 1995) that suggest that mitigating factors tend not to enter in to the assessment process. One issue that one social worker drew attention to be the emotional difficulty mothers find themselves in when the abuse has been perpetrated by a sibling. What often appeared as a lack of support for the girl could be seen as a misunderstanding by the mother of the emotional needs of her children. A daughter who appeared to be surviving the trauma of being sexually abused by her brother could appear to be in less need of emotional support than an abusive son who appeared weak and lacking self-control. The social worker's view was that this type of situation benefited no one. The girl was not receiving the emotional support she needed, and the boy was not being made to confront the consequences of his actions. The social worker was in a sense very critical of mothers in this situation, arguing that they were legitimising the abusive behaviour of their sons by expending their time and energies on them to the detriment of their sisters, effectively rewarding abusive behaviour. She felt very strongly that this constituted maternal collusion in the abuse. Although one can understand the frustration that the social workers felt in these circumstances, this perception does seem to show a lack of understanding of the difficult position of mothers in that situation.

The majority of the cases, however, involved the sexual abuse of girls by a father figure, and this had profound emotional consequences for other family members. The social workers spoke of siblings being torn between love for their fathers and attempting to support their sisters. In one case the brother of a girl who had been raped by her father spent the whole of the court case sobbing inconsolably as he felt utterly torn.

> He wanted to stay around his father. When it got down to it he told his sister that if he had to choose between his father and his sister, he would be with his sister. I think that would probably be right, because he was very supportive to her (SW).

Siblings were also affected in other ways. If there was a sibling in the house and there was no evidence of abuse being perpetrated against her/him it was not uncommon for supervised contact to be put in place with the abusing father. This contact often deteriorated over time. Social workers saw this as partly a function of supervised contact and the unnaturalness of it. They also pointed to cases where the attitude of siblings to the abuser changed as they began to realise the enormity of what he had done. They also pointed to the key role that mothers played, in that as mothers grew angrier with the perpetrators this was often reflected in the feelings of their non-abused children.

Social workers illustrated through reference to specific cases the complexities involved in the emotional responses of mothers when the abuse had been perpetrated by a father figure. Mothers exhibited shame that they had allowed the abuse to happen, some mothers felt that they also had suffered and felt extreme anger towards the perpetrator for what he had done to them, others became quite distraught at the potential outcome of losing their partner upon whom they were either financially or emotionally dependent. Renvoize (1993) makes the point that such a degree of maternal emotional turbulence can place enormous pressure on the mother of an abused child even to the point of suppressing any disclosure. Some mothers showed a contradictory set of emotions, revolving around turbulent relations with their daughters. On the one hand they would make every attempt to support their daughters, often in inappropriate ways by letting them do as they pleased, and on the other hand ending up in frequent violent arguments with them and blaming them for the break up of the family. When such unstable relationships manifested themselves the social workers perceived girls as being at increased risk.

The research also uncovered issues of maternal inhibition in talking about sexual matters to daughters, something the social workers saw as potentially placing some girls at risk. In cases where this had been a factor in the development of the abuse the social workers worked with the mothers to assist them in overcoming their inhibitions. They also pointed out that the brittle nature of parental emotions when abuse has occurred meant that they needed to be very circumspect in their actions. This was made very clear in a case that the key worker referred to as being 'very unusual' in that the abuse was by the father of an adopted father. The blood relatives of the grandfather throughout the case consistently exonerated his behaviour and blamed the girl. The father blamed himself entirely for the abuse to the point that he suggested to the social worker that everything would have been alright if he had never met his wife and married her and thus never adopted the child.

> I've never come across that before. I imagined that he would perhaps feel very sort of hurt by his own family's reaction, but I've never come across somebody taking it so far to be blaming himself in the way he has done (SW).

Both parents wanted to do whatever was necessary for their daughter to come through the abuse and be able to make normal sexual relations in adult life, but for some time they resisted social services offers of help in the belief that they could give their daughter the support she needed without the intervention of any other agency. Although, in this case, the intervention proposed by the social worker was purely voluntary, and comprised advice, assistance and guidance, this degree of parental resistance underlines some of the issues highlighted by Farmer and Owen (1995) in terms of parental resistance to participation in child protection conferences and other statutory aspects of the process. Principally, the parents, in this particular case, felt that their capacity as care givers and protectors to their child was being questioned, and they feared a loss of control over aspects of their family life. After some time they came to social services and requested help that was duly given. The social worker praised the emphasis her own training placed on client choice. She made the point that the help parents actively requested was valued more and therefore of far more use than help that might have been placed upon them, which may have served only to exacerbate their feelings of guilt and thus undermine their own efforts at supporting the girl.

The Perpetrator

One of the problem areas for social workers was that of working with the perpetrators. On occasions this was related to the difficulty the worker had in actually attempting to work with someone that (s) he knew had behaved in such an abusive manner. This difficulty seemed to be greatest in those social workers with the least experience and in those cases where they found the abuse particularly repellent. The central focus of their difficulties, however, was in the area of the interpenetration of resources and the criminal justice system. The point was repeatedly made by social workers that there was no infrastructure of services to which they could refer perpetrators. There were very few resources available to assist adolescent or adult perpetrators to learn to accept responsibility (Kopp, 1988; Kettle, 1990; Afnan and Smith, 1992); thus the attitude of the mother was seen as a crucial factor in terms of the future behaviour of the perpetrator. The only help that was generally on offer to perpetrators came if they were convicted and either imprisoned or made subject to a probation order. Farmer and Owen (1995) report that treatment for adult perpetrators was seen within the child protection network as the responsibility of the probation service. The social workers in this study did not entirely endorse that view. Rather, they perceived the situation in terms of a paucity of resources, seeing the probation service, as offering what little help for perpetrators that was available. In effect, unless a conviction was secured, the only help available to perpetrators was that which could be offered by the social workers themselves. Central to this work were attempts to persuade perpetrators to acknowledge the abuse and accept responsibility. The social workers found this particularly difficult, as perpetrators tended on the whole to resist acknowledgement. Some of the social workers saw this as inevitable, as perpetrators would deny the abuse in order to prevent themselves being prosecuted. [9] The social workers pointed to cases where individuals had originally admitted the abuse and then on the advice of a solicitor denied it. Some social workers saw this as an indication of the potential disbenefits to the abused girl of the criminal justice system. Perpetrators will consistently deny the abuse and put pressure onto the family that can lead the girl to retract her allegations, leaving social services in a very difficult position in respect of such things as Care Orders and Supervision Orders. In other words they saw elements of the criminal justice system in this respect increasing the level of risk for the girl. If the girl did not recant, but the perpetrator continued to deny the abuse, he would receive no help. In some cases where the perpetrator refused to leave the family home, the social workers had to make use of voluntary arrangements or Care Orders for the removal of the girl.

The concept of a confrontational process caused some worries for the social workers in other respects. A not uncommon recommendation of Initial Child Protection Conferences was that a risk assessment be carried out with the perpetrator. The social workers reported a variety of responses from perpetrators to risk assessments. Some would cooperate fully, most would not. The refusal to cooperate tended to take two forms; out and out refusal to cooperate at all, the perpetrator simply seeing the social worker as an enemy, and initial cooperation in the immediate aftermath of being accused gradually being replaced by a more uncooperative attitude. The social workers pointed out that a great deal of their work with perpetrators didn't confront the abuse at all, it was simply in terms of ensuring the practical arrangements of the perpetrators accommodation.

The social workers saw the lack of services for perpetrators who were not convicted meaning that the activities of these men could not be controlled or monitored with any degree of efficiency. Some social workers believed that perpetrators were well aware of this and thus those who were not convicted would on many occasions attach themselves to another family and place other young people at risk. Their managers also expressed concern, primarily about finding ways to ensure the safety of the girl, whilst not totally excluding the perpetrator from any involvement in child care and protection plans. This view seemed to reinforce some of the tensions in child protection demonstrated by Fox-Harding (1991), in that they were attempting to articulate a central role for the state in child protection, whilst simultaneously holding to a concept of the family as being the central institution for the care and protection of children. The managers were also acutely concerned over issues to do with false allegations of sexual abuse against foster parents. This may have had less to do with the prevalence of false allegations, and more to do with a fear of not 'getting it right' as far as their organisation was concerned.

The social workers also saw serious problems in terms of perpetrator denial. In those cases where the perpetrator admitted the abuse it was either because the evidence was overwhelming from the girl and other family members, or admission was followed by denial in an attempt to prevent a criminal prosecution. The social workers, to some extent, implicated the mothers in the perpetrators' processes of denial as in several cases perpetrator denial went hand in hand with a social worker perception of maternal non-belief or ambivalence. The social workers found this frustrating and tending to hamper their attempts to confront the issues and provide the appropriate therapeutic intervention for the girls.

The social workers, both in their accounts of specific cases and in their recollections of past cases, also pointed to perpetrators rationalising the abuse, claiming in various ways that the whole thing was a mistake. This element of mistake appeared to take various forms. Firstly, the actions of the alleged perpetrator had been misunderstood or deliberately taken out of context by the girl. Wattam (1992) emphasises that such a reaction by a perpetrator can on occasions be more than simply an excuse, and that they can construct their own behaviour as being nurturing or educating. The social workers reported perpetrators arguing that the girl had genuinely misunderstood what was going on and had placed a negative connotation on innocent actions, or the girl had deliberately used an ambivalent incident to try and make trouble for the perpetrator. This latter attempt at explanation emerged in only two cases, both of which involved an adopted child. In each case it was accompanied by statements pertaining to the girl not being 'family'; in one case not being familiar with the idiosyncrasies of the behaviour of family members, and in the other case, in terms of the girl already being 'damaged goods', a troublemaker.

The second rationalisation of the situation that social workers reported being offered by perpetrators was that they had engaged in inappropriate sexual activity with the girl, but their actions had been a consequence of mistaken identity:

> He [perpetrator] worked shifts and she [girl] used to go and get in bed with him now and again, and he said he thought it was his wife, he made a mistake and touched her (SW).

Several perpetrators, whilst admitting specific incidents, attempted to distance themselves from blame by placing the responsibility back onto the adolescent girl, by claiming that they had been led on or seduced. This particular modality of blaming the victim appears to have a long history (Gordon 1988), and was often accompanied by a claim by the perpetrator that he was under the influence of drink at the time and thus was not in full control of his actions. There appeared to be a remarkably high degree of acquiescence in this idea by other family members and the authorities. In several cases the girl's mothers accepted that specific incidents had occurred, but accepted that the blame lay with their partner being drunk, and if he had been sober this would never have happened. One needs to examine this acquiescence from the point of view of mothers and realise that it gives them a way of avoiding the horrific conclusion that their partner has violated their daughter. The position of the authorities in the shape of the criminal justice system is less understandable, and is best illustrated by a specific example. A social worker gave an account of a case wherein a man repeatedly sexually abused his teenage son and daughter over a number of months, always when under the influence of alcohol. He was convicted and imprisoned. Whilst in prison he was treated for his alcohol abuse, but not for his sex offending. The treatment for alcohol abuse, but not for sex offending, seems to draw upon two distinct themes. Firstly, as far as child abuse, including sexual abuse is concerned, alcohol abuse has been long been seen as a risk factor (Greenland, 1987, for example). Secondly, there is a widely held view that recidivism rate for sex offenders cannot be seriously reduced by treatment. The research on treatment success is inconclusive. Furby *et al* (1989) in a review of clinical studies, for example, concluded that there was no evidence that treatment reduced offending, yet other studies (Maletsky, 1980, 1991; Marshall and Barbaree, 1988) showed significant reductions in the recidivism rates of child sexual abusers. Prentky and Burgess (1990) concurred with the view that treatments can be effective and argued that treatment programmes would be a more cost-effective way of dealing with sexual abuse than imprisonment. The social workers were far from impressed by the idea that the perpetrator could utilise drunkenness as an excuse for abusive activities, preferring to see the sexual abuse of children and adolescents as being consequent upon a personality disorder in certain men.

> It is often used as an excuse, and of course it is a disinhibitor, but it depends on underlying personality traits (SW).

Another trait that was identified by the social workers amongst some perpetrators was that of a disproportionate need to be in control. This is theorised in various ways in the psychological and sociological literature, and can be seen in terms of the maintenance of structured power relations between individuals (Giddens, 1984), or an extreme manifestation of the operation of the processes of patriarchy (Miles, 1992), or in terms of an 'authoritarian personality' (Adorno *et al*, 1950). However it is theorised, the empirical evidence is similar. Several of the perpetrators of sexual abuse against their daughters were men who displayed a great need to be in control. This reflects the testimony of many adult survivors of child or adolescent sexual abuse (Women's Resource Centre, 1989; Renvoize, 1993). This authoritarianism often manifested itself in terms of physical chastisement or a proliferation of rules of conduct within the family, even down to who and what could be spoken of in the family home. The general behaviour of these men was felt by the girls concerned to be as abusive as the sexual assaults, as in each case it denied them their autonomy. In some cases what happened to the girl was a mirror of what had been happening to her mother over a relatively long period, the overriding image being of a man attempting to control absolutely the members of his family. In some cases, the configuration of sex and violence as forms of control became clear in that the sexual abuse was always prefigured by a physical assault. These men almost always had a preferred vision of themselves as being particularly respectable and correct. Survivors accounts suggest that this is not unusual (Women's Resource Centre, 1989). This created some problems for the social workers in that these men were so entrenched in their attitudes that risk assessment work with them was almost impossible.

The Degree of Cooperation and Level of Participation of the Family

The invocation to partnership is clearly stated in government policy guidance (DoH, 1991c, para: 1.4), and the establishment of a working partnership between social worker and parents was noted by Sharland *et al* (1995) as central to successful child protection intervention. Farmer and Owen (1995) make clear the importance of developing enough common ground between the family and the social worker to develop a feasible child protection plan, with the caveat that when the abused is an adolescent the importance of this partnership diminishes somewhat in favour of a closer working relationship between the social worker and the young person.

Family participation and working in partnership, has become the focus of some research (Marsh and Fisher, 1992; Owen, 1992), although the move towards a participatory model in child protection has been slower to develop than in other areas of social work (Croft and Beresford, 1990; Barnes and Wistow ed., 1992). The difficulties attendant on developing working partnerships with the family in child abuse cases has long been recognised. The importance of establishing a good working relationship with the family of an abused child was recognised as long ago as the Lester Chapman Inquiry (Berkshire County Council, 1979), and continues to be seen as crucial. In a summary of recent research (DoH, 1995), this 'ecological' view is reiterated within a perspective that perceives of the child as a 'consumer' of child protection:

> Children like services they see as being directed towards their needs, but their protection is also enhanced by dealing with the health, economic and relationship problems that beset families. Welfare and protection should be complementary (DoH, 1995, Pg.48).

Participation of the Perpetrator in the Child Protection Process

Although not as influential to social work practice, a feminist critique of the family dysfunction model of child sexual abuse has developed, deriving from the fact that the vast majority of child sexual abusers are male, arguing that child sexual abuse can be visualised best not in terms of pathological families or individuals, but in terms of a function of societal attitudes and power relations. This tends to root child sexual abuse within the parameters of the workings of patriarchy. However, the cultural attitudes and material manifestations of the workings of patriarchy do not remain fixed. Rather, they adapt through time as an integral element of cultural change. The 1980s witnessed a significant cultural change in British society. [10] It would not be unreasonable to see one element of the cultural shift in terms of a growth in selfishness and a loosening of societal responsibilities and constraints. If one also takes into the equation a changing labour market with degrees of uncertainty of employment for significant numbers of men, and the psychological threat that posed to their expression of masculinity, one can see the ingredients for an increased prevalence in child sexual abuse. Men are more likely to be in the home for longer periods, traditional expressions of masculine autonomy are increasingly circumscribed, and the social taboos on specific behaviours are weakened by an overarching societal attitude of self-interest. However, as the true incidence of child sexual abuse is not known, one can only speculate as to the real effect of this cultural shift on child sexual abuse.

The major critique of the family dysfunction model offered by feminists is that sexual offenders abuse women and children because they are able to behave in this way with little potential cost to themselves (Gelles, 1983), and family dysfunction explanations of abuse can reinforce the privileged position of the perpetrator through their tendency to remove some of the responsibility from the perpetrator and diffuse it across the whole family. Further, the overemphasis on attempting to maintain the family can place the girl back into a situation of risk (Macleod and Saraga, 1988, 1991). These concerns are refuted by Bentovim (1988) who claims that within the family dysfunction model some families are diagnosed as not being suitable for treatment as the prognosis for them is too poor.

The social workers did little to encourage perpetrator participation in the child protection process, beyond attempts to persuade perpetrators to remove themselves from the family home. When perpetrators attended Child Protection Conferences, the social workers saw them as attending but not participating. Further, the social workers tended towards a view that there was no useful purpose to be served in perpetrators attending Child Protection Conferences. Indeed, some of them saw perpetrator attendance as detrimental in that it could act to intimidate other family members.

Family Participation in the Child Protection Process

The invocation to partnership operates as an important organising feature of the child protection process in several aspects of the work. One central aspect is the concept of working in partnership with the families of abused children. The social workers found a degree of difficulty in several cases in accomplishing any form of partnership with parents. They cited several reasons for this. A recurring feature was the problem of trust. Several of the mothers in cases where the father figure was the abuser tended to focus the problems besetting the family, and the potential break-up of the family, on the social worker or social services generally. Similar processes of parental hostility to social workers have been noted elsewhere (Cleaver and Freeman, 1995; Farmer and Owen, 1995), in terms of both abusers and non-abusing parents feeling anger at what they saw as a loss of confidentiality as the various professionals transformed their specific family problems into a child protection case, often incorporating a sense of injustice in non-abusing parents at their loss of control once the child protection process was instigated. The social workers saw this presenting a serious block on familial participation in the process.

This lack of family participation manifested itself primarily in two ways. Firstly mothers would cooperate in terms of attending conferences and reviews, but as observers rather than as active participants:

> She [the mother] was never in partnership. We never worked together as joint work with family and workers. She was there as a sounding block really and she was there to be given information and to be invited to things. She was very much 'I'll come, but you can do the work. There's no way I'm joining you in this.' (SW).

Secondly, there were cases within which mothers and other family members were simply uncooperative and refused even to participate at any level at all, something that during the course of several cases deteriorated into open conflict between the social worker and the mother. The view of those social workers that had experienced this type of response was to equate it with a lack of maternal belief of the girl's allegations. It would not be unreasonable to make that inference, but there may well be other issues that need examining. Mothers in this situation can often be caught between the conflicting claims of their partners and their child (Farmer and Owen, 1995), and their reactions could be misinterpreted by social workers (Sharland *et al*, 1995). There have been great strides made in attempting to involve the families of abused children in Child Protection Conferences and other aspects of the child protection process in recent years, but wider questions of the distribution of power within professional-client relationships may well need to be addressed further. Research points to several points within the process wherein the parents of abused children feel a lack of control. Katz (1995) points to parents being too distressed and uninformed at the time of initial investigations and the Initial Child Protection Conference to make a worthwhile contribution. The structuring of relationships within Child Protection Conferences creates an us and them scenario (Cleaver and Freeman, 1995), with family members feeling that they don't understand what is happening (Farmer and Owen, 1995), although as Bell (1993) found in Leeds, those parents that did attend conferences had a better idea of what was going on and had their views better represented than those who did not. Farmer and Owen (1995) also discovered that parents found child protection plans frightening as they felt that they signified unrestricted access for social workers into their private lives, and they also feared the consequences of a lack of feedback in that they were unsure if they were doing the right thing.

The mothers of sexually abused adolescent girls were already emotionally vulnerable as a consequence of the position they were in. Their sense of inadequacy as far as protecting their daughters may well have been exacerbated by the attentions of social workers and the mobilisation of official child protection procedures. If one adds to that the dominant role of the welfare professionals within conferences and reviews, the attitude of some of the mothers and other family members becomes a little more understandable. The anger and lack of cooperation they exhibited may well reflect a very real sense of impotence, yet successful partnership requires empowerment. Biehal and Sainsbury (1991) and Marsh and Fisher (1992) stress the need for consent, negotiation and agreement at all stages if cases are to result in successful outcomes, and Sharland *et al* (1995) found that the attitudes and behaviour of social workers at the initial investigation stage, and the success or otherwise of developing a working partnership, had a crucial influence on the outcomes of cases.

The social workers tended to draw upon a rationalist and normative discourse of parenting when discussing questions of family involvement in the child protection process:

> There's not a reliable family member who would have been good as a resource at that time that we could have used (SW).

The social workers also made clear that the degree of cooperation and participation could change over time. Relatively uncooperative families became more cooperative as the social worker developed a closer personal relationship with the mother and other family members. A similar pattern seemed in evidence in those families that were relatively cooperative at the outset of the process, and gradually became less cooperative. In other words, the relationship that developed between the social worker and the mother and other family members could be seen as a crucial factor in the degree to which the family cooperated with social services and the degree of participation of those families in aspects of the process, such as attendance at conferences and reviews and in drawing up a child protection plan. This concurs with the findings of Farmer and Owen (1995). Clearly other factors were also at work. Social workers identified issues such as initial belief in the allegation being offset by 'emotional blackmail' (SW) by the perpetrator, or initial denial being displaced by the realisation that this awful thing had really occurred. Although not always aware of the circumstances that caused the levels of cooperation and participation to increase or decrease, the social workers clearly understood through experience that initial familial attitudes to cooperation often changed over time, although they remained aware that the families within which abuse had occurred were often volatile and unpredictable (Packman and Randall, 1989; Hallett, 1995). From a practical perspective, social workers were aware that there were serious difficulties in attempting to develop any long term child protection strategies in the immediate aftermath of disclosure, as it tended take some time for families to come to terms with the allegations, and it was very difficult to know to what degree the mother and other family members believed the girl's allegations. The level of belief/non-belief was a critical factor in a whole range of issues in respect of the level of cooperation and participation of the family in developing a child protection plan.

Social workers made the point that at the time of the initial investigation the emotional state of the family and that of mothers in particular varied immensely, although they saw a definite correlation between the state of mind of the mother and the status of the alleged abuser. If the allegations were against someone outside the family the initial reaction to social services taking an interest was often one of relief and satisfaction. This was rarely the case, however, when the allegation was being made against the father or other close family member. In such cases the initial reaction of the mother tended to be either one of disbelief, anger or depression. Social workers were of the view that apart from ensuring the safety of the girl it was important that the social worker should step back a little at this stage to enable the mother and other non-abusing family members to work through their denial, to enable them to act as real participants in any child protection plan.

The procedures were thought to be very beneficial to the process in this respect. Child protection plans, for example, have to be written down and agreed by all parties (DoH, 1991c, paras. 5.17.1 - 5.17.4). The social workers felt this ensured the girls' families were aware what was expected of them and of the social worker and any other agencies that were involved, and thus minimised the capacity of families to act otherwise. It also minimised the capacity of social services to act otherwise, and therefore enhanced the degree of trust between the social worker and the families. Child protection plans were one aspect of the procedures that the social workers found very helpful.

> You are expecting family participation, and you have something written down there that can be looked at. You can't have one without the other (SW).

The level of cooperation that social workers experienced from families in general and mothers in particular didn't always change over time. Some of the mothers of the abused girls simply refused to participate from the outset and could not be persuaded otherwise. This tended to be accompanied by expressions of doubt as to the girl's story, and these cases were seen by social workers to be those within which the level of risk for the girl remained consistently high, as they were very often those cases wherein the mother refused to break contact with the alleged perpetrator. Social workers also found in those more entrenched cases that a lack of cooperation with social services was often also reflected in a lack of cooperation by mothers and other family members with other agencies such as the education authority.

A specific feature of non-cooperation that was identified by the social workers was that of the displacement of blame for the crisis in the family away from the perpetrator not onto the girl, but onto the social worker. The consequences of this were visualised in various ways. Most of the social workers saw this type of attitude as constituting a serious stumbling block to any form of family participation in the child protection process, as relations of trust could not develop between the worker and the family. Others saw it as an opportunity to commence family participation as they saw it as acting to protect the girl from becoming the locus of blame for the family's ills.

The social workers also took account of the level of understanding of the mother both in terms of the seriousness of the abuse and in terms of their understanding of elements of the child protection process. This manifested itself in two distinct ways, both of which had an impact upon the ways in which social workers attempted to draw the mothers into an involvement in the process of protecting the girls. Firstly, social workers cited an inability on the part of mothers to grasp the separation of various actions and issues within specific cases as preventing them from working with social services in developing a protection plan for the girl concerned. In one case the social worker reported that the mother visualised the social worker as being the principal proponent in the removal of her daughter and the arrest of her husband, although in reality she had signed the accommodation paper herself and the only involvement the social worker had in the arrest of her husband was in accompanying the police officers to the family home. In sum she saw the social worker as the primary mover in the break-up of her family.

> ...she can't intellectualise it...she sees that we did the accommodation and we did the arrest, and she can't split the two up (SW).

The social worker saw this as a problem associated with a fairly poor level of cognitive skill on the part of the mother, although he also felt that a complete separation of the social work and criminal justice aspects of child protection would have obviated this problem to some degree.

It is important to point out at this stage that the social workers gave accounts of several cases where mothers and other family members not only cooperated throughout the progress of specific child protection cases, but were active participants in child protection plans, and cooperated closely with other agencies, including direct liaison with schools.

Issues of Confidentiality

The issues that social workers confronted in respect of families resisting intervention were often quite complex. In some cases this resistance revolved around issues of confidentiality and the stigma attached to being investigated for child abuse. The research (Birchall with Hallett, 1995) points to the iatrogenic effects of intervention as a possible factor in risk assessment, but one that seems rarely to be taken into account. The inclusion of the iatrogenic effects of intervention on the family as a risk factor again begs the question as to who is the client, yet the procedural framework for intervention is clearly founded on a recognition that families can and do suffer stigma if they are investigated (DoH, 1991c, para. 5.11.3), even if it is found that no abuse has occurred. The social workers were acutely aware of this difficulty, and the difficulty attendant upon carrying out their statutory duties to investigate every referral without causing problems for 'innocent' families and/or the non-abusing members of families within which abuse had occurred. Their view, was that as high degree of confidentiality as possible be maintained at all times from the initial investigation onwards, although their accounts made clear that in practice this did not always occur.

Issues of confidentiality also penetrated the social workers' thinking when working with the perpetrators in adolescent sexual abuse cases. Although in many cases neighbours and colleagues of the perpetrator remained unaware of any issues of sexual abuse that he was involved in, social workers made the point that, however discreet they and the police were in their dealings with the perpetrator and his family, people in the area soon came to be aware that something was going on. Although in none of the cases discussed did they suggest that any confidentiality had deliberately been breached by either themselves or the police, in some cases confidentiality for the perpetrator was breached through insensitivity of action? Social workers reported, for example, accompanying police officers to families' homes in order to effect an arrest of the perpetrator. Although the police officers were not in uniform this kind of activity tended to attract the attention of neighbours and could hardly be seen as discreet.

One social worker, who accepted that there are arguments that suggest that due to the nature of his actions the perpetrator has abdicated his right to confidentiality, pointed to the very real problems that she encountered working in child protection in a Garrison town. She saw the interplay between social services and the Army welfare system when child sexual abuse had been alleged being invested with problems stemming from the lack of confidentiality inherent within the Army welfare system. In civilian life as a child protection case develops the social worker will not take it upon himself/herself to inform the perpetrator's employer, except in those circumstances where he enjoys a privileged access to young people in his employment. This would be both a denials of his human rights and contrary to any due process model of criminal justice in that it could place him in a prejudicial position in an area of life within which his conduct had not previously been questioned. The scenario within the Army is very different. When informed of child abuse allegations SAAFA social workers are obliged to inform the Welfare Officer of the Garrison. If the allegation is made to social services the social worker concerned is placed in a difficult position. The Children Act stresses the needs of the child as being the paramount concern at all times (Children Act, 1989 s.1 (1)). In order to gain access to the family and to arrange preventative or therapeutic work, and to organise the initial investigation process and possibly initiate criminal proceedings, the social worker needs to inform SAAFA or the Army Welfare Officer who will arrange time off for the soldier concerned. That time off is arranged through the line command system meaning that the soldier's immediate superior becomes aware of the allegations. The social worker made the point that this placed the soldier in physical danger as knowledge of the allegations then became widespread amongst his comrades. This served to become the horns of a dilemma for social workers. Should (s)he inform the Army of the allegations so that preventative and therapeutic work could take place with the girl and her family and by doing so place the perpetrator at such a level of physical risk that he may choose to leave the Army without necessarily having a job or home to go to, or should (s)he take no action leaving the girl at some degree of risk within an abusive situation. To some extent this mirrors in very sharp relief the more commonplace problem facing social workers in child protection every day. The question to be answered is how are the best interests of the child to be served? It would appear, within the context of military personnel accused of abuse, that a lack of confidentiality within the military makes the problem a far more difficult one to solve.

There are other issues of confidentiality that impinge on the process. Social workers made clear that both in terms of the girl, her family, and the perpetrator, information was shared with professionals from other agencies only insofar as it was pertinent to their involvement in the case. One needs to be somewhat circumspect about this kind of comment, however. A great deal of information is shared at Initial Child Protection Conferences and Reviews, and it is not altogether clear whether every member of such a conference or review needs to be privy to all the information.

The 'Problem' of Participation

Family participation in the child protection process is clearly a very complex issue. There are many levels of conflict and cooperation between families and social workers, and varying degrees of family participation in the child protection process. The level of cooperation and participation can change over time for a variety of reasons. A further twist to the tale comes from the accounts of social workers regarding those mothers whose attitude towards participation and cooperation appeared to oscillate throughout the case. One social worker, for example, pointed to a case she was dealing with where she found the mother both a very honest and very difficult woman to deal with, primarily because at one level she cooperated as she wanted to do the best for her daughter, yet on another level she resisted the social worker's efforts. The social worker saw this resistance deriving from the mother minimising the realities of the abuse and thus failing to see how such a little thing could have such serious consequences for her and her family.

One of the clear messages to emanate from the workers accounts is that it is one thing for governmental policy to invoke concepts of partnership between families and social services, but it is quite another to implement that partnership. The social workers had to confront a wide range of issues in attempting to work in partnership with the families of sexually abused adolescent girls, whilst retaining the basic concept of how best to involve various family members in developing ways in which to protect the girl and further her best interests (Farmer, 1993).

Summary

The influence of the girls' families on the social workers' actions revolved around two distinct yet related aspects; the use of issues relating to the family as risk factors for the girls, and issues relating to the participation of the family in the child protection process.

The key family factors in the social workers' risk assessments were those concerned with the constitution or formation of the family unit, the relationships within it and the quality of parenting. The risk assessments also routinely called upon deeply embedded professional concepts of 'cycles of abuse'. Offsetting these various risk factors, the social workers drew upon concepts of family and neighbourhood support systems. Running throughout the social workers' risk assessments was a very powerful patriarchal discourse of mothering. Although mothers were not routinely blamed in an overt sense for the sexual abuse of their daughters, they tended to be seen as guilty by omission. They had failed to protect their daughters. It did appear that, apart from the girls' themselves, the central focus of the process was firmly fixed on the mothers (Merrick, 1996).

The perpetrators were not ignored, however, Their remaining presence in the family home was clearly seen as a very serious risk factor. However, the degree of risk they posed at any time was difficult for the social workers to assess, as the perpetrators tended not to admit the abuse, through fear of conviction and imprisonment, and generally refused to undergo risk assessments. The social workers seemed to have contrasting perceptions as to what sort of men sexually abuse children and adolescents, although they all tended to refer to perpetrators in terms of some kind of pathology. This view of the perpetrators as aberrant men reflects a professional social work ideology that prioritises individual responsibility over social-structural considerations, whilst also serving to distance the social workers from the perpetrators. There are two elements to this distancing. Firstly, it can be seen as a function of professionalism to create role distance between self and client (Goffman, 1971; Toren, 1972). This again raises the issue as to who exactly is the client in child protection cases, although the minimal amount of work carried out with perpetrators would suggest that if they are clients at all then they are seen as relatively unimportant ones. Secondly, the creation of role distance serves to insulate the social worker from certain self-imputations of guilt or anxiety. For female social workers this creates a qualitative difference between the perpetrators and their own male family and friends, thus constraining potential anxieties they may have in terms of their own daughters. For male social workers the creation of this role distance can serve to insulate them from issues that may emerge in terms of the interpenetration of their own modalities of sexual arousal and their experiences of parenting [11].

In terms of the influence on social workers actions of issues relating to family participation in the child protection process, the analogy with elements of Twigg's typology of carers (Twigg, 1992; Twigg and Atkin, 1994) is apt. Parents and other non-abusing members of the immediate and extended family are seen variously in terms of resources, co-workers and co-clients. Issues such as maternal ill-health and disability were clearly addressed in some cases, suggesting that mothers were seen as co-clients with needs to be met if there was to be a successful outcome to the case. Members of the extended family and friends and neighbours were clearly seen by the social workers as contributing to the child protection process, but were rarely involved in any decision-making. In effect they can be seen in terms analogous to Twigg's concept of carers as a resource. The most powerful analogy with Twigg's model, however, was in respect of mothers and non-abusing members of the immediate family. In accordance with procedural invocations to partnership, the social workers made every effort to incorporate them into the child protection process as co-workers. There were clearly several real difficulties in achieving partnership, or even a degree of cooperation. The social workers made clear that there were barriers of distrust and conflict to be overcome, including parental perceptions of a loss of control and a lack of confidentiality in respect of their privacy. However, in many cases non-abusing members of the family (and sometimes perpetrators) were prepared to cooperate with the process, sometimes to the point of active participation. The social workers saw the central actor in this process as the mother, although the actions and attitudes of other family members were also granted some significance. The importance the social workers placed on the mother perhaps reflects an overemphasis on the mother's role, but is well founded in that issues of maternal belief and support are central to the recovery process. Twigg's final category, that of the superseded carer, is less applicable in this area of child protection, as the rationale informing child protection recognises the family as the 'natural' locus for the care and protection of children (DoH, 1991c).

Finally, the division of family elements into risk assessment factors and cooperation and participation is only analytical, and does not suggest a linear process with fixed boundaries at each stage. The social workers were not only carrying out formal risk assessments, but also engaging in risk assessment at all time during the process. Further, the degree and quality of family participation in the child protection process and the quality of family cooperation were intimately implicated in the degree of risk the social workers perceived as being present for the girls.

7 The worker and practice

Introduction

Social worker child protection practice in cases of the familial sexual abuse of adolescent girls is shaped by a multiplicity of factors relating to administrative requirements and governmental injunctions. However:

> Formally prescribed procedures did not account for the observed differences in practice (Gibbons *et al*, 1995).

Woodhouse and Pengelly (1991) suggest that the preoccupation with rules, procedures and professional status has served to insulate the professional from thinking too deeply about the realities of sexual abuse 'with its compulsive and repulsive aspects' (Pg.234).

Issues relating to the girl and her family serve to shape the practice of social workers, not least in that social workers routinely employ 'moral' or 'value' judgements in respect of the girl's character and behaviour and the quality of the parents (mothers) protection skills (Higginson, 1990; Thorpe, 1991, 1994). However, the process of 'making a referral' is an interactive process (Wattam, 1992), and the current research points to the central role of interactions involving the social workers in accomplishing a whole series of outcomes in terms of the girls' recovery, partnership with the family and interagency coordination. This suggests that various personal attributes that the social worker brings to these interactions will have a significant bearing upon those outcomes. In other words certain personal attributes of the social workers and issues important to them on a professional and personal level will significantly influence their child protection practice.

Following arguments to emerge from the sociology of knowledge (Lave, 1986), Sibeon (1991) makes clear that some of the things that happen in the social work area office may be unique to that office at the level of personal biographies or personalities. One remains aware that the personal attributes or characteristics of each social worker and issues that preoccupy them will be different, and some will be of greater significance than others. Those attributes and issues of greatest significance can, however, be placed into five broad categories; the individual capacities and limitations the worker feels (s)he has to carry out specific tasks, her/his amount of experience in child protection generally and sexual abuse in particular, the relevance and degree of training (s)he has had in terms of the issues and practices concerned with child protection in cases of sexual abuse, her/his perceptions of personal safety in specific situations arising out of the child protection process, and the importance (s)he attaches to issues arising from the gendered interactions inherent in the child protection process.

The question this chapter seeks to confront is the ways in which these various 'personal' factors contribute to the workers' management of personal and professional 'risk' and the influence they have on their child protection practice.

Training and Experience

Pithouse (1987) indicates social workers tend to accomplish their day to day tasks through reference to 'rarely stated motives and taken for granted assumptions' (Pg.2). Some of their intervention preferences will stem directly from aspects of the individual workers personality and his/her general life experiences. However, as these preferred intervention practices are related to some extent to the worker's level of self-confidence in working in specific ways, and her/his self-perceived levels of knowledge and expertise in specific areas, it is clear that aspects of professional training and experience have a significant part to play.

The social workers' training comprised two distinct elements; the initial training and education they received in qualifying, and their ongoing in-service training and professional development education. All the social workers were qualified, yet their experience of initial training was very diverse. There appeared to be a different emphasis on sexual abuse at different educational institutions, and at different times. Most of the social workers who had trained since the Cleveland Inquiry (1988) explained that sexual abuse issues had formed a significant part of their courses, whereas for those who had trained prior to Cleveland sexual abuse had formed little if any part of their training. Some of those who had trained post-Cleveland also pointed to little sexual abuse training in their initial qualification due to student choice. Their courses had been modular, and they had opted for other modules.

The degree of understanding the social workers had of child sexual abuse had a clear impact upon how useful they felt their initial training had been in terms of dealing with specific sexual abuse cases. Some of those whose initial training had contained little or no sexual abuse elements felt that the issues surrounding sexual abuse and child protection practice were so specific that their initial training was of little or no value to their sexual abuse work. Those for whom sexual abuse issues had been a more central part of their training saw some value in the training, but with serious caveats

I think it is good grounding, but it is just theoretical until you do it (SW).

They saw their initial training as useful up to a point but felt it placed too great an emphasis on initial investigations and not enough on ongoing intervention strategies.

From a practical viewpoint the social workers saw their ongoing in-service training as more useful. This contradicts research (Farmer and Owen, 1995) that found social workers relatively dissatisfied with their in-service training. In-service training is an integral part of child protection work. All of the workers had been on several courses relating to sexual abuse. The courses fell into two categories. Some were 'compulsory', such as specific training in video interviewing and initial investigations that the workers had to do before they could participate in video interviews or go out on initial investigations. Other courses did not have the same 'compulsory' overlay; rather they were put in place to improve worker skills in specific areas and/or to increase the workers' knowledge base. These were seen as particularly important by those workers whose initial training had lacked a sexual abuse component, whilst those whose training had included sexual abuse also saw them as useful in updating their understanding as 'things change so often as you go along' (SW).

Although the social workers in both local authorities saw benefits in the in-service courses and saw management as taking ongoing training seriously, they did express some concern. Some social workers saw ongoing training, in similar ways to initial training, as concentrating too heavily on the entry process. They felt that there was too much training in respect of initial investigations to the detriment of ongoing aspects of child protection. This reflects earlier findings (Farmer and Owen, 1995) that showed a feeling amongst social workers that they were undertrained for some of the issues they had to confront, despite a great deal of in-service training. Other workers saw problems of financial prudence as diminishing the quality of in-service training. A particular example of this in one of the local authorities was the withdrawal of the authority from a joint venture with a local university in respect of a post-qualifying diploma, and its replacement with in-house training modules.

The social workers were also concerned that however much training was made available and however good it might be, much of the value of it was lost through the pressure of overbearing caseloads that denied workers the time and space to put ideas into practice. Despite these worries they tended to find their in-service training useful at least in a general sense. A clear problem emerges here, similar to that highlighted by the tranch of Department of Health research into the child protection process published in 1995. In the summary of findings of that research (DoH, 1995) it was claimed that despite the substantial amount of in-service training taking place, the limited nature of that training, along with several other factors, left social workers less aware of certain child protection issues than they ought to have been.

The key issue in terms of training was that the social workers felt that it prepared them for the work in a general sense, but it didn't really prepare them for the reality of individual cases. However, they felt that without the training the very process of thinking through the case might not have been possible. One worker in respect of a specific case put this quite bluntly:

I couldn't have done it without the training (SW).

The social services managers saw a close relationship between training and experience.

I think training is an introduction to ideas in a sense. Social workers then need to go on and see for themselves how that relates (Manager).

The level of experience of the social workers in the sample varied considerably. Some had been working in child protection for ten years or longer, others two years or less. What clearly emerged from their accounts was the importance of experience. This manifested itself in a number of ways. The most important aspect of experience that the social workers stressed was that each case is unique. In a sense this emphasised both the centrality of professional experience in developing the self-confidence necessary to accomplish the child protection task, and the limitations of experience in that the next case may present problems or raise issues that the worker had not previously confronted. The major benefit of substantial experience appeared to be that workers came to expect the unexpected, and were very aware of the great diversity of cases that could come under the rubric of adolescent sexual abuse. One social worker, who had recently had a case involving a girl with a learning disability, summed up the situation.

> No two cases are alike. I've worked with another girl with learning disabilities and it was nothing like this one. It was a completely different approach, a different technique, everything (SW).

Another social worker stressed that in some ways every case is a learning process and that, to some extent, the way one proceeds he personality of the 'performer' with experience (Goffman, 1971) and leads to greater confidence in accomplishing that role even in novel situations.

It was not only experience in child protection that was seen as valuable. Aspects of experience in other areas of social work and beyond were also seen to some extent to be of value in dealing with specific cases Several of the workers in the sample had come into child protection from other areas of social work and saw this as a positive benefit from two distinct standpoints. Those who had worked in mental health services felt their experience useful in that it tended to raise issues of the relationship between parental mental health problems and child abuse. At a more general level, one worker pointed out that working in one area of child care informs one's work in another. This she saw as helping her to see her child protection task in a more 'ecological' way than some of her colleagues. Other workers were less sure of the use value to their child protection work of previous experience in other aspects of child care, such as residential work, although this may have had less to do with the lack of use value of such work *per se*, than the fact that they were involved in this work prior to the implementation of the Children Act, and prior to the 'discovery' of the prevalence and consequences of child and adolescent sexual abuse. One social worker, for example, explained that when she worked in residential childcare in the 1980s she had to deal with two cases of suspected sexual abuse. Any knowledge she derived in respect of sexual abuse at that time came from her experience of those cases, as she found little in the child care manuals and other professional texts. This seemed to be a fairly common theme, several workers pointing to badly handled cases in the past, wherein they had worked with a distinct lack of understanding of the issues involved.

At a more specific level, workers pointed towards experience in specific aspects of child protection. They spoke of the need for experience in video interviewing, as times would arise when the girl would simply not be responding and one would need to know how to proceed to get the interview back on course. They also pointed to the practicalities of working in specific environments. It was only through experience that they knew exactly what resources and facilities were available to them to refer girls and/or perpetrators to. As one worker, who had previously worked for another authority, pointed out these differed according to locality, as did the general drift of policy and preferred intervention strategies. In other words, a particular dimension of experience was the specific experience of working in a particular locality for a particular agency.

Experience not only assisted social workers in accomplishing their child protection tasks, but it also seriously influenced their attitudes to specific clients and their understanding of specific cases. In some workers experience seemed to have bred cynicism, something that was also seen as a problem by managers who saw social workers as coming into the profession with idealistic notions of 'helping' and then being rapidly reduced to the crisis management of severe family problems. Social worker experience also appeared to foster a whole series of multiple assumptions. Cooper and Ball (1987) point to the problem of myths in social work practice. Drawing upon Charles (1983) Cooper and Ball (1987) suggest that there are multiple myths that social workers in child abuse work can fall prey to that ignore the complexity of family situations within which abuse occurs, the capacity of individuals and families to hide the abuse from the social worker's gaze, and the capacity of children to find ways of communicating the realities of their abuse. Cooper and Ball (1987) see these myths founded upon a variety of factors, including workers holding fast to a narrow conception of what constitutes abuse, an over-involvement with a family that can lead to the worker failing to notice deterioration over time, and a belief that if something goes wrong someone else will notice and raise the alarm. Cooper and Ball (1987) make the significant point that it is not necessarily the social workers that are to blame for their misconceptions. Rather they argue that the responsibility should lie:

> ...with their supervisors who are detached enough to ask the right questions and to both support and monitor their staff Cooper and Ball, 1987, Pg.88).

One worker referred to the likelihood of false accusations arising from marital rifts, and another repeatedly used the phrase 'Its a classic case' (SW), a phrase that concurrently implies a concept of typicality in adolescent sexual abuse cases that is completely at odds with the notion of uniqueness, whilst imputing a whole series of assumptions about human behaviour and 'types' of people. One worker felt that from her experience she had detected a class element in child protection in terms of sexually abused girls. She suggested that middle-class girls were less likely than working class girls to report the abuse, and more difficult to obtain a full disclosure from. This she saw as a consequence of middle-class mores.

> We instil an element of restraint in kids, and the more middle-class they are, the more that restrain is there, to the point where they accept things they shouldn't accept (SW).

These disparate assumptions clearly have a common thread that resonates with Pithouse's (1987) contention that:

> ...assumptions about clients are steeped in a common-sense theory that arises from the practical experience of doing the job (Pithouse, 1987, Pg.81)

Experience plays a significant part in the development of this professional 'common-sense' and the gradual submersion of a more inquisitive or idealistic approach. At the time of initial professional education and early in any career, an individual will grapple with the various theoretical constructs and professional themes upon which her/his profession relies. Any professional actions (s)he takes will thus be amenable to discussion and discursive reflection, forming a significant part of her/his 'discursive consciousness' (Giddens, 1976, 1984). As (s)he becomes more experienced in the profession those themes and constructs will become tacit (Hardiker, 1981), a part of her/his 'practical consciousness' (Giddens, 1976, 1984), leading to non-reflexive routinised professional actions. In other words, through experience the individual will become inculcated into embedded modes of professional attitude that are beyond question.

When speaking of specific cases it became clear that social workers do see all cases as unique, but are influenced in their intervention strategies by the outcomes they have achieved in what they perceive of as similar cases in the past. The more unusual a case appeared to be the less certain social workers were how best to achieve what they saw as an optimum outcome for the client.

> This was an unusual case...I think given another way we'd still end up with a pig's ear, because I don't know we could have actually offered as an agency anything that would have helped...[the girl] much more (SW).

The social workers felt that many things were of value in helping them in their interventions, not least procedural guidelines and the quality and extent of their training, but in the final analysis they saw no substitute for experience.

At one level it is relatively easy to become aware of the influence of training and experience on the way the social workers approached particular cases; they gave straightforward statements of how a particular course or experience of previous similar cases led them to act in particular ways. At another level it is very difficult to see the ways in which training and experience have been brought to bear on specific cases, as both training and experience combine together with a multiplicity of other factors to create the professional persona of the worker with his/her own particular preferences for working in certain ways rather than others. Pithouse (1987) refers to 'common-sense' theory drawn both from the formal knowledge base of the profession and the practical experience of working within the setting itself. It is clear that issues of training and experience impact directly upon the modes of practice of individual social workers in terms of the acquisition of specific child protection skills. Training and experience also serve another function. They serve to create the child protection social worker. As Marx (1844, 1977) contended thinking and being are analytically distinct, but are always 'in unity with each other' (Pg.93). One can see therefore that through his/her initial training, experience and in-service training the individual is originally transformed from lay person to social worker and is constantly being reinforced in that role. As Sibeon (1991) points out, social work 'contains both oral and written traditions' (Pg.44). Experience and training can thus both be seen as modalities of transmission of the 'core' values and working methodologies of social work practice, including those values of professional autonomy and individualised self-reliant working practices. They serve to inculcate the individual into a particular professional world view. That is not to say that individual social workers cannot hold heterodox views and challenge existing practice methodologies. The 'language habits' (Sapir, 1966) of social work are not restrictive in the way that 'Newspeak' (Orwell, 1949) is restrictive. They are not overtly exclusionary. Rather they tend to form a particular framework within which problem solving is accomplished.

Individual Capacities and Limitations of the Worker

The social workers in the sample were aware that as individuals their practice could differ from that of their colleagues.

> There are individual ways of working and we are very aware that we work in different ways and sometimes we will disagree. We all have different personalities (SW).

In general differences of approach were seen as being endemic to the social work enterprise, and related to the varying personal and professional strengths and weaknesses of individual social workers.

> We all have our own vices and our specialities really and go our own way (SW).

However, the meanings the social workers ascribed to such differences varied considerably, the social workers perceptions of individual differences of approach as either beneficial or detrimental to the accomplishment of their child protection tasks depending to a great extent upon procedural imperatives and management attitudes. It became clear from the social workers accounts that cases were allocated in terms of different criteria in different area offices. In some offices there was a simple system of allocation based on the available time and space that individual social workers had in respect of the amount and complexity of the cases they were already carrying. Other offices allocated cases with more thought to the individual skills, capacities and preferences of the social workers in the team.

This social worker perception of local management differences of attitude towards personal skills and preferences was reflected at a higher management level. One senior manager stressed the importance of differential skills and matching cases to workers on the basis of the workers' specific capacities. A completely opposite view emerged from an interview with another senior manager, who perceived of child protection far more rigidly as a system, and spoke almost solely in terms of fixed procedures and identified what he saw as a problem for his department in that some social workers did not always work strictly to the rules.

At the more specific level of individual skills and capacities some social workers pointed to cases where their own limitations had clearly shaped their practice in various ways. They gave accounts of cases where they had called for assistance from a colleague or were asked by a colleague for assistance when the original worker felt unable to deal with the special needs of a client or the relationship between the worker and the girl or her family was problematic. The degree to which the social workers accepted differing skills and capacities and assisted each other varied considerably across different area offices. The common denominator in seeking assistance from a colleague seemed to be a problem of worker confidence in specific situations. This was exemplified in one particular case where the social worker felt her client would benefit from counselling, but she lacked the confidence to give that counselling.

> I didn't feel skilled enough to undertake it and I didn't want to botch it. I thought if I botch it I could make it ten times worse for her (SW)

The social worker felt herself caught in a 'double bind' in that she felt that whatever she did in this situation would be detrimental to the girl's recovery process. She felt that she had begun to develop a good relationship with the girl over time and that it would be counterproductive to bring in another worker to counsel the girl as the new worker would have to build up such a relationship, setting the whole process back several weeks. However, she lacked any confidence to counsel the girl herself. Although she had been trained in counselling skills, she had never counselled anyone before, and she had little experience of sexual abuse work. It also became clear from her account, that she was unsure if she believed the girl, and was afraid that she might transmit her scepticism to the girl during counselling with serious consequences if the girl's allegations were true. As all her colleagues had full caseloads the girl was never counselled.

At a more general level several social workers stressed that many girls and their families tended to assume that the social workers would have 'all the answers' (SW). The social workers found this very stressful, especially when the girl and her family were trying to find their role within the process. The imputation of that level of expertise onto the social worker in such situations can be seen as part of the process of transference (Herman, 1994; Hooper *et al*, 1997) that could later emerge in the form of great anger towards the social worker when (s)he was unable to display such omnipotence. Some social workers experienced similar problems when working with perpetrators. They found that perpetrators tended to try and manipulate them in order to minimise the threat (of acknowledgement, prosecution etc.) to themselves. Most of the social workers found working with perpetrators the most difficult aspect of child protection, particularly if the abuse had been 'really horrendous' (SW). Some social workers spoke of being extremely stressed and of this aspect of the work having a serious effect on them personally. Some female social workers who had worked intensively with either the girls or the perpetrators spoke of feeling as if they had experienced the abuse, clearly indicating that elements of countertransference could impact upon the process.

There appeared to be some relationship between financial restrictions in welfare expenditure and levels of social worker anxiety over differential skills and capacities. The withdrawal of the police from most initial investigations and the lack of resources in social services departments that often prevented a second social worker going out on initial investigations left some social workers feeling exposed and lacking anyone to talk things through with on the spot. This reflected a wider concern amongst some social workers that there was not enough sharing of knowledge within the area office, leaving them too reliant upon their own knowledge base alone. Although factors such as supervision and peer support and advice were central elements in the operation of area offices[1], the sharing of knowledge was severely circumscribed, Colleagues would only give advice when it was requested. The concept of individual practice autonomy appeared to disallow the free flow of advice and information in case it could be misinterpreted as criticism[2].

Earlier research (Farmer and Owen, 1995) contends that this is a consequence of both a lack of time to discuss things with colleagues and a 'macho' culture within some offices that severely discouraged the open expressing of feelings. This was not the case with all the social workers in the sample, however. It needs to be made clear that different area offices had differing degrees of knowledge sharing. Whereas in some offices there seemed to be very little in the way of discussing individual cases, in other office there was a great deal of informal discussion of cases. In some very difficult cases this was carried a little further.

> We sometimes spend part of a team meeting discussing a specific case if we find that it is needed, and actually have a proper directed discussion (SW).

The office within which this level of case discussion seemed to be most developed was one in which the team had been together a long time, suggesting that the capacity to place your perceived weaknesses in front of colleagues may depend to some extent upon the quality of relationship you have with them. This accords with Goffman's (1971) concept of the 'backstage' area in his dramaturgical perspective of interaction wherein the members of a 'team' can relax and drop their 'performances'. Retaining Goffman's concept of the 'team' with shared goals and perspectives, this specific office appeared to have a particular view of differential skills and approaches to the child protection task. One worker commented that the major benefit of team discussions was to have colleagues affirm one's intervention strategies. Whilst acknowledging the fact that one 'can't take personality out of the work' (SW), she pointed out that the team were 'all on the same wavelength' (SW) and that she would find it difficult to work with a newcomer with different ideas. At the other extreme social workers in another areas office expressed concern that their area office did not function as a team. One worker, who had come from a background in residential care found great difficulty in accepting that although different workers had different abilities, there was no working concept of mutuality that allowed them to draw upon each others capacities to the overall benefit of the team.

To a degree the sense of a 'shared team perspective' and a reluctance to welcome heterodox thinking can be seen to relate to a professional or institutional form of defence against the enormous anxieties child protection work in this field engenders. Woodehouse and Pengelly (1991) lucidly trace the contours of these anxieties and defences and show the serious problems they create for effective inter-agency collaborative working. They illuminate three basic strands in terms of the great anxieties social workers feel in working in child sexual abuse, and the defences they employ to manage such anxieties. Firstly, child protection work in general creates anxieties for social workers in that they are being asked to take responsibility for the protection of children from harmful parents. The facts in child abuse cases are often confusing and inconclusive. Social workers feel impelled to intervene, but are often far from sure that they are benefiting the child and can often blame themselves in anticipation of doing the wrong thing. Woodhouse and Pengelly (1991) found social workers in their sample had their professional self-esteem undermined:

> ...not only from outside but from within, by anxiety that they might be perpetrating the very failures of parenting which they were committed to making good (Woodhouse and Pengelly, 1991, Pg.177)

These anxieties were added to by the high rate of referrals from other parts of the child protection network that were seen to be unloading the problem onto them. This led to defensive behaviour in inter-agency relations; social workers dealing with their anxieties and conflicts of feelings by turning the blame for those feelings onto other agencies, creating serious difficulties in terms of collaborative work.

The second theme the Woodhouse and Pengelly (1991) map out is the basic psychodynamic problem of triangular relationships. They point to the fact that triangular relationships can lead to 'splitting' and seriously inhibit collaborative work. The problem of managing these triangular relationships whilst also being seen as the legitimate authority to deal with child abuse leads to social workers and other agencies rigidifying their structures and practices and modes of thought to the detriment of collaboration.

The third theme Woodhouse and Pengelly (1991) bring out is that of the specifics of sexual abuse. They make the point that it arouses strong emotions and the consequences of 'getting it wrong' are great.

> A dimension is added to both anxieties and defences by child sexual abuse. And in a field so characterised by uncertainty, the implications of 'not knowing' ...become too fearful to contemplate. Integrity and autonomy, institutional as much as professional, can be threatened by uncertainties which in reality should be seen as relevant and inescapable (Woodhouse and Pengelly, 1991, Pg.234)

Some area offices were less rigid in their acceptance of 'new' ways of thinking about child protection cases and sexual abuse in particular. Some social workers spoke of the benefits they gained from the presence of students on placement with them, in that they gained insights from the students, that can clearly be seen to derive from the students exposure to more recent thinking on the subject allied to their lack of inculcation into the specifics of the culture of the particular office. Nevertheless, implicit in all the social workers' accounts was the view that only professional social work perspectives on child abuse had any real validity.

The current research clearly reflects earlier findings that individual capacities and limitations have a significant effect on social work practice.

> [Social workers] apply their own preferred modes of intervention: that is the skills and relationships they feel most comfortable with (Pithouse, 1987, Pg.15)

How individual social workers, area offices and senior managers dealt with these individual skills and limitations varied considerably, and were located within their interpretations of the legislation and local procedures. There was a general awareness that no two workers would approach a case in exactly the same way, and many of the social workers were of the view that different outcomes would result from similar cases with different workers. This perhaps emphasises the inexact nature of the social work enterprise in general and the child protection process in particular, and points to the methodological difficulties in linking social work inputs with client outcomes. As far as the social workers in the sample were concerned, differential outcomes were not seen in terms of better or worse.

Social workers can work in very different ways and be equally effective (SW).

Risk and Personal Safety

The accomplishment of their child protection task exposed social workers to a degree of risk in terms of their own personal safety, and this was a matter of concern to all the social workers. The issues associated with personal risk to social workers working within child protection is a conspicuous absence in the child protection research literature, perhaps reflecting a research preoccupation with systems evaluation and child-centred studies. The research that does examine social worker perspectives (for example, Pithouse, 1987) tends to perceive of social workers only in their professional role without reference to broader aspects of their thinking as individuals. The risk to social workers in child protection contains both a psychological and a physical element.

The psychological risk is that associated with the holding of often horrendous details of abuse disclosed to them by clients. Social workers gave accounts of physical and other symptoms they experienced as a direct result of the psychological strain they felt in such circumstances. One worker referred to routinely getting home and 'reaching for the paracetamol and the sherry bottle' (SW) in attempts to unwind from the pressure. At the level of individual situations this may well suffice, although some social workers referred to the repeated intensity of such experiences as leading to 'burn out' and even likened the experience to post-traumatic stress disorder. To a great extent this risk was obviated through processes of informal supervision and peer support that enabled individual workers to be 'de-briefed' in such circumstances. However, these processes of support were not always readily available, and some area offices seemed to have better 'de-briefing' procedures in place than others. Different social workers also had different stress thresholds. leaving some at far greater risk than others. Herman (1994) notes the risks inherent for professionals in working closely with the victims of any kind of trauma. She makes the point that the process of countertransference that can occur as a result of the professional's attempts to empathically understand the victim's responses to her traumatic experiences can lead to the professional beginning to experience both psychological and somatic symptoms that are similar to those endured by the victim.

A great deal of what has come to be known as 'burn-out' clearly relates to the high degree of stress of such experiences for social workers. The problem is perhaps greater in respect of child and adolescent sexual abuse than it is in terms of other forms of abuse in that it can also force both male and female social workers to confront either their own personal experiences of unwanted sexual contact or aspects of their own sexuality they find disturbing.

As far as physical risk was concerned, the issues were far more straightforward. Physical risk for the social workers was primarily associated with conducting initial investigations alone. Initial investigations were seen by all the social workers as potential flashpoints as they constituted going into the unknown with little knowledge of what they might find. In some area offices there was a policy of ensuring that individual social workers never went on an initial investigation alone. If the police were not willing to go then another social worker would accompany the duty worker on the investigation. To some extent this was to provide a 'second pair of eyes' to improve the efficiency of the investigation, but equally it was to attempt to ensure the personal safety of the worker. One impact of this was that initial investigations could be delayed until a colleague was free to accompany the duty worker. It also had the consequence of taking another worker away from the office and adding to the general pressure on time associated with overloaded caseloads.

Personal safety was also considered on a more routine basis with the operation of 'information' boards showing where social workers had gone and at what time they expected to return. For most of the social workers personal safety was a major preoccupation. One made the point that as well as informing her colleagues where she was going she would also ask them to come and get her if she did not return, even if out on a routine visit in an ongoing case.

> There are situations where you know a client quite well, but there's that sort of underlying vulnerability. Personal protection is important (SW).

Not all area offices operated in this way. Other offices routinely sent workers out even on initial investigations alone, something several social workers found extremely stressful,

> ...because you really don't know what you are going to find when you get there (SW).

Some workers saw a real problem of resources impacting on safety as it was simply not always possible for a second person to accompany them to visit clients. Some partial solutions were put in place in some teams such as issuing workers with pagers or mobile phones, though this itself was seen to create problems in that when issued with mobile phones or pagers they found themselves being contacted in respect of other cases when out on a visit, impacting negatively on their abilities to concentrate on the case they were dealing with. [3]

Issues of Gender

Resource constraints also impacted closely on issues of gender, as there were times when a male worker, for example, felt that it would be beneficial to have a female colleague accompany him and vice versa, again as it would not be clear what they would find and to whom the girl and her family would best respond, yet the pressure of individual workloads often made this impossible.

There were wider concerns over gender amongst child protection social workers. The issues as they saw them were not clear-cut. Some felt that due to the nature of sexual abuse it should only be female social workers that dealt with it, at least in respect of working with the girl. This view reflects, to some extent, elements on one side of an ongoing debate within the child protection literature in respect of the complex configuration of masculinity, gendered power relations, and the psychological effects of child sexual abuse. From a social psychological perspective Jones (1991) argues that, in respect of young children, the interactions between male social workers and female victims of child sexual abuse can be seen as power relations that serve to replicate the asymmetrical power relations inherent in the original abuse. Frosh (1988) also subscribes to this view to some extent, although he clearly sees a place for men within the child protection process for sexually abused children, albeit a severely circumscribed one. The basic tenor of Frosh's (1988) argument is that the child protection process can be chronologically divided into two distinct elements. The first of these elements, which comprises the bulk of social services child protection effort, from the initial investigation through to the disclosure interview and the child protection conference, he terms the validation process. He argues that, as the research and practice evidence overwhelmingly points to child sexual abusers as male, then it is very likely in any individual case that the child has been abused by a man. He then argues that aspects of the validation process, in particular the disclosure interview, can be very emotionally intense for the child. In order to minimise the degree of distress the process can cause to the child, and to maximise the potential for eliciting information about the abuse from the child, he argues against male involvement. He does not see it, however, in terms of a blanket removal of men from this stage of the process. Indeed, for the very reasons argued above, Frosh's (1988) optimal person to conduct the disclosure interview and take the lead within the validation process would be an adult the child knew well and trusted, irrespective of gender.[4] Frosh, however, accepts that in reality the person working with the abused child during this element of the process will rarely be a person the child knows well, and he thus argues that unless there is convincing evidence to the contrary, one should assume the abuser is male and thus assume that the child will approach consequent encounters with men with at least some degree of uncertainty. He thus concludes that in practice it is preferable as a general rule that female workers conduct this aspect of the process. Frosh (1988) acknowledges that any future therapy may well be enhanced by the inclusion of male workers during the validation process in terms of rebuilding connections of trust between the child and men generally, but argues that the risk of distress to the child is too great.

Where Frosh (1988) does see a role for men is in the second element of the process, that of therapy. Firstly he sees a role for men in the direct counselling of abusers, in that they can provide them with an alternative, non-abusive, version of masculinity. This is not, however, unproblematic. Firstly, work with abusers is granted very low priority and little of it is done. Secondly, although Frosh (1988) implicitly acknowledges the plurality of masculinities through his belief that the worker can present an alternative to the abuser, he appears to take the masculinity of the male worker himself as unproblematic and non-abusive, failing to acknowledge the two-way process of interaction that may involve any influences the abuser may bring to bear on the worker. Frosh (1988) also sees a role for male workers in the counselling of non-abusive fathers, in ways that mirror those for abusers, in terms of confronting some of their uncertainties in respect of their sexuality. Similar criticisms can be made in that again Frosh (1988) fails to acknowledge the possibilities of the client's masulinity influencing that of the social worker. As far as direct counselling of the child is concerned Frosh (1988) finds it altogether more complex. He argues for the co-presence of male and female workers, making two powerful arguments. Firstly, the presence of a male worker can act to prevent the working through of feelings developing into an anti-male collusion, and secondly, the presence of a female worker can act as a buffer to protect the child against too intense a level of contact with a man too soon after the abuse.

Frosh (1988) makes one very important point in terms of the individual therapy of sexually abused children that the social workers tended to routinely agree with. He argues that in the final analysis there are very real problems in being over-prescriptive in terms of the gender of the therapist, arguing that the best guide must be the expressed wishes of the child concerned,

> ...as lack of recognition of their desires is precisely one of the destructive characteristics of child sexual abuse (Frosh, 1988, Pg.10).

Pringle (1995) takes up some of the issues that Frosh (1988) does not confront. He argues that the male worker's version of masculinity cannot be assumed. Pointing to the literature that suggests significant numbers of welfare workers will have been abused themselves (Glaser and Frosh, 1993) and that equally significant numbers of welfare workers may have at some time been abusers (Pringle, 1993), and recent public scandals relating to child sexual abuse within residential settings, he suggests that some abusive men may well gravitate towards child protection work in ways similar to those in which they move into residential care work. He thus makes the key point that male workers working with abusers, for example, need to confront their own feelings and tendencies to oppress in order to avoid colluding in the abusers' rationale for their actions. In general terms, Pringle (1995) argues far more strongly than Frosh (1988) for the exclusion of men working alone at all stages of the process both with sexually abused children and with abusers.

One of the problems that both Frosh (1988) and Pringle (1995) then face is the burden placed on female workers if male workers are to be circumscribed in their activities. Frosh (1988) argues that women professionals require proper support and supervision in their work and that resources must be made available to prevent those women from carrying too high a caseload. Pringle (1995) comes to similar conclusions, arguing that there is a pressing need to confront patriarchal tendencies within the various welfare professions, and afford a high status to the child protection work carried out by women. He also argues for the need to ensure that those aspects of the work that ought to be carried out by female workers are only done within the context of freedom of choice for those women and at a recognised salary level.

Although the social workers in the sample did not articulate it with any degree of precision, they tended to see the involvement of men in the early stages of the child protection process as possibly unethical and counterproductive in terms of developing a useful child protection plan. Many also felt that only a woman could really understand what a sexually abused girl had been through, though there was nothing in their accounts that suggested any agreement with either Pringle or Frosh that male social workers could pose any kind of risk to sexually abused girls. A countervailing view also emerged in that it was seen as beneficial for the social worker to be male. One (female) social worker suggested that she knew of girls that,

> ...have actually found it beneficial to talk to a male, because early on they may need to realise that not all men are abusers (SW).

She did go on to say that in her experience gender issues could be very complicated. She pointed to cases of boys who had been sexually abused finding it impossible to disclose to a male, but being able to talk to a female. This clearly reflects some of the points raised by Frosh (1988), and does not contradict his argument for the routine use of female workers at the validation stage. It also points to the complex ways in which patriarchal ideologies operate, and the complex of meaning within which sexist practices have their being (Harvey, 1990). For a boy or young man to admit to another man that he has been raped, for instance, is for him to lose his grasp on elements of his masculinity. The interweaving of elements of personal experience and of cultural expectations that go to form both dominant and subordinate forms of masculinity that can cause this loss of masculine identity can be seen as holding a mirror to the masculinities of the child sex abusers and male social workers.

> Masculinity is always bound up with negotiations about power, and is therefore always experienced as tenuous (Roper and Tosh, 1991).

Although the social workers expressed a variety of views on how gender impacted upon their practice, the dominant view was that where possible the gender of the key worker should be an integral part of client choice, in that some girls simply felt more at ease talking to a woman, others to a man. What was clear, however, was that male social workers in particular were very aware of gender as a potential issue. Male social workers spoke of occasions when they called upon female colleagues to conduct aspects of ongoing counselling with the girls concerned, whereas no examples of female workers eliciting similar help from male colleagues emerged. To some extent this relates to normative views of child protection as a primarily female task, and the gendered structuration of child protection work. It also reflects an appreciation by male social workers that sexual abuse is a problem *of* males *for* females, to the extent that the men were uneasy about their participation in child protection for that particular client group.

> There are men who feel they are not the most appropriate person to deal with [a female adolescent] sexual abuse investigation (SW).

Summary

The social workers' child protection practice was influenced by factors relating to the workers themselves along three distinct trajectories.

Firstly, there were issues pertaining to their training and education. Those whose original training was prior to the Cleveland Inquiry (1988) found that their original training provided them with no significant knowledge base for their work with sexually abused children and adolescents. Those who qualified after the Cleveland Inquiry felt themselves better informed, although they found their initial training and education relatively unhelpful in any practical sense. Rather, their original training provided them with a fairly theoretical knowledge base upon which to build through in-service training and experience in the work. A significant problem became apparent, in that not only was the period at which social workers qualified a factor in the levels of theoretical knowledge about sexual abuse, but the form and place of qualification was also a factor. Some social workers had, as students, been able to choose not to follow sexual abuse modules. Given the increasing information that is coming to light, in terms of, for example, the prevalence of sexual abuse in residential homes (*Panorama*, BBC, 10.3.97), it would seem appropriate that sexual abuse training ought to be a compulsory part of all social worker training.

The social workers found their in-service training much more useful in a practical sense, although they felt it concentrated to too great a degree on the entry process, with not enough attention being paid to ongoing work such as aftermath work. The role of training and education in qualifying and in-service training can clearly be seen to be different, although both serve the function of transforming the lay person into the professional child protection worker. The function of training in qualification can clearly be seen as initiating the student into the general knowledge base of the profession, whereas in-service training is primarily concerned with the development of practical competences. In these terms both initial and in-service training can be seen as essential elements in learning to do the job. They can be also be seen as elements in a process of inscription into a professional child protection social work culture at two levels. Initial training, through exposure to the accepted knowledge base of the profession, inscribes the student into the general culture of professional social work, as central to any process of knowledge transmission is the transmission of cultural norms and values (Gerth and Mills, 1954). In-service training carries this process a little further in that it serves both to inscribe the fledgling social worker into the specific norms and values of sexual abuse child protection work, and reinforce those norms and values in more established workers.

Secondly and closely associated with training was experience. Experience was greatly valued by the social workers; much of their practical knowledge was derived from their experience of previous cases. Two practical elements of experience were clearly important. The experiential knowledge of the setting (child protection work in general, and the area office in particular), and knowledge of what resources were available. Experience also served a similar function to training in terms of the transmission and reinforcement of professional norms and values, leading social workers to internally reject heterodox child protection perspectives. In this respect it was clearly assisted by processes of formal and informal supervision and peer support[5].

Thirdly, in part due to differences in training and experience, the social workers' practice was circumscribed by their own perceptions of their particular skills and limitations. This led to varying degrees of confidence in performing particular tasks within the process. The levels of overall professional confidence of individual social workers was to a large extent determined by the ways in which particular area offices managed those differential skills and limitations.

Underlying these three themes were the social workers' perceptions of the significance of gender issues in the child protection process for sexually abused adolescent girls, and issues of their own personal safety.

Gender was not seen as a major issue by the social workers, although several female social workers felt uneasy in respect of working with perpetrators, in that they could sometimes feel threatened or intimidated. Similarly the male social workers were uneasy in terms of working directly with sexually abused girls. This seems to reflect issues surrounding male dominance in gendered interactions generally, in the everyday reproduction of patriarchal social structures (Westwood, 1984; Liddle and Joshi, 1986; Jagger, 1988). Although issues of gender influenced the social workers actions, they were interpenetrated by a powerful discourse of client choice that clearly operated as some form of professional rubric. The girls were seen as 'nearly adult' and as such their choice of key worker, for example, tended to override any issues of gender interaction that concerned the social workers.

Issues relating to personal safety emerged from the social workers accounts that had some influence on practice. Firstly, social workers felt themselves at a degree of psychological risk from working in a field as potentially traumatic as child and adolescent sexual abuse. Taken in conjunction with resource issues such as excessive caseloads, this suggests that the social workers would routinely be exercising their various skills and capacities at a less than optimum level. One consequence of this would be the delivery of a child protection service to sexually abused adolescent girls that is of a poorer quality than it ought to be. Secondly, workers felt themselves to be at some degree of physical risk, especially when going out on initial investigations. The ways in which different area offices managed this risk varied, and the ways in which they managed this risk had a direct impact upon the social workers perceptions of the degree of risk, although the interpenetration of this issue with questions of limited resources meant that in many cases the sense if risk involved could not be entirely removed. Sometimes social workers had go out on visits alone.

In general it can be seen that certain personal factors are important in child protection practice for this client group, not least in that the complex of training, experience and personal attributes that each worker brings to the role will be different from that of any other worker.

8 Conclusion

Introduction

This study commenced with the aim of developing our understanding of the various factors that influence social workers' child protection practice in cases involving the familial sexual abuse of adolescent girls.

- Administrative procedures
- Injunctions to coordination with other agencies
- The girl herself
- The girl's family
- The training and experience of the social worker

All of these factors were influential to a greater or lesser degree in different cases. The effect of the individual factors, was, however, far from straightforward. There was clearly a great deal of interaction between these various factors, sometimes complementary, sometimes conflictual. At times the intersection between various influential factors left the social workers with conflicting notions of how to proceed, as they felt impelled in different directions at once.

Summary of Findings

The principal findings of the research can be summarised in terms of a series of tensions inherent within the child protection process in cases involving the familial sexual abuse of adolescent girls that served to influence the ways in which the social workers ascribed 'meaning' to specific cases and thus influenced the ways in which they proceeded.

- The organisational needs of social services departments vs. the needs of social workers as child protection practitioners

This was apparent in terms of general organisational imperatives that prioritised initial 'crisis management' work over and above ongoing aftermath work and the importance attached to procedures. One notes, however, that this was not a simple one way process of constraint on practice as these levels of prioritising and ascriptions of procedural importance were interpreted differently and varied from area to area. The key point was that they provided boundaries for the intervention strategies of social workers and were perceived by those social workers to a greater or lesser extent as constraining their practice. The structure of the process itself also left many social workers with concerns over their capacity to meet the long-term needs of girls around the age of fifteen or sixteen, because of their anxieties over transitional arrangements consequent upon girls reaching the upper age limit of the child protection arrangements.

- The workings of aspects of interagency coordination.

At the level of referral, the social workers were less suspicious of referrals from other professionals than from members of the public. However, it was clear that there was a significant degree of interagency distrust or rivalry within the child protection network. This distrust was not across the board. The social workers, for example, enjoyed good relationships with professionals from education. They had less successful relationships with many professionals from the health services. There was a tendency to be suspicious of the motives of psychiatrists and psychologists when they gave reasons why they could not work with particular girls, and many social workers were clearly annoyed at the attitudes of some consultants and GPs at Child Protection Conferences. Much of their annoyance relates back to aspects of the legislation and its consequent procedures. Social Services social workers recognised themselves as the lead professionals in specific cases, but found many medical professionals unwilling to accept their lead in coordinated intervention strategies. In many ways, this involves issues of ownership of child abuse as a phenomenon. Although elements of a medical model of child sexual abuse remained apparent in the social workers thinking, particularly the ways in which they pathologised perpetrators as deviant, they did tend towards a more 'social' model that recognised a multiplicity of factors beyond the physical nature of the sexual practices themselves. Some medical practitioners, however, held to a more rigid medical model of child sexual abuse, a model which granted them as doctors the legitimate expertise. This would tend to question the commitment of all professionals in the child protection network to the mandate for coordination.

- Between child protection social work and the operation of the criminal justice system.

This tension emerged at a multiplicity of points within the process, relating to initial investigations, joint video interviews, and the rationale for prosecution/non-prosecution. This tension was so great that most of the social workers felt they were pursuing a completely different agenda within child protection to that being pursued by the police and the courts, to the point that the issues of decriminalising child sexual abuse came into some accounts. The social workers' concerns in this area reflect a wider debate both within social work and academia, in terms of the problematic interface between social work and the criminal justice system in the child protection process (Prior *et al* 1997, Wattam, 1997b, DoH and Welsh Office, 1997). King and Trowell (1992) argue that there is a real problem in child protection emanating from the legal system's need for closure and definitive once and for all conclusions.

> ...while the answers to these pressing questions may resolve the immediate legal problems and allow the case to be closed, they do not tackle the issues of the long-term welfare of children which lies concealed behind the facade of legal rhetoric (King and Trowell, 1992, Pg.51).

Following the arguments of Parton (1991) and Parton *et al* (1997) further argue that:

> The need to present a convincing case in court overrides help for children (King and Trowell, 1992, Pg.72).

However, the degree of tension between the social workers and the criminal justice system (especially the police) varied immensely. The closer the interpersonal relationship between individual social workers and police officers, the more successfully coordinated intervention strategies were achieved.

- Tensions in terms of the clients.

The first of these raise the question as to who exactly was the client in these cases, and that question was not successfully resolved. The social workers intervention strategies appeared to rest upon a level of contradiction or confusion as to who exactly were the clients. The sexually abused girls clearly were clients. The rationale for intervention rested on notions of effecting change to terminate or prevent recurrence of their abuse. However, some aspects of risk assessment, although ostensibly to manage the levels of risk for the girls, appeared in terms of risk or potential risk to the mother. It was also clear that specific aspects of some intervention strategies were aimed at resolving issues for family members other than the girl herself[1]. Non-abusing family members, mothers in particular, could best be seen in some cases as 'co-clients' (Twigg, ed., 1992; Twigg and Atkin, 1994).

- Tensions between the social workers' normative professional views as to the best interests of the girls concerned, and elements of client choice in terms of the girls' role in any decision-making process within the child protection process.

This was apparent in a multitude of ways. Girls made decisions in terms of accommodation and in terms of continuing relationships with the perpetrators that the social workers felt put them at risk, and they often refused therapeutic and other help, that social workers were convinced was in their best interests. Underpinning this tension were issues relating to adolescent sexual abuse itself, particularly the psychological consequences that often left girls in no fit state to make judgements as to what were their own best interests. Yet, as a loss of autonomy is a feature of any abusive relationship (Herman, 1994), it may be that the exercise of client choice could in itself be therapeutic, that actions the girls took that were not in their best interests physically were perhaps in their best interests psychologically.

The tensions that became apparent between the social workers and the police and the courts, and those between the social workers and aspects of client choice were intimately configured with the crucial element of the age of the girls. The courts utilised chronological age as a proxy for maturity, and tended to see all girls over twelve as 'nearly adult'. This impacted on the social workers practice as it significantly shifted the balance within the social worker-client relationship in favour of the client, at least in terms of the law. As both the criminal law and the civil law play significant roles in shaping the environment for child protection interventions, this had a considerable influence on the general social worker-client relationship. The tension was more complex than that, however. It was apparent that there was an internal conflict within some social workers that left them torn between concepts of empowerment and client choice on the one hand, and the protection of vulnerable children on the other.

- Tension derived from the chronic underfunding of social services child protection work.

The therapeutic needs of the girls were not being met to the satisfaction of many of the social workers, principally through the operation of resource constraints[2]. In other words both the social workers professional standards were not being met and the clients needs not being met due to mileage limitations, overweighted caseloads and deficits in the quality of in-service training.

Conclusions and Recommendation

The interplay between these various tensions make plain the need for significant changes in the ways in which social services child protection is organised for sexually abused adolescent girls. Further they suggest a redeployment of resources and changes in a series of interagency relationships.

Large numbers of children are filtered out of the child protection process at an early stage (Wattam, 1997a; Gibbons, 1997), suggesting that a significant number of children enter the child protection process that need not be there. This suggests that professionals from other agencies, such as GPs and teachers should be made more aware of the signs of actual abuse rather than the conditions of risk of abuse, across all forms of child abuse. This would entail a reversal in the trend that has seen a socio-medical model of child abuse gradually replaced by a socio-legal model of child protection (Parton et al 1997). This would lead to the system itself being less 'swamped' (Gibbons, 1997), releasing social workers to deal with those referrals that remain in a more thorough manner.

Parton (1997) argues that there should be a refocusing on need rather than risk within child care and protection as a more useful deployment of resources and that the emphasis within child care and protection should be refocused on prevention. He argues for a greater commitment to Section 17 and Part Three of the Children Act, 1989, in terms of providing resources for families with children in need. Parton's argument can be seen to derive from anxieties over the gradual trend towards child protection procedures, clear rules and the professional valorisation of child protection to the detriment of processes of assessing need and supporting families in trouble (Hearn, 1997). Wattam (1997a) suggests the development of less formal structures such as 'drop-in' centres for children and families with open access policies that would focus on the resolution of various intrafamilial issues outside any legalised process of allegations and blaming. Thorburn et al (1997), suggest that taking a broader view without focussing too narrowly purely on specific abusive incidents may go some way towards ensuring greater cooperation in any child protection initiatives by both the child and the parents. These provisions make a great deal of sense in terms of the prevention of neglect and physical injury. however, given the specific aetiology of sexual abuse, one would see such a reordering of priorities as of minimal value.

The principal benefit that would be gained in terms of sexual abuse work both from a reordering of priorities in child protection generally from crisis intervention to family support modalities of preventing children in need falling into the category of risk, and in terms of making other professionals more aware of the signs and symptoms of actual abuse rather than the conditions of risk, would be that it would release social workers from conducting initial investigations into a significant number of families where it was not required, whilst also considerably reducing the large number of physical abuse and neglect cases. This would give social workers more time to work on sexual abuse cases. As pressure of time management due to overburdened caseloads was seen by the social workers as a significant factor in the problems they encountered with their work, this would have the effect of considerably reducing their anxieties. In effect, it would represent a redeployment of resources rather than additional resources that would reduce the incidence of physical injury and neglect cases whilst providing social workers with more time to accomplish their child protection task in cases of child sexual abuse.

The relationship between child protection social workers and professionals from other agencies also needs to be addressed. Firstly, there is a clear need for joint training of social workers and other members of the child protection network, especially in terms of the ways in which the mandate to coordination is interpreted. In those areas where joint police/social service training took place there were tangible benefits of mutual understanding and coordinated intervention strategies. Joint training thus needs to be extended to cover all the different agencies in the child protection network. This training would need to clarify exactly the role of each of the agencies in the child protection network and enhance the mutual understanding of the different organisational needs of the agencies concerned. There may well be a significant resource implication in this as it would need to be preceded by relatively intensive single agency training in terms of professionals from different agencies coming to terms with their own professional and organisational 'defences' of their discipline boundaries (Woodhouse and Pengelly, 1991), to enable them to meaningfully participate in joint training programmes. Joint training itself would offer more than a sharing of expertise and a mutual understanding on a professional basis, however. Significant benefits for coordination would derive from such training through the development of better interagency interpersonal relationships.

Significant difficulties remain, however. There is the considerable problem of the relationship between the therapeutic needs of sexually abused young women and the operation of the criminal justice system. Lees (1997) points to aspects of objectification in the portrayal of women's bodies in rape trials. This clearly represents elements if an intersection between patriarchal cultural definitions of femininity and the reductionist tendencies of the law to define objects, persons and actions in precise terms outside the complexities of social interaction, definitions that claim to be 'unified and superior' to any competing knowledge claims. (Smart, 1989). Victim responses in rape and sexual assault cases are thus afforded little significance compared to exact descriptions of specific acts. The law is also exact in what it counts a crime, thus discounting many sexually abusive incidents endured by women (Kelly and Radford, 1996). Several consequences flow from this in terms of child or adolescent sexual abuse. Firstly, the need to provide exact detail of events and actions can be both difficult and traumatic for the girls concerned. Secondly, the law acts as a modality of assessing the abuse purely in terms of material practices, whereas a therapeutic approach needs to focus to a much greater extent upon the consequences of events, actions and environments, whether or not the law deems them criminal. Thirdly, implicit in a legal approach is the concept that the perpetration of sexual abuse is deviant; feminist concerns over sexual abuse as integral to wider issues of the operation of patriarchal structures and practices are simply seen as 'illegitimate' knowledges. This calls into question the value of criminal proceedings. Despite the therapeutic advantages that conviction can bring, one would on balance like to see the current trend towards non-prosecution continue, as the law is perhaps the least appropriate way of dealing with sexual abuse.

These various recommendations clearly point to changes in terms of prioritising issues in child care and protection generally that would have implications for child protection in sexual abuse cases, and changes in child protection practice specifically in terms of sexual abuse work. From a social worker perspective these changes would serve to ameliorate some of the tensions inherent in the execution of their sexual abuse child protection tasks. However, they do not deal with the central issue; the specificity of working with adolescent girls.

Firstly, in terms of worker competence and the specificity of adolescence, time must be made available for social workers to acquaint themselves with adolescent sexual abuse and child protection research, and in-service training needs to be improved to include theoretical as well as practical elements.

Secondly, the serious problem of constraints on aftermath work because of the upper age limit of the child protection process needs to be confronted. As an immediate measure a great deal of conflict between social workers and sexually abused adolescent girls could be resolved by the introduction of transitional arrangements to move the girls through into adult services between the ages of sixteen and eighteen. This would be of considerable benefit, although issues concerning relationships of trust between the social worker and the girl that are central to concerns over the continuity of care would still remain. From a longer term perspective the reduction in social worker caseloads as a consequence of the reordering of priorities towards family support services (Parton, 1997; Thorburn *et al*, 1997; Wattam, 1997a), could be taken as an opportunity for a reorganisation within social services.

Special adolescent sexual abuse teams should be developed that operate according to the child protection procedures in just the same ways as area teams will in respect of younger children. However, once the upper age limit of child protection is reached and girls are removed from the Child Protection Register, the involvement of the adolescent sexual abuse unit social worker will continue in terms of aftermath work for as long as the social worker and the young woman feel it is needed.

Clearly, the cost of providing such teams in every area may well prove prohibitive. It would thus be more appropriate to provide these units to cover a wider geographical area. Although this would entail greater distances for these social workers to travel, there would be distinct advantages in terms of continuity of care for sexually abused adolescent girls and young women. Further, many of the social workers expressed a preference for working with younger or older children[3], and felt more or less competent with specific age groups. There are also the benefits of specialised teams per se in that they tend to focus more clearly on their shared objectives (Adair, 1986). Thus such an initiative would provide three tangible benefits; the continuity of aftermath care for sexually abused adolescent girls for as long as it was appropriate, the development of specialised teams committed to adolescent sexual abuse work, and the opportunity for social workers to specialise in an area of child protection where they feel most competent.

None of these recommendations is particularly radical and none will fully resolve the tensions inherent in child protection work with sexually abused adolescent girls. However, if implemented, they would go some way towards reducing levels of social worker stress and enhance their own sense of professional competence. They would also go some way towards providing the level of service delivery that sexually abused adolescent girls deserve.

Notes

Chapter One

1. For a fuller discussion of children's rights and their relationship to issues of child protection see Chapter Five.

2. This is evident in terms of questions relating to the up bringing or property of a child, the need for speedy decisions (s.1 (2), DoH, 1991a, para. 1.8), as delay in resolving questions pertaining to a child's welfare can be detrimental to the child, the welfare checklist (s.1 (3)), that lists the factors such as the wishes of the child, his/her physical and emotional needs and any harm (s) he has suffered or is likely to suffer, that should be taken into account when determining any question relating to the child's welfare, and the principle of non-intervention (s.1(5)), whereby an order will only be made if it is better than no order at all.

3. Although the word never appears in the text of the Act, examples of partnership recur throughout the text, such as parental responsibility being held by more than one person (s.1 (5)), consultation prior to making a care order (s.35 (11)), the recognition that children may refuse medical or psychiatric examination (s.43 (8)), and the recognition that social services should as certain the wishes of a child they are looking after and his/her parents before any decisions are made in respect of the child (s.22(4)).

4. This emphasis on the family and the need for working in partnership with them is seen throughout the act in various guises; the position of unmarried fathers, grandparents and other relatives is enhanced ((s.10 (7), DoH, 1990a).

Chapter Two

1. Clearly, the inductive categorization of respondents accounts is part and parcel of a process of deriving social scientific 'meaning' from the everyday 'meanings' social workers' attached to their actions. However, as both Giddens (1993) and Schutz (1972) have made clear, there are limits to the inductive process. The social researcher does not come to a research project without some form of existing perspective or view on the question (s) he is researching. Rather, the existing research into those questions and adjacent or related issues, and the general social scientific understanding of the researcher will form part of his/her meaning complex. In other words, the understanding the researcher develops from the accounts of the social workers must to some extent be experientially derived (Kant, 1953; Rock, 1979). The process of moving from the accounts given by respondents to a sociological analysis of those accounts requires the researcher to develop social scientific constructs out of the 'everyday' constructions of meaning of the respondents (Giddens, 1993; Schutz, 1972; Weber, 1964; Winch, 1958). One of the problems to be accounted for here was specific to the

respondent status. Social work training engages with some elements of sociology and many of the respondents were in fact sociology graduates prior to entering social work. This meant that in places they invoked elements of social theory both in terms of justification and rationale for their actions. It was thus important to be vigilant in accepting their use of various sociological perspectives in constructing their frames of meaning for their actions, whilst not necessarily subscribing to those theoretical perspectives.

Chapter Three

1. See Chapter Six.

2. See Chapter Six.

3. One need to be aware of the role group work can play in recovery process and the limitations of that role. Hooper *et al* (1997) in their examination of groups for women survivors of sexual abuse from an attachment theory perspective, review the research and highlight many benefits that can act as a powerful corrective to the emotional traumas associated with sexual abuse. They see a whole range of benefits to be derived from such groups. Membership of such a group can diminish the individual's sense of isolation, and can lead the individual into re-evaluating her own experience in the light of the testimony of others. Membership of such groups can help the individual to release anger, firstly in a compassionate sense in terms of the injustice done to other members of the group, and later, after recognising the similarities between her own experience and that of others, on her own behalf. In other words, group membership can lead to a reduction of self-blame and enable the individual to place the blame for her abuse in the hands of her abuser. Group members who are further down the road of recovery can act as role models, enabling individuals to see that it is possible to overcome the abuse. The various members of the group each serve to validate the emotional responses of one another and give tacit permission to share their experiences, itself a powerful corrective to secrecy and denial, and membership of the group as a form of solidarity can act as a safe base from which the individual can attempt to reconnect with the outside world. Groups for survivors of sexual abuse do, however, have limitations. Firstly, before joining the group, all its members will be strangers to the individual. Thus only those willing to disclose their abuse in a public setting will feel able to join. Joining a group represents a 'strange situation' with concomitant problems for the individual, and the psychological/emotional stress of listening to others emotions and stories of their experiences may be too much for many to bear. Indeed, such groups are inappropriate for those for whom increased stress poses particular risks, such as those who are suicidal, psychotic, drug or alcohol dependent or with a severe psychopathology. There is also the danger that membership of a group exclusively for survivors of sexual abuse could reinforce a focus on that aspect of experience to too great an extent, diminishing the capacity of individuals to connect with the wider community and reinforcing the sense of survivor of sexual abuse not as an experience but as an identity. Herman (1994) in charting the process of recovery from child sexual abuse and other traumas suggests that different types of therapeutic group are appropriate at different stages in the process. She argues

that in the early stages one to one therapy is far more useful to bring the survivor to a point where she becomes able to cope with strangers and their stories. She also argues that groups need to change their focus through time, the early stages being devoted primarily to education and only later moving towards the sharing of experiences to help stimulate the sense of remembrance and loss suffered by trauma survivors. It is only at the final stage of the process that Herman (1994) suggests that conflict should be confronted and emotions given a freer rein. She also argues that there are substantial benefits to be derived in the final stages of recovery through membership of heterogeneous groups of survivors of varying traumas as a useful stage in facilitating reconnection to the wider community.

4. For a fuller discussion of the various benefits and disbenefits of short-term and long-term groups for survivors of sexual abuse see Hooper *et al* (1997)

5. See Chapter Five.

6. See Chapter Five.

7. See Birmingham City Council, for example (cited in Leeds City Council, Project Management Group, 1992).

8. The 'cycle of abuse' concept tends to present itself in a variety of forms. In terms of child sexual abuse the argument is that women whose children are sexually abused by men were themselves sexually abused as children (Faller, 1989; Goodwin et al, 1981). It is often pathologised both in professional thinking and in terms of public and political debate as some form of social 'disease' transmitting across generations (Vizard and Tranter, 1988b). Feminist researchers have developed a series of criticisms of this view. Firstly, the sample groups in the research the concept derives from contained only those families known to child protection agencies, yet prevalence research (Kelly et *al*, 1991; Russell, 1984) suggests that only around 5 per cent of incidents come to the attention of child protection agencies. Secondly, although some research has found higher rates of sexual abuse amongst women whose children have been sexually abused, compared with population as a whole (Faller, 1989; Goodwin *et al*, 1981), others have found rates comparable to that of the general population (Deblinger *et al*, 1993) Thirdly Kelly *et al* (1991) found in the UK that 59 per cent of young women and 27 per cent of young men reported some form of sexually intrusive experience prior to the age of eighteen, suggesting that childhood sexual abuse, rather than being seen as a 'pathology' that transmits across generations of women in 'sick' families, is better characterized as a relatively commonplace female experience. Some feminists argue that the persistence of the concept of 'cycle of abuse' as an 'explanation' of childhood and adolescent abuse is intimately configured with the professionalisation of child protection work and its consequent domination by male experts (Hudson, 1992). Drawing on Hooper (1987, 1992) and Macleod and Saraga, 1988), Hooper (1995) sees the concept of 'cycle of abuse' as owing "more to professional and patriarchal ideologies than to empirical validity" (Hooper, 1995, Pg.349). Hooper (1995) goes on to point out that despite attempts to 'discover' the relationship between women's own history of childhood sexual abuse and their degree of support for their own children once

sexual abuse has been revealed (de Jong, 1988; Gomes-Schwartz *et al*, 1990, Myer, 1984), no clear evidence has emerged. Hooper (1995) and other feminists are not only critical of the relative invalidity of the concept as an explanation for child and adolescent sexual abuse, a concept that implies a causal link without any explanation of the mechanisms involved (DiSabatino, 1989), they are also critical of the effects the widespread acceptance of the concept can have on women whose children have been abused. Hooper (1995) argues that it legitimates the intervention of mental health professionals into the lives of mothers and children, whereas only serious intervention with abusive men will act towards reducing the sexual abuse of children. She also stresses the disempowering nature of a discourse of 'cycle of abuse', in that it can act to pathologise those women who have been abused in childhood or adolescence with the implication that they may be dangerous to their own children. Given the 'undiscovered' nature of most incidents of child sexual abuse and the long-term lack of appropriate therapeutic services for those incidents that did develop into child protection cases, the process of recovery for many of these women will be incomplete. The stigma, guilt and self-blame associated with a history of childhood sexual abuse may remain with them, only to be exacerbated if their own children are sexually abused and professional discourse implies a causal link. Hooper (1995) also suggests that the persistence of the discourse of 'cycle of abuse' may well inhibit women with a history of child sexual abuse from revealing it to mental health professionals for fear of having their parenting skills judged in a discriminatory fashion. Hooper's (1995) major criticism of the 'cycle of abuse' concept is that it offers both women and professionals "a seriously distorting lens" (Hooper, 1995, Pg.352) of interpretation of the copresence of childhood sexual abuse in women and their children, that directs attention towards the past rather than confronting the issues involved with the current abusive situation.

9. See Chapter Five.

10. See Chapter Seven.

11. See Chapter Four.

12. See Chapter Four

13. Hooper (1995) argues that the myth of false allegations and the various stereotypes surrounding sexual violence act towards creating difficulties for women and girls in defining their experiences as abusive, leaving a situation where girls may adopt coping strategies of minimizing or forgetting the abuse they have been subject to.

14. This was a particularly significant issue in respect of service families when the fathers were temporarily posted abroad.

15. See Chapter Five.

16. See Chapter Five.

17. See Chapter Seven.

Chapter Four

1.One notes that examples of innovative work in the voluntary sector (e.g. Rape Crisis sexual abuse counseling) led to social worker referrals that could be said to express novel elements of statutory/voluntary sector collaboration, indicating the potential for radical coordination within child protection. Although such innovative work could not be said to constitute coordination, the opportunities for referral it offers social workers can be seen as an added dimension to interagency interactions.

2. See Chapter Seven.

3. See Chapter Seven.

4. See also Farmer and Owen (1995) for social worker concerns over the involvement of police detectives in child protection.

5. From a personal perspective, a thirteen year old boy who was a friend of the family who had been sexually abused by a neighbour was refused counseling despite his mother's repeated requests, as he waited for the prosecution of his abuser. As the court case became immanent, he became more and more withdrawn and eventually committed suicide.

6. cf. Case managers in other aspects of social work.

7. See Chapter Five.

Chapter Five

1. This process exists in the Netherlands in respect of adolescents engaging in sexual activities. In Dutch law children over the age of twelve are entitled to engage in sexual intercourse, but between the ages of twelve and sixteen their parents are entitled to prevent them exercising this right. If the parents refuse permission, the child can take them to a national tribunal, the Children's Council, which will make a legally enforceable judgement, based on evidence from all concerned parties, as to whether the parent's refusal was reasonable. The Dutch seem to have managed to incorporate an element of adolescent self-determination within a framework that acknowledges the differential development of adolescents and pays due regard to child protection (Veerman, 1992). Older children are both freed from unnecessary parental restrictions whilst still being protected from sexual exploitation by adults.

2. See Chapter One.

3. This probably derives from social workers perceiving sexual abuse in terms of addictive behaviour that is both compulsive and deviant, and their realization that

sexual abuse tends to be repetitive and ongoing (Women's Resource Centre, 1989), the victims being primarily female (Thorpe, 1994), and tending to know the perpetrator (Gibbons *et al*, 1995), and that sexual abuse takes place in specific environments that grant the perpetrator the opportunity to abuse (Finkelhor, 1979).

4. The social workers did not believe that the actions of the police/CPS always enhanced aspects of the girls' safety. They sometimes found the insistence in bringing a prosecution as acting against the best interests of the girl in terms of her ongoing protection needs. They saw the development of a prosecution case as bringing too much pressure on the girl and her family and expressed great concern in terms of a failed prosecution resulting in lost protection opportunities in that information that was used to support a prosecution case that was unsuccessful may have been better used to support an application for a Care Order or a Supervision Order - See Chapter Four.

5. The sociological concept of a career is one that articulates closely to the everyday accepted concept of an employment career. It is the movement through time of an individual in a particular sphere. One can, for example have a housing career as one goes through life moving from one form of accommodation to another, or a substance abuse career that traces the development through time of an individual's use of alcohol, controlled drugs and other substances. A girl's protection career can thus be seen as her movement through the child protection process over time. This may well articulate closely to, but needs to be distinguished from, what may well be a parallel 'care career' that can also be traced through time and may involve elements of home living, fostering and institutional care.

6. See Chapter Four.

7. See Chapter Four.

8. See Gibbons *et al*, (1995), Wattam, (1997a).

9. See Chapter Six.

10. The social workers were not unanimous in their own attitudes towards the girls' participation in Child Protection Conferences, although most of them were in favour. The Research literature (Merchant and Luckham, 1991; Birchall with Hallett, 1995) would tend to imply that this divergence of view with a majority in favour is reflected nationally.

11. See Chapter Seven

12. Archard (1993) compares this to oriental perceptions of life as a continuous process. Oriental perceptions thus have no end status of adulthood or full maturity, rather individuals can be more or less mature than others and any individual can continue to mature through life. This suggests that oriental thought is more amenable to issues of maturity, whereas western thought tends to revolve around concepts of capacities and competences that are relatively rigidly attached to chronological age.

13. See Chapter Four.

14. This is a significant point. The girl's use of talk on sexual matters in a group situation cannot be taken as an indicator of knowledge, rather it is better seen as being the argot of that specific age and gender defined group. The different forms of talk the girls employed in individual and group sessions can be seen as 'situated talk' (Mills, 1940; Gerth and Mills, 1954) aimed at a particular audience (Goffman, 1971) within a particular power-knowledge relation (Foucault, 1980, 1990).

15. One notes the problems of distinguishing between consent and coercion, particularly if the girl has not developed to a fully adult level of cognitive capacity.

16. See Criminal Justice Act, 1991, and Criminal Justice and Public Order Act, 1994, and current initiatives on electronic tagging, youth custody and parenting classes.

17. See Chapter Four.

18. See Chapter Three.

19. The concept of typification was developed by Keddie (1971) as a modality employed by teachers of categorizing pupils according to their approximation to certain 'ideal types' (Weber, 1978).

20. This does not preclude the physical separation of the girl and the perpetrator as the central theme in protection

21. See also Fisher (1995) in terms of social worker knowledge base being principally derived from experience and 'official' literature rather than from reading of research and other associated literature.

Chapter Six

1. See Chapter One.

2. Waterhouse and Carnie (1992) developed a further amendment to this general type of model in their study of fifty-one child sexual abuse cases in Scotland. They derived a set of criteria for the assessment of risk that divided into two distinct areas. Their primary criteria could be seen as 'social' criteria and articulated closely to factors relating to parental and familial characteristics. They added to this a secondary, clinical, set of criteria, based upon medical signs and symptoms that would confirm or refute the abuse.

3. It is important to differentiate between the roles of wife and mother. In a great deal of sociological discourse the concepts of wife and mother are conflated. In

some Marxian conceptualizations (Zaretsky, 1976, for example) the roles of wife and mother are seen as reproducing the (male) workforce on a daily and a generational basis. What differentiation there is between women's roles within the family in capitalism is not spelt out specifically in terms of wife and mother. Rather, women's twin roles within the family are the daily reproduction of the workforce through the management of food, shelter and sexual and emotional fulfillment for the man of the family, and the generational reproduction of the workforce through the bearing of children and the inculcation within those children of the cultural norms of the society. In either case woman are seen not as economic producers, but as economically dependent upon men. Feminists have noted the high level of economic dependency of women on men, but have sought to confront the underlying structural and ideological themes that create this level of dependence. Further they have questioned malestream assumptions that this economic dependence translates to forms of emotional dependence, exposing much of what is seen as 'natural' in masculinity and femininity as the ideological constructs of male domination. Many feminists in the early days of the women's movement (Firestone, 1970; de Beauvoir, 1972; for example) saw male-dominance as deriving from the biological given of female child-bearing and the nurturance of young children which displaced women from the public spheres of economic and political production into the private sphere of human reproduction. Both sociological and technological arguments were put forward to suggest that the historical necessity for this gendered division of labour had passed. Crucially, it was the role of mother that was seen as being at the centre of female oppression. Later feminist work (Choderow, 1978; Daly, 1978), whilst maintaining the centrality of motherhood in defining the difference between men and women, began to question the social and cultural values placed on the different emotional and moral attributes of men and women, arguing that essential nature of motherhood to human existence should be valued more highly. Although Daly's (1978) celebration of female-centredness appears as the complete antithesis of Firestone's (1970) call for the technological replacement of natural motherhood, both analyses still maintain motherhood as a crucial defining feature in patriarchal structures of male-dominance and female oppression. Incorporating some of the perspectives of Daly (1978) and Rich (1977) in terms of the ideological structures a patriarchal society creates out of the differences between male and female attributes, and deriving to some degree from Ruddick's (1984) concept of 'maternal thought' as nurturing and fostering change, Johnson (1988) reaches very different conclusions. She argues strongly that it is not motherhood, but marriage that are the key to women's relationship to men, acting as a paradigm for male dominance in a more general way. She contends that as mothers women are 'strong'. Mothering involves the care and nurturance of others and as such is the complete antithesis to dependence. As mothers, women have others who are dependent on them. The crucial problem Johnson (1988) sees for mothers is that they are also often wives. "Through marriage mothers become wives, and this basic element of kinship systems places males in control of women. Yet marriage in all cultures is also often mandatory or made strongly preferable to other alternatives" (Johnson, 1988, Pg.40). The role of wife is completely different to that of mother. Women as wives are expected to remain in a position of subservience to their husbands. Clearly the form of this subservience differs greatly across different societies. Johnson (1988) makes the point that in western societies female submission to men must be subtle, but none the less it remains a cultural imperative. "Female superiority as a wife in virtually all aspects runs counter to the implicit rule that adult heterosexual relationships are to be male dominated" (Johnson, 1988, Pg.40). In the final analysis, for Johnson (1988) it is not women's mothering that lies at the centre of male-dominance, but the "constraint on women in this society to define themselves in terms of their relationship to men" (Johnson, 1988, Pg.9). In other words the real problem for women is not mothering but marriage. Not only does Johnson's (1988) analysis shed some light on the forces behind patriarchal divisions in society, it also alerts us to the everyday tensions inherent in being both a wife and mother.

4. See also Farmer and Owen (1995), Pg.197.

5. See also Farmer and Owen (1995), Pp.236-237.

6. See Madge (1983), for example.

7. See Chapter Three.

8. cf. Finkelhor (1984) and the overcoming of internal inhibitions.

9. There is a great deal of heuristic force in such a perception. The CPS Code for Crown Prosecutors takes a relatively hard line on sex offending generally, and those found guilty of a sexual offence against a minor will normally be imprisoned (Sampson, 1994). Sex offenders in general, and those convicted of offences against children or adolescents in particular, if imprisoned can be in some physical danger. In order to protect such prisoners from assault by other inmates many are subject to Rule 43, which acts to segregate them from other prisoners. In effect this often means that they are locked in their cells for up to twenty three hours a day with no access to recreational or educational facilities (Sampson, 1994).

10. There was a significant shift in patterns of entertainment, the theatre, cinema, and spectator sport being supplanted to a great extent by home entertainments such as satellite television, video and computer games. The revolution in information technology began to open up the possibilities for many people of working from home. Free market principles began to be applied to elements of the welfare state, and a visible shift began to take place that shifted long established principles of communitarian responsibility for welfare back onto the individual. Public participation in political and civic life diminished considerably, and trades union membership fell. In other words, there was a considerable cultural shift towards privatisation.

11. See Erooga (1994), for problems experienced by male social workers when working with sexual abuse perpetrators.

Chapter Seven

1. See Chapter Three.

2. To what extent individual autonomy of practice is a reality is another matter, as the child protection enterprise is clearly located within a framework of legislation, governmental directives, local policy and administrative procedures and issues surrounding mandated interagency coordination.

3. See Chapter Three.

4. Compare with Furniss (1991) and the importance of the role of 'trusted person' as child's fixed point of trust in the transition from the everyday world to the world of child protection process.

5 See Chapter Three.

Chapter Eight

1. See Chapter Six.

2. See also Bamford (1990) and Kelly (1991).

3. See Chapter Seven.

Bibliography

Abel, G.G., Becker, J.V., Cunningham-Rathner, J., Routeau, J., Kaplan, M. and Reich, J. (1984) 'The Treatment of child Molesters: A Manual', Unpublished manuscript, University of Columbia

Adair, J (1986) *Effective Teambuilding*, Pan, London

Adams, P., Berg, L., Berger, N. Duane, M., Neill, A.S., and Ollendorf, R. (1972*), Children's Rights: towards the liberation of the child*, Panther, London

Adams-Tucker, C. (1982) 'Proximate effects of sexual abuse in childhood: a report on 28 children', American *Journal of Psychiatry*, 139, Pp.1252-1256

Adorno, T.W. *et al* (1950) *The Authoritarian Personality*, Harper and Row, New York

Afnan, S. and Smith, J. (1992) 'Working together? A survey of current child sexual abuse practice', *Newsletter of Association of Child Psychology and Psychiatry*, 14, (1), pp. 11-16

Aiken, M., Dewar, R., Di Tomaso, N., Hage, J. and Zeitz, G.(1975*) Coordinating Human Services*, Josey-Bass, San Francisco,Ca.

Aldrich, H.E. (1972) 'An organisational environment perspective on cooperation and conflict between organisations in the manpower and training system', in Neghandi, A. *Interorganisation Theory*, Kent State University Press, Kent, Ohio

Aldrich, H.E. (1976) 'Resource dependence and interorganisational relations', *Administration and Society*, 7, Pp.419-454

Aldrich, H.E. (1979) *Organisations and Environments*, Prentice Hall, Englewood Cliffs, N.J.

American Academy of Pediatrics Committee on Child Abuse and Neglect (1991), 'Guidelines for evaluation of sexual abuse of children', *Pediatrics*, 87, pp. 254-260

Anderson, E. and Clarke, L (1982) Disability *in Adolescence*, Methuen, London

Angelou, M. (1984) I *Know Why The Caged Bird Sings*, Virago, London

Archard, D. (1993) *Children's Rights and Childhood*, Routledge, London

Aries, P. (1962) *Centuries of Childhood*, Penguin, Harmondsworth

Armitage, P. (1983) 'Joint working in primary health care', *Nursing Times*, 79, 28, Pp.75-78

Bagley, C. (1995) *Child Sexual Abuse and Mental Health in Adolescents and Adults*, Avebury, Aldershot

Bagley, C. and Ramsey, R. (1986), 'Sexual abuse in childhood: psychosocial outcomes and implications for social work practice', *Journal of Social Work and Human Sexuality*, 4 Pp.33-47

249

Bamford, T. (1990) *The Future of Social Work*, Macmillan, London

Barnes, J.A. (1979) *Who Should Know What? Social Science, Privacy and Ethics*, Cambridge University Press, Cambridge

Barnes, M. and Wistow, G. ed. (1992) Researching *User Involvement*, Nuffield Institute

Barrett, S. and Hill, M. (1984) 'Policy bargaining and structure in implementation theory', *Policy and Politics*, 12, Pp.219-240

Barth, R.P. and Berry, M. (1987) 'Outcomes of child welfare services since permanency planning', *Social Services Review*, Vol.61, pp. 71-90

Bass, E. and Thornton, L. eds. (1983) *I Never Told Anyone: Writings by Women Survivors of Child Sexual Abuse*, Harper and Row, New York

Becker, J. (1991) 'Working with perpetrators', in Murray, K. and Gough, D. eds. *Intervening in Child Sexual Abuse*, Scottish Academic Press, Edinburgh

Becker, S. and Macpherson, S. eds. (1988) Public Issues, *Private Pain: Poverty, Social Work and Social Policy*, Social Services Insight Books, London

Bell. M. (1993) 'Parental Involvement in Initial Child Protection Conferences in Leeds', University of York

Benedict, L.L.W., and Zautra, A.A.J. 'Family environmental characteristics as risk factors for childhood sexual abuse, (1993) *Journal of Clinical Child Psychology*, 22 (3) Sep. 93, Pp.365-374

Benjamin, M. (1981) 'Child Abuse and the interdisciplinary team: panacea or problem?' in Irving, H. ed. *Family Law: an interdisciplinary perspective*, Caswell, Toronto, Canada

Benson, J.K. (1975) 'The interorganisational network as a political economy', *Administrative Science Quarterly*, 20, Pp.229-249

Benson, , J,K. (1982) 'A framework for policy analysis', in Rogers, D.L. and Whetten, D.A and associates *Interorganisational coordination: theory, research and implementation*, Iowa State University Press, Iowa

Bentovim, A. 'Who is to blame' (1988) *New Statesman*, 5th August

Bentovim, A., Elton, A., Hildebrand, J., Tranter, M. and Vizard, E. (1988) *Child Sexual Abuse within the Family: Assessment and Treatment; The Work of the Great Ormond Street Sexual Abuse Team*, Wright, London

Bentovim, A. and Boston, P. (1988) 'Sexual Abuse - Basic Issues - Characteristics of Children and Families', in Bentovim, A., Elton, A., Hildebrand, J, Tranter, M., and Vizard, E. eds. *Child Sexual Abuse within the Family: Assessment and Treatment; The work of the Great Ormond Street Sexual Abuse Team*, Wright, London

Bentovim, A. and Vizard, E. (1988) 'Sexual abuse, Sexuality and Childhood', in Bentovim, A., Elton, A., Hildebrand, J, Tranter, M., and Vizard, E. eds. *Child Sexual Abuse within the Family: Assessment and Treatment; The work of the Great Ormond Street Sexual Abuse Team*, Wright, London

Berkshire County Council (1979) *Lester Chapman: Report of an Independent Inquiry commissioned by the County Councils and Area Health Authorities of Berkshire and Hampshire*

Berliner, L. (1991a) 'Interviewing Families', in Murray, K. and Gough, D.A., eds. *Intervening in Child Sexual Abuse*, Scottish Academic Press, Edinburgh

Berliner, L. (1991b) 'Treating the effects of sexual assault', in Murray, K. and Gough, D.A., *Intervening in Child Sexual Abuse*, Scottish Academic Press, Edinburgh

Besharov, D.J. (1987) 'Contending with overblown expectations', *Public welfare*, Winter, Pp.7-11

Biehal, N., Clayden, J., Stein, M. and Wade, J. (1995) *Moving On*, HMSO, London

Biehal, N. and Sainsbury, E. (1991) 'From values to rights in social work', *British Journal of Social Work*, 21, pp. 245-257

Birchall, E. (1989) 'The frequency of child abuse' in Stevenson, O. ed. *Child Abuse: Public Policy and Professional Practice*, Harvester Wheatsheaf, London

Birchall, E. with Hallett, C. (1995) *Working Together in Child Protection: Report of Phase Two, a survey of the experience and perceptions of the six key professions*, HMSO, London

Birns, B. and Meyer, S-L. (1993) 'Mothers' role in incest: dysfunctional women or dysfunctional theories?' *Journal of Child Sexual Abuse*, 2 (3) Pp.127-135, 137-143

Blaikie, N. (1993) *Approaches to Social Enquiry*, Polity Press, Cambridge

Blyth, E. and Milner, J. (1990) 'The process of interagency work', in Violence Against Children Study Group, *Taking Child Abuse Seriously*, Unwin Hyman, London

Boddy, M. and Fudge, C. eds. (1984) *Local Socialism*, Macmillan, London

Bond, J., Cartlidge, A., Gregson, B., Philips, P., Bolam, F. and Gill, K. (1985) *A study of interprofessional collaboration in primary health care organisations*, University of Newcastle upon Tyne Health Care Research Unit, Newcastle

Boon, C. (1984) 'Betrayal of trust: Father-daughter incest' *Tellus*, 5 (winter), Pp.17-19

Booth, T.A. (1981) 'Collaboration between the health and social services: Part 1, A Case Study of joint planning', *Policy and Politics*, 9,1,Pp.23-49

Bowlby, J. (1988) *A Secure Base: Clinical Applications of Attachment Theory*, Rourledge, London

Brearly, P. (1982) *Risk and Social Work*, Routledge, London

Breckenridge, J. and Bereen, R. (1992) 'Dealing with mother-blame: workers responses to incest and child sexual abuse', in Breckenridge, J. andCarmody, M. eds. *Rethinking the Family: Some Feminist Questions*, Longman, New York

Bridge, J. Bridge, S. and Luke, S. (1990) *Blackstone's Guide to the Children Act 1989*, Blackstone, London

Briere, J. (1984) 'The long-term effects of childhood sexual abuse: defining a post-sexual-abuse syndrome', paper presented to 3rd National Conference on the Sexual Victimisation of Children, Washington, DC.

Briere, J.N. (1992) *Child Abuse Trauma*, Sage, London

Briere, J. and Runtz, M. (1987) 'Post-sexual abuse trauma: Data and implications for clinical practice', *Journal of Interpersonal Violence*, 2, pp.367-379

Brook, E. and Davis, A. (1985) *Women, the Family and Social Work*, Tavistock, London

Brown, A. (1984) *Consultation: An Aid to Successful Social Work, Community Care Practice Handbook*, Heinemann Educational Books, London

Browne, A. and Finkelhor, D. (1986) 'Initial and long-term effects: a review of the research' in Finkelhor, D. and associates ed. *A Sourcebook on Child Sexual Abuse* , Sage, Newbury Park, Ca.

Browne, K., Davies, C. and Stratton, P. eds. (1988) *Early Prediction and Prevention of Child Abuse*, Wiley, London

Bryman, A. (1988) *Quantity and Quality in Social Research*, Unwin Hyman, London

Cain, M. ed. (1989) *Growing Up Good: Policing the Behaviour of Girls in Europe*, Sage, London

Campbell, B. (1988) *Unofficial Secrets*, Virago, London

Cann, A.J. (1989) 'Child Abuse Reporting and Investigation: Policy Guidelines for Decision-Making' , *Child Abuse Review*, 3, 2, pp.27-30

Carter, P., Jeffs, T. and Smith, M. eds. (1989), *Social Work and Social Welfare, Yearbook 1*, Open University Press, Milton Keynes

Carter, P., Jeffs, T. and Smith, M. eds. (1990), *Social Work and Social Welfare, Yearbook 2*, Open University Press, Milton Keynes

Carter, P., Jeffs, T. and Smith, M. eds. (1991), *Social Work and Social Welfare, Yearbook 3*, Open University Press, Milton Keynes

Challis, L., Fuller, S., Henwood, M., Klein, R., Plowden, W., Webb, A., Whittingham, P and Wistow, G. (1988) *Joint Approaches to Social Policy: Rationality and Practice*, Cambridge University Press, Cambridge

Charles, J. (1983) 'Dangerous Misconceptions', *Community Care*, 1st December

Children Act 1989

Choderow, N. (1978) *The Reproduction of Mothering*, University of California Press, Los Angeles

Cleaver, H. and Freeman, P. (1995) *Parental Perspectives in Cases of Suspected Child Abuse*, HMSO, London

Cleveland County Council (1988) *Report of the Committee of Inquiry into Child Abuse in Cleveland 1987*, DHSS Cmnd 412, London, HMSO, 1988

Cloke, C. and Davies, M. eds. (1995) *Participation and Empowerment in Child Protection*, Pitman Publishing, London

Clyde, J. (1992) *The report of the inquiry into the removal of children from Orkney in February 1991*, HMSO, Edinburgh

Cohen, P. (1986), *Rethinking the Youth Question*, Working Paper 3, Post 16 Education Centre, London

Coleman, J. (1976), *The Nature of Adolescence*, Methuen, London

Coleman, J. ed. (1992) *The School Years: Current Issues in the Socialization of young People*, Routledge, London

Coleman, J.C. and Hendry, L. (1990) *The Nature of Adolesence*, 2nd edition, Routledge, London

Colwell Report (1974) *Report of the Committee of Inquiry into the Care and Supervision provided in relation to Maria Colwell*, HMSO, London

Conte, J. (1990) 'The incest offender: An overview and introduction', in Horton *et al* eds. *The Incest Perpetrator*, Sage, London, Pp.19-28

Conte, J. and Schuerman, J. (1987) 'Factors associated with an increased impact of child sexual abuse', *Child Abuse and Neglect*, 11, pp.201-211

Cook, K.S. (1977) 'Exchange and power in networks of interorganisational relations', *The Sociological Quarterly*, 18, Pp.62-82

Cooper, D.M. and Ball, D. (1987) *Social Work and Child Abuse*, Macmillan, London

Cooper, I. and Cormier, B. (1982) 'Inter-generational transmission of incest', *Canadian Journal of Psychiatry*, 27, pp. 231-235

Coote, A. ed. (1992) *The Welfare of Citizens: Developing New Social Rights*, IPPR, London

Corby, B. (1987) *Working with Child Abuse*, Open University Press, Milton Keynes

Corby, B (1993) *Child Abuse: Towards a Knowledge Base*, Open University Press, Buckingham

Corby, B. and Mills, C. (1986) 'Child abuse: risks and resources' *British Journal of Social Work*, 16, pp.531-542

Cornwell. J. (1984) *Hard-Earned Lives:Accounts of Health and Illness from East London*, Tavistock, London

Courtois, C. (1979) 'The incest experience and its aftermath' *Victimology: An International Journal*, 4, pp.337-347

Creighton, S. (1984) *Trends in Child Abuse*, NSPCC, London

Creighton, S. (1992) *Child Abuse Trends in England and Wales, 1983-1990*, NSPCC, London

Creighton, S. and Noyes, P. (1989) *Child Abuse Trends in England and Wales 1983-1987*, NSPCC, London

Crittenden, P. (1988) 'Family and Dyadic Patterns of functioning in Maltreating Families' in Browne, K. *et al Early Prediction and Prevention of Child Abuse*, Wiley, Chichester

Croft, S. and Beresford, P. (1990) *From Paternalism to Participation: Involving People in Social Services*, Joseph Rowntree Foundation, York

Dale, P. Davies, M., Morrison, T. and Waters, J. (1986), *Dangerous Families: Assessment and Treatment of Child Abuse*, Tavistock, London

Daly, M. (1978) *Gyn/Ecology: The Metaethics of Radical Feminism*, Beacon, Boston

Dartington, T. (1986) *The limits of altruism: Elderly mentally-infirm people as a test case for collaboration*, King Edward's Hospital Fund for London, London

Davies, M. ed. (1991) *The Sociology of Social Work*, Routledge, London

David, M (1991) 'Putting on an Act for Children?' in Maclean, M. and Groves, D. *Women's Issues in Social Policy*, Routledge, London

Davies, B. (1977) 'Agency collaboration or worker control?' *Youth and Society*, 22 Pp.3-6

Dawson, P. and Stevens, R. (1993) 'Applications for secure accommodation - a further twist in the labyrinth' *Justice of the Peace*, 157 (48) 27 Nov. Pp.761-762

Deblinger, E., Hathaway, C.R., Lippman, J. and Steer, R. (1993) 'Psychosocial characteristics and correlates of symptom distress in nonoffending mothers of sexually abused children', *Journal of Interpersonal Violence*, 8 (2) Pp.155-168

Dempster, H. (1993) 'The Aftermath of Child Sexual Abuse: Women's Perspectives' in Waterhouse, L. ed. *Child Abuse and Child Abusers: Protection and Prevention*, Jessica Kingsley, London

Department of Health (1988) *Protecting Children: A Guide for Social Workers Undertaking a Comprehensive Assessment*, HMSO, London

Department of Health (1990a) *Principle and Practice*, HMSO, London

Department of Health (1990b) *Survey of Children and Young Persons on Child Protection Registers, Year Ending 31 March 1989*, HMSO, London

Department of Health (1991a) *Guidance and Regulations, vol.1*, HMSO, London

Department of Health (1991b) *Guidance and Regulations, vol.2*, HMSO, London

Department of Health (1991c) *Working Together under the Children Act 1989*, HMSO, London

Department of Health (1991d) *Working with Sexual Abuse: Guidelines for Trainers and Managers in Social Services Departments*, HMSO, London

Department of Health (1992) *Survey of Children and Young Persons on Child Protection Registers, Year Ending 31 March 1991, England, Provisional Feedback*, HMSO, London

Department of Health (1993) *Report on the Children Act 1989*, HMSO, Cm. 2144, London

Department of Health (1994) *Survey of Children and Young Persons on Child Protection Registers, Year Ending 31 March 1993*, HMSO, London

Department of Health (1995a) *Child Protection: Messages from Research*, HMSO, London

Department of Health (1995b) *The Challenge of Partnership in Child Protection: Practice Guide*, HMSO, London

Department of Health, *Caring For People*, Cmnd 849

Department of Health and Welsh Office (1997) *People Like Us: The report of the review of safeguards for children living away from home*, HMSO, London

Department of Health and Social Security (1973) *Report of the Committee of inquiry into the care and supervision provided in relation to Maria Colwell*, HMSO, London

Department of Health and Social Security (1982) *Child Abuse: A Study of Inquiry Reports 1973-1981*, HMSO, London

Department of Health and Social Security (1985a) *Review of Child Care Law: Report to Ministers of an Interdepartmental Working Party*, HMSO, London

Department of Health and Social Security (1985b) *Social Work Decisions in Child Care: Recent Research Findings and Their Implications*, HMSO, London

Department of Health and Social Security (1987) *The Law on Child Care and Family Services*, Cm.62 HMSO, London

Department of Health and Social Security and Welsh Office (1988) *Working Together: a guide to arrangements for interagency cooperation for the protection of children from abuse*, HMSO, London

de Jong, A. (1988a) 'Childhood sexual abuse precipitating maternal hospitalization', *Child Abuse and Neglect*, 10, pp. 541-553

de Jong, A. (1988b) 'Maternal responses to the sexual abuse of their children', *Pediatrics*, 81, pp. 14-21

de Young, M. (1982) *The Sexual Victimization of Children*, McFarland, Jefferson, NC

de Young, M. (1991a) 'Women as mothers and wives in paternally incestuous families: Coping with role conflict', *Child Abuse and Neglect*, 18, pp. 83-85

de Young, M. (1991b) 'Immediate maternal reactions to the disclosure or discovery of incest', *Journal of Family Violence*, 9, pp. 21-33

Dingwall, R. (1986) 'The Jasmine Beckford Affair', *Modern Law Review*, 49, 4, Pp.489-507

Dingwall, R. (1989) 'Some problems about predicting child abuse and neglect', in Stevenson, O. ed. *Child Abuse: Public Policy and Professional Practice*, Harvester Wheatsheaf, London

Dingwall, R., Eekelaar, J. and Murray, T. (1983) *The Protection of Children: State Intervention and Family Life*, Blackwell, Oxford

Dobash, R.E. and Dobash, R.P. (1979) *Violence Against Wives: A Case Against the Patriarchy*, The Free Press, New York

Dobash, R.E. and Dobash, R.P. (1992) *Women, Violence and Social Control*, Routledge, London

Dobash, R., Carnie, J. and Waterhouse, L. (1993) 'Child Sexual Abusers: Recognition and Response' in Waterhouse, L. ed. *Child Abuse and Child Abusers: Protection and Prevention*, Jessica Kingsley, London

Domoney, L., Smale, G. and Warwick, J. (1989) *Shared Care: Towards developing partnership between health and Social Services staff and the people they serve. Final Report. HEA Feasibility Study*, National Institute for Social Work, London

Donzelot, J (1979), *The Policing of Families*, Hutchinson, London

Driscoll, J. and Evans, L. (1992) 'An Evaluation of the Participation of Parents and those with Parental Responsibility in the Child Protection Process in Suffolk', Suffolk, Social Services Department, Ipswich

Driver, E. and Droisen, A. eds. (1989) *Child Sexual Abuse: Feminist Perspectives*, Macmillan, London

Duckett, J. (1977) 'The coordination of welfare and health services in Australia', *Australian Journal of Social Issues*, 12, 3, Pp.188-199

Dunleavy, P. (1980) *Urban Political Analysis*, Macmillan, London

Eekelaar, J. and Dingwall, R. (1990) *The Reform of Child Care Law: A Practical Guide to the Children Act 1989*, Tavistock/Routledge, London

El-Faizy, M. (1994) 'Let down by the law', *The Guardian*, 20th August

Elton, A. (1988) 'Assessment of Families for Treatment', in Bentovim, A., Elton, A., Hildebrand, J, Tranter, M., and Vizard, E. eds. *Child Sexual Abuse within the Family: Assessment and Treatment; The work of the Great Ormond Street Sexual Abuse Team*, Wright, London

Erikson, E. (1968) *Identity, Youth and Crisis*, W.W. Norton & Co., New York.

Erickson, M., Egeland, B. and Pianta, R. (1989) 'Effects of maltreatment on the development of young children', in Cicchetti, D and Carlson, V. eds. *Child Maltreatment: Theory and Research on the Causes and Consequences of Child Abuse and Neglect*, Cambridge University Press, Cambridge

Erooga, M. (1994) 'Where the professional meets the personal', in Morrison, T., Erooga, M. and Beckett, R.C. eds. *Sexual Offending Against Children: Assessment and Treatment of Male Abusers*, Routledge, London

Everson, M. and Boat, B. (1989) 'False allegations of sexual abuse by children and adolescents' *American Academy of Child and Adolescent Psychiatry*, 28, (2) Pp.230-235

Everson, M., Hunter, W., Runyon, D., Edelsohn, G. and Coulter, M. (1989) 'Maternal support following disclosure of incest', *American Journal of Orthopsychiatry*, 59, pp. 197-207

Faller, K. (1989a) 'Why sexual abuse? An exploration of the intergenerational hypothesis', *Child Abuse and Neglect*, 13, Pp.543-548

Faller, K.C. (1989) *Child Sexual Abuse: An Interdisciplinary Manual for Diagnosis, Case Management and Treatment*, Macmillan, London

Farmer, E. (1993) 'The Impact of Child Protection Interventions: The Experiences of Parents and Children' in Waterhouse, L. ed. *Child Abuse and Child Abusers: Protection and Prevention*, Jessica Kingsley, London

Farmer, E. (1997) 'Protection and child welfare: striking the balance', in Parton, N. ed. *Child Protection and Family Support: Tensions, Contradictions and Possibilities*, Routledge, London

Farmer, E. and Owen, M. (1995) *Child Protection Practice: Private Risks and Public Remedies*, HMSO, London

Farmer, E. and Parker, R. (1991) *Trials and Tribulations*, HMSO, London

Farson, R. (1978) *Birthrights*, Penguin, Harmondsworth

Finkelhor, D. (1979) *Sexually Victimised Children*, The Free Press, New York

Finkelhor, D. (1984) *Child Sexual Abuse: New Theory and Research*, The Free Press, New York

Finkelhor, D. (1986) 'Prevention: A Review of Programs and Research', in Finkelhor, D. with Araji, S., Baron, L., Doyle Peters, S. and Wyatt, G.E. *A Sourcebook on Child Sexual Abuse*, Sage, London

Finkelhor, D. (1986) 'Abusers: Special Topics', in Finkelhor, D. with Araji, S., Baron, L, Peters, S.D. and Wyatt, G.E. *A Sourcebook on Child Sexual Abuse*, Sage,London

Finkelhor, D. (1991) 'The Scope of the Problem' in Murray, K and Gough, D.A. *Intervening in Child Sexual Abuse*, Scottish Academic Press, Edinburgh

Finkelhor, D. (1996) 'Long-term effects of sexual abuse', paper delivered at Child Abuse and Neglect Conference, Dublin, August

Finkelhor, D. and Baron, L. (1986) 'High Risk Children' in Finkelhor, D. with Araji, S., Baron, L., Peters, S.D. and Wyatt, G.E. *A Sourcebook on Child Sexual Abuse*, Sage, London

Finkelhor, D. and Browne, A. (1988) 'Assessing the Long-Term Impact of Child Sexual Abuse: A Review and Conceptualisation', in Hotaling, G.T., Finkelhor, D., Kirkpatrick, J.T. and Straus, M.A. eds. *Family Abuse and its Consequences*, Sage, London

Firestone, S. (1970) *The Dialectic of Sex*, Bantam, New York

Fisher, M. (1990), *Parental Participation in Case Conferences: Social Work in Partnership*, University of Bradford

Fisher, T. (1995) *A Systematic Knowledge Base in Child Protection: What Knowledge do Social Workers Use?* Department of Social Policy and Social Work, University of York, February

Fisher, T., Bingley Miller, L. and Sinclair, I. (1995) 'Which Children are Registered at Case Conferences', *British Journal of Social Work*, 25, Pp.191-207

Foucault, M. (1977), *Discipline and Punish: The Birth of the Prison*, Allen Lane, London

Foucault, M. (1980) 'Truth and Power', in Foucault, M. *Power/Knowledge: Selected Interviews and Other Writings 1972-1977*, Harvester Wheatsheaf, London

Foucault, M. (1980) *Power/Knowledge*, Harvester Wheatsheaf, London

Foucault, M. (1978,1990) *A History of Sexuality Vol.1*, Penguin, London

Fox-Harding, L. (1991a) 'The Children Act 1989 in Context: Four Perspectives in Child Care Law and Policy', *Journal of Social Welfare and Family Law*, No.3, Pp.179-193, and No.4, Pp.285-302

Fox-Harding, L. (1991b) *Perspectives in Child Care Policy*, Longman, London

Freeman, M.D.A. (1983) *The Rights and Wrongs of Children*, Francis Pinter, London

Freeman, M. (1989) 'Principles and processes of the law in child protection' in Stainton Rogers, W. *et al* eds. *Child Abuse and Neglect: Facing the Challenge*, Batsford/Open University Press, London

Freeman, M.D.A. (1992) *Children, Their Families and the Law: Working with the Children Act*, Macmillan, London

Frosh, S. (1988) 'No Man's Land?: the Role of Men Working with Sexually Abused Children', *British Journal of Guidance and Counselling*, 16, Pp.1-10

Frost, N. and Stein, M. (1989) *The Politics of Child Welfare*, Harvester Wheatsheaf, London

Frothingham, T.E., Barnett, R.A.M., Hobbs, C.J. and Wynne, J.A. (1993), 'Child sexual abuse in Leeds before and after Cleveland', *Child Abuse Review*, Vol.2, pp. 23-34

Fuller, R. (1992) *In Search of Prevention*, Avebury, Aldershot

Furby, L. Weinrott, M.R. and Blackshaw, L. (1989) 'Sex offender recidivism: a review', *Psychological Bulletin*, 105 (1) Pp.3-30

Furniss, T. (1983) 'Family process in the treatment of intra-familial child sexual abuse', *Journal of Family Therapy*, 5, Pp.263-278

Furniss, T. (1991) *The Multi-Professional Handbook of Child Sexual Abuse: Integrated Management, Therapy, and Legal Intervention*, Routledge, London

Gadsby Waters, J. (1992) *The Supervision of Child Protection Work*, Avebury, Aldershot

Galligan, D. (1992) 'Procedural Rights in Social Welfare' in Coote, A. ed. *The Welfare of Citizens: Developing New Procedural Rights*, IPPR, London

Gavey, N., Florence, J., Pezaro, S. and Tan, J. (1990) 'Mother-blaming, the perfect alibi: Family therapy and the mothers of incest survivors', *Journal of Feminist Family Therapy*, 2, pp. 1-25

Gelles, R.J. (1983) 'An exchange/social control theory' in Finkelhor, D., Gelles, R.J., Hotaling, G.T. and Straus, M.A. eds. *The Dark Side of Families*, Sage, Beverly Hills

Gerth, H and Mills, C.W. (1954) *Character and Social Structure*, Routledge and Kegan Paul, London

Giaretto, H. (1982) *Integrated Treatment of Child Sexual Abuse*, Palo Alto Science and Behaviour Books, California

Gibbons, J. (1997) 'Relating outcomes to objectives in child protection policy', in Parton, N. ed. *Child Protection and Family Support: Tensions, Contradictions and Possibilities*, Routledge, London

Gibbons, J., Conroy, S. and Bell, C. (1993) *Operation of Child Protection Registers, Report to the Department of Health*, Social Work Development Unit, University of East Anglia

Gibbons, J., Conroy, S. and Bell, C. (1995) *Operating the Child Protection System*, HMSO, London

Giddens, A. (1976) *New Rules of Sociological Method*, Hutchinson, London

Giddens, A. (1984) *The Constitution of Society*, Polity Press, Cambridge

Giddens, A. (1993) *New Rules of Sociological Method, 2nd Edition*, Polity Press, Cambridge

Gil, D. (1970) *Violence against Children*, Harvard University Press, Cambridge, Mass.

Gilbert, N. (1992) 'Social Constraints on Primary Prevention: The Case of Child Sexual Abuse' in Otto, H-U. and Flosser, G. eds. *How to Organize Prevention*, de Gruyter, Berlin

Giller, H., Gormley, C. and Williams, P. (1992) *The Effectiveness of Child Protection Procedures*, Social Information Systems Ltd.

Glaser, B. and Strauss, A. (1967) *The Discovery of Grounded Theory*, Aldine, Chicago

Glaser, D, and Frosh, S, (1993) *Child Sexual Abuse, 2nd Edition*, Macmillan, London

Glick, I. and Kessler, D. (1980) *Marital and Family Therapy*, Grune and Stratton, New York

Goffman, E. (1971) *The Presentation of Self in Everyday Life*, Pelican, London

Gomes-Schwartz, B., Horowitz, J.M. and Cardarelli, A.P. (1990) *Child Sexual Abuse: The Initial Effects*, Sage, London

Goodwin, J., McCarthy, T. and DiVasto, P. (1981) 'Prior incest in mothers of abused children', *Child Abuse and Neglect*, 5, pp. 87-95

Gordon, L. (1988) *Heroes of Their Own Lives: The Politics and History of Family Violence*, Virago, London

Gordon, M. (1989) 'The family environment of sexual abuse: A comparison of natal and stepfather abuse' *Child Abuse and Neglect*, 13, Pp.121-130

Gough, D. (1993) 'The Case For and Against Prevention' in Waterhouse, L. ed. *Child Abuse and Child Abusers: Protection and Prevention*, Jessica Kingsley, London

Gough, D., Boddy, F., Dunning, N. and Stone, F.(1987) *A longitudinal study of Child Abuse in Glasgow, Volume 1: the children who were registered*, University of Glasgow: Social Paediatric and Obstetric Research Unit.

Greenland, C. (1987) *Preventing CAN Deaths: An International Study of Deaths Due to Child Abuse and Neglect*, Tavistock, London

Griffin, C. (1985) *Typical Girls? Young Women from School to the Job Market*, Routledge and Kegan Paul, London

Griffin, C (1993) *Representations of Youth: the study of youth and adolescence in Britain and America*, Polity Press, Cambridge

Gruber, K. and Jones, R. (1983) 'Identifying determinants of risk of sexual victimization of youth', *Child Abuse and Neglect*, 7, Pp.17-24

Hall, L. and Lloyd, S. (1989) *Surviving Child Sexual Abuse*, Falmer, London

Hall, R., Clark, J., Giordano, P., Johnson, P. and van Roekel, M. (1977) 'Patterns of interorganisational relationships, *Administrative Science Quarterly*, 22, Pp.457-474

Hallett, C. (1989) 'Child abuse inquiries and public policy', in Stevenson, O. ed. *Child Abuse: Public Policy and Professional Practice*

Hallett, C. (1993) 'Working Together in Child Protection' in, Waterhouse, L. ed. *Child abuse and Child Abusers*, Jessica Kingsley, London

Hallett, C. (1995) *Interagency Coordination in Child Protection*, HMSO, London

Hallett, C. and Birchall, E. (1992) *Coordination and Child Protection: a Review of the Literature*, HMSO, Edinburgh

Hallett, C. and Stevenson, O. (1980) *Child Abuse: Aspects of Interprofessional Co-Operation*, George Allen and Unwin, London

Hansard, House of Commons, 29th June, 1987

Hardiker, P. (1981) 'Heart or head: the function and role of knowlege in social work', *Issues in Social Work Education* 1 (2) pp. 85-111

Hardiker, P., Exton, K. and Barker, M. (1991) *Policies and Practices in Preventative Child Care*, Avebury, Aldershot

Harvey, L. (1990) *Critical Social Research*, Unwin Hyman, London

Haugaard, J. J. and Reppucci, N. D. (1988) *The Sexual Abuse of Children*, Jossey-Bass, London

Heard, D.H. and Lake, B. (1997) *The Challenge of Attachment for Caregiving*, Routledge, London

Hearn, B. (1997) 'Putting child and family support and protection into practice', in Parton, N. ed. *Child Protection and Family Support: Tensions, Contradictions and Possibilities*, Routledge, London

Helfer, R.E. and Schmidt, R. (1976) 'The community-based child abuse and neglect program' in Helfer, R.E. and Kempe, C.H. eds. (1976) *Child Abuse and neglect, the family and the community*, Balinger, Cambridge, Mass.

Hendessi, M. (1992) *4 in 10: Report on Young Women who become Homeless as a Result of Sexual Abuse*, CHAR, London

Heraud, B. (1970) *Sociology and Social Work*, Pergamon, London

Herman, J. (1981) *Father-Daughter Incest*, Havard University Press, Cambridge, Mass.

Herman. J. (1994) *Trauma and Recovery: From Domestic Abuse to Political Terror*, Harper Collins, London

Herman, J. and Hirschman, L. (1977) 'Father-daughter incest', *Signs*, 2, Pp.735-756

Hevey, D. and Kenward, H (1989) 'The Effects of Child Sexual Abuse' in Stainton Rogers, W. *et al* eds. *Child Abuse and Neglect: Facing the Challenge*, Batsford/Open University Press, London

Higginson, S. (1990) 'Under the influence', *Social Work Today*, 22 (14), pp. 20-21

Higginson, S. (1992) 'Decision-making in the assessment of risk in child abuse cases', M.Phil Thesis, Cranfield Insitute of Technology

Hill, M. (1990) 'The manifest and latent lessons of child abuse inquiries' *British Journal of Social Work*, 20, 3, Pp.197-214

Hjern, D. (1982) 'Implementation research: the link gone missing', *Journal of Public Policy*, 2, 3, Pp.301-308

Holt, J. (1975) *Escape From Childhood*, Penguin, Harmondsworth

Home Office and Department of Health (1992) *Memorandum of Good Practice on Video Recorded Interviews with Child Witnesses for Criminal Proceedings*, HMSO, London

Homan, R. (1991) *The Ethics of Social Research*, Longman, London

Hooper, C-A. (1987) 'Getting him off the hook', *Trouble and Strife*, 12, Pp.20-25

Hooper, C-A, (1992) *Mothers Surviving Child Sexual Abuse*, Routledge, London

Hooper, C-A. (1995) 'Women's and children's experiences of sexual violence: Rethinking the links', Women's Studies International Forum, Vol.18, Pp.349-360

Hooper, C-A. (1996) 'Men's violence and relationship breakdown: Can violence be dealt with as an exception to the rule', in Hallett, C. ed. Women and Social Policy, Harvester Wheatsheaf, London

Hooper, C-A. and Humphreys, C. (1998) 'Women whose children have been sexually abused: Reflections on a debate', *British Journal of Social Work*

Hooper, C-A., Koprowska, J. and McClusky, U. (1997) 'Groups for women survivors of childhood sexual abuse: the implications for attachment theory', *Journal of Social Work Practice*

Howe, D. (1986) *Social Workers and Their Practice in Welfare Bureaucracies*, Gower, Aldershot

Howe, D. (1990) 'The client's view in context', in Carter, P., Jeffs, T, Smith, M. eds. *Social Work and Social Welfare: Yearbook 2*, Open University Press, Milton Keynes

Howe, D. (1991a) 'The Family and the Therapist; Towards a Sociology of Social Work Method' in Davies, M. ed. *The Sociology of Social Work*, Routledge, London

Howe, D. (1991b) 'Knowledge, Power, and the Shape of Social Work Practice' in Davies, M. ed. *The Sociology of Social Work*, Routledge, London

Hudson, A. (1989) 'Troublesome Girls: towards alternative definitions and policies' in Cain, M. ed., *Growing Up Good: Policing the Behaviour of Girls in Europe*, Sage, London

Hudson, A. (1992) 'The child sexual abuse 'industry' and gender relations in social work', in Langan, M. and Day, I. eds. *Women, Oppression and Social Work*, Routledge, London

Hudson, B. (1984) 'Femininity and Adolescence', in McRobbie, A. and Nava, M. eds. Gender and Generation, Macmillan, London

Hudson, B. (1989) 'Collaboration in Social Welfare: a framework for analysis' *Policy and Politics*, 15, Pp.175-182

Humphreys, C. (1992) 'Disclosure of child sexual assault: implications for mothers', *Australian Social Work*, 45, 3, Pp.27-35

Illich, I. (1976) *Limits to Medicine: Medical Nemesis*, Penguin, London

Independent 24.2.94

Jagger, A.M. (1988) *Feminist Politics and Human Nature*, Rowman and Littlefield, Towata, NJ

James, J., Womack, W. and Strauss, P. (1978) 'Physical reporting of sexual abuse of children', *Journal of American Medical Association*, 240, Pp.1145-1146

Johnson, M.M. (1988) *Strong Mothers, Weak Wives: The Search for Gender Equality*, University of California Press, London

Johnston, J. (1992) *Mothers of Incest Survivors: Another Side of the Story*, Indiana University Press, Bloomington, Indiana

Jones, D.P.H. (1991) 'Interviewing Children', in Murray, K. and Gough, D.A. *Intervening in Child Sexual Abuse*, Scottish Academic Press, Edinburgh

Jones, D, and McGraw, J.M. (1987) 'Reliable and fictitious accounts of sexual abuse of children', *Journal of Interpersonal Violence*, 2, pp. 27-45

Jones, D. and Seig, A. (1988) 'Child sexual abuse allegations in custody or visitation disputes', in Nicholson, B. ed. *Sexual Abuse Allegations in Custody and Visitation Disputes*, American Bar Association, Washington DC

Jones, J., George, E., Goldsmith, L, Hussell, C. and Llewellyn, G. (1986) *Child Abuse Policy, Practice and Procedures*, London Borough of Westminster

Jones, M.A. (1985) *A Second Chance for Families*, Child Welfare League of America, New York

Jordan, B. (1997) 'Partnership with service users in child protection and family support', in Parton, N. ed. *Child Protection and Family Support: Tensions, Contradictions and Possibilities*, Routledge, London

Joseph, Y. (1995) 'Child protection rights: can an international declaration be an effective instrument for protecting children', in Cloke, C. and Davies, M. *Participation and Empowerment in Child Protection*, Pitman Publishing, London

Justice, B. and Justice, R. (1979) *The Broken Taboo: Sex in the Family*, Human Sciences Press, New York

Kadushin, A. (1977) *Consultation in Social Work*, Columbia University Press, New York

Kant, I. (1953) *Critique of Pure Reason*, Macmillan, New York

Katz, I. (1995) 'Approaches to empowerment and participation in child protection', in Cloke, C. and Davies, M. eds. *Participation and Empowerment in Child Protection*, Pitman, London

Keddie, N. (1971) 'Classromom Knowledge' in Young, M.D.F. *Knowledge and Social Control*, Collier, London

Kelly, A. (1991) 'The "new" managerialism in the social services' in Carter, P., Jeffs, T. and Smith, M. eds. *Social Work and Social Welfare, Yearbook 3*, Open University Press, Milton Keynes

Kelly, L. (1988) *Surviving Sexual Violence*, Polity Press, Cambridge

Kelly, L and Radford, J. (1996) "Nothing really happened': the invalidation of women's experiences of sexual violence', in Hester, M., Kelly, L and Radford, J. eds. Women, *Violence and Male Power*, Open University Press, Buckingham

Kelly, L., Regan, L. and Burton, S. (1991) *An Exploratory Study of the Prevalence of Sexual Abuse in a Sample of 16-21 Year Olds*, Child Abuse Studies Unit, Polytechnic of North London

Kelly, L., Wingfield, R., Burton, S. and Regan, L. (1995) *Splintered Lives: Sexual Exploitation of Children in the Context of Children's Rights and Child Protection*, Child and Woman Abuse Studies Unit, University of North London

Kendall-Tackett, K.A., Williams, L.M. and Finkelhor, D. (1993) 'Impact of sexual abuse on children. A synthesis and review of recent empirical studies', *Psychological Bulletin*, 113, 1, Pp.164-180

Kersten, J. (1989) 'The institutional control of girls and boys' in Cain, M. ed., *Growing Up Good: Policing the Behaviour of Girls in Europe*, Sage, London

Kettle, J. (1990) *Survey of Treatment Facilities for Abused Children and of Treatment Facilities for Young Sexual Abusers of Children*, National Children's Home, London

Kimmel, A.J. (1988) *Ethics and Values in Applied Social Research*, Sage, Newbury Park, Ca.

King, M. (1996) *A Better World for Children: Explorations in Morality and Authority*, Routledge, London

King, M. and Trowell, J. (1992) *Children's Welfare and the Law: The Limits of Legal Intervention*, Sage, London

Kirk, S.K. (1998) 'Influences on social workers' child protection practice in cases involving the familial sexual abuse of adolescent girls', D.Phil. thesis, Department of Social Policy and Social Work, University of York (unpublished)

Kirkwood, C. (1993) *Leaving Abusive Partners: From the Scars of Survival to the Wisdom for Change*, Sage, London

Kopp, F.H. (1988) *Remedial Intervention in Adolescent Sex Offences: Nine Program Descriptions*, Safe Society Press, Orwell

Kubler-Ross, E. (1970) *On Death and Dying*, Tavistock, London

La Fontaine, J. (1990) Child Sexual Abuse, Polity Press, Cambridge

Lakatos, I. (1970) 'Falsification and the methodology of scientific research programmes', in Lakatos, I. and Musgrave, A. eds. *Criticism and the Growth of Knowledge*, Cambridge University Press, Cambridge

Lane, S. (1991) 'The sexual abuse cycle', in Ryan, G. and Lane, S. eds. *Juvenile Sexual Offending: Causes, Consequences and Correction*, D.C. Heath, Lexington

Langmade, C.J. (1983) 'The impact of pre- and post pubertal onset of incest experiences in adult women as measured by sex anxiety, sex guilt, sexual satisfaction and sexual behavior', *Dissertation Abstracts International*, 44, 917B

Lasch, C. (1977) *Haven in a Heartless World: The Family Besieged*, Basic Books, New York

Lave, J. (1986) 'The values of quantification', in Law, J. ed. *Power, Action and Belief: A New Sociology of Knowledge?* Routledge and Kegan Paul, London

Lealman, G.T., Haigh, D., Phillips, J.M., Sloan, J. and Ord-Smith, C. (1983) 'Prediction and prevention of child abuse - an empty hope', *The Lancet*, 8339, pp. 1423-1424

Leeds City Council, Project Management Group (1992) *Children in Need Project Report*, 26th October

Lees, C.A. (1981) 'Do Life Events Contribute to Rape Victim Vulnerability', paper presented at the 8th Annual Conference for Women in Psychology, Boston, March

Lees, S. (1986) *Losing Out: Sexuality and Adolescent Girls*, Hutchinson, London

Lees, S. (1996) 'Unreasonable doubt: The outcomes of rape trials', in Hester, M., Kelly, L and Radford, J. eds. *Women, Violence and Male Power*, Open University Press, Buckingham

Lees, S. (1997) *Ruling Passions: Sexual Violence, Reputation and the Law*, Open University Press, Buckingham

Levine, S. and White, P. (1961) 'Exchange as a conceptual framework for the study of interorganisational relationships', *Administrative Science Quarterly*, 5, Pp.583-601

Liddle, J. and Joshi, R. (1986) *Daughters of Independence: Gender, Caste and Class in India*, Red Books, London

Lincoln, Y.S. and Denzin, N.K. (1994) 'The fifth moment', in Denzin, N.K. and Lincoln, Y.S. *Handbook of Qualitative Research*, Sage, London

Lipsky, M. (1980) *Street-level Bureaucracy*, Russell Sage, New York

London Borough of Greenwich (1987) *A Child in Mind: Protection of Children in a Responsible Society. Report of the Commission of Inquiry into the Circumstances Surrounding the Death of Kimberley Carlile*, London Borough of Greenwich

Lonsdale, G. (1991) 'A Survey of Parental Participation at Initial Child Protection Case Conferences'

Macfarlane, K. (1978) 'Sexual abuse of children', in Chapman, J.R. and Gates, M. eds. *The Victimisation of Women*, Sage, Beverly Hills, Ca.

Macleod. M. and Saraga, E. (1988) 'Against Orthodoxy', *New Statesman*, 1st July

Macleod, M. and Saraga, E. (1991) 'Clearing a path through the undergrowth: a feminist reading of recent literature on child sexual abuse', in Carter, P., Jeffs, T. and Smith, M.K. eds. *Social Work and Social Welfare*, Open University Press, Milton Keynes

Madge, N. (1983a) 'An Introduction to Families at Risk' in, Madge, N. ed. *Families at Risk*, Heinemann, London

Madge, N. (1983b) 'Identifying families at risk', in Madge, N. ed. *Families at Risk*, Heinemann, London

Maletsky, B.M. (1980) 'Self-referred vs. court referred sexually deviant patients: Success with covert sensitization', *Behaviour Therapy*, 11, pp. 306-314

Maletzky, B.M. (1991) *Treating the Sexual Offender*, Sage, Newbury Park

Marsh, P. and Fisher, M. (1992) *Good Intentions: Developing Partnership in Social Services*, Joseph Rowntree Trust, York

Marshall, W.L. and Barbaree, H.E. (1988) 'The long term evaluation of a behavioural treatment program for child molesters', *Behaviour Research and Therapy*, 26, (6), Pp.499-511

Marx, K. (1968) 'The Eighteenth Brumaire of Louis Bonaparte' in Marx, K. and Engels, F. *Selected Works in One Volume*, Lawrence and Wishart, London

Marx, K. (1977) *The Economic and Philisophic Manuscripts of 1844*, Lawrence and Wishart, London

May, T. (1993) *Social Research: Issues, Methods and Process*, Open University Press, Buckingham

McIntyre, K. (1981) 'Role of mothers in father-daughter incest: A feminist analysis', *Social Work*, 26, pp. 426-466

McKeganey, N.P. and Hunter, D.J. (1986) 'How 'they' decide: exploring professional decision-making' *Research, Policy and Planning*, 6,1, Pp.15-19

McLachlan, G. ed. (1981) *Matters of moment*, OUP, London

Merchant, A. and Luckham, S. (1991) 'A Study of Parental and Child Participation in CP Conferences in mid-Essex'

Meiselman, K. (1978) *Incest*, Jossey-Bass, San Francisco

Merrick, D. (1996) *Social Work and Child Abuse*, Routledge, London

Miles, M.B. and Huberman, M. (1984) *Qualitative Data Analysis*, Sage, Beverley Hills, Ca.

Miles. R. (1992) *The Rites of Man: Love, Sex and Death in the Making of the Male*, Paladin, London

Mills, C. W., (1940) in Manis, J.G. and Meltzer, B.N. eds. (1972) *Symbolic Interaction, 2nd Edition*, Allyn and Bacon, Boston

Mitterauer (1992) *A History of Youth*, Blackwell, Oxford

Monck, E., Sharland, E., Bentovim, A., Goodall, G., Hyde, C. and Lwin, R. (1995) Child Sexual Abuse: A Descriptive and Treatment Study, HMSO, London

Moore, J.G. (1992) *The ABC of Child Protection*, Ashgate, Aldershot

Moran-Ellis, J. (1996) 'Close to Home: The Experience of Researching Child Sexual Abuse', in Hester, M., Kelly, L, and Radford, J. eds. *Women, Violence and Male Power*, Open University Press, Buckingham

Morrison, T. (1994) 'Context, constraints an considerations for practice', in Morrison, T., Erooga, M. and Beckett, R.C. eds. *Sexual Offending Against Children: Assessment and Treatment of Male Abusers*, Routledge, London

Morrison, T., Blakey, C., Butler, A., Fallon, S. and Leith, A. (1990) *Children and Parental Participation in Case Conferences*, NSPCC, London

Morrison, T., Erooga, M. and Beckett, R.C. eds. (1994) *Sexual Offending Against Children: Assessment and Treatment of Male Abusers*, Routledge, London

Mrazek, P., Lynch, M. and Bentovim, A. (1981), 'Recognition of child sexual abuse in the United Kingdom', in Mrazek, P. and Kempe, C. eds. *Sexually abused children and their families*, Pergammon, Oxford

Mulford and Rogers (1982) 'Definitions and models', in Rogers, D. and Whetten, D. *Interorganisational coordination: theory, research and implementation*, Iowa State University Press, Iowa

Murcott, A. (1980) 'The social construction of teenage pregnancy', *Sociology of Health and Illness*, 2(1), pp.1-23

Murray, K. and Gough, D.A. (1991) *Intervening in Child Sexual Abuse*, Scottish Academic Press, Edinburgh

Myer, M. (1984) 'A new look at mothers of incest victims', *Journal of Social Work and Human Sexuality*, 3, Pp.47-58

Nash, C.L. and West, D.J. (1986) 'Sexual molestation of young girls: a retrospective survey', in West, D.J. ed. *Sexual Victimisation*, Gower, Aldershot

Nasjleti, M. (1980) 'Suffering in silence: the male incest victim', *Child Welfare*,59. pp.269-275

Nava, M (1984) 'Drawing the Line: A Feminist Response to Adult-Child Sexual Relations', in McRobbie, A. and Nava, M. eds. *Gender and Generation*, Macmillan, London

Nelson, B. (1984) *Making an issue of child abuse: political agenda setting for social problems*, University of Chicago Press, Chicago

Nelson, S. (1987) *Incest: Fact and Myth*, Strathmullion, Edinburgh

North Yorkshire ACPC (1991) 'Family Participation in Child Protection Conferences'

Norton, A. and Rogers, S. (1981) 'The health service and local government services' in McLachlan, G. ed.*Matters of moment*, OUP, London

Oakley, A. (1980), *Women Confined: Towards a Sociology of Childbirth*, Martin Robertson, London

Oates, R., Forest, D. and Peacock, A. (1985) 'Self-esteem of abused children' *Child Abuse and Neglect*, 9 Pp.159-163

O'Hagan, K. (1989) *Working with Child Sexual Abuse*, Open University Press, Milton Keynes

Ollendorf, R. 'The rights of adolescents'(1972) in Adams, P., Berg, L., Berger, N. Duane, M., Neill, A.S., and Ollendorf, R., *Children's Rights: towards the liberation of the child*, Panther, London

Oliver, J.E., (1993) 'Intergenerational transmission of child abuse: rates, research and clinical implications' *American Journal of Psychiatry*, 150 (9) Sep. Pp.1315-1324

Oppenheimer, R., Howells, K., Palmer, R.L. and Chaloner, D.A. (1985) 'Adverse sexual experience in childhood and clinical eating disorders: a preliminary description', *Journal of Psychiatric Research*, 19, 2/3. Pp.357-361

Orbach, S. (1997) 'Revenge Tragedy', *Guardian Weekend*, August 16th

Orwell, G. (1949) *Nineteen Eighty-Four*, Penguin, London

O'Toole, R., Turbett, P. and Nalepka, C. (1983) 'Theories, professional knowledge and diagnosis', in Finkelhor, D., Gelles, R., Hotlaing, G. and Straus, M. eds. *The Dark Side of Families*, Sage, Beverly Hills, Ca.

Otto, H-U and Flosser, G. eds. (1992), *How to Organize Prevention*, de Gruyter, Berlin

Owen, M. (1992) *Social Justice and Children in Care*, Avebury, Aldershot

Packman, J. (1993) 'From prevention to partnership: child welfare services across three decades' *Children and Society*, 7 (2), Pp.183-195

Packman, J. and Randall, J. (1989) 'Decision-making at the gateway to care', in Stevenson, O. ed. *Child Abuse: Public Policy and Professional Practice*, Harvester Wheatsheaf, London

Palmer, R.L., Oppenheimer, R., Dignon, A. *et al* (1990) 'Childhood sexual experience with adults reported by women with eating disorders: an extended series', *British Journal of Psychiatry*, 156, Pp.699-703

Panorama, BBC, 10.3.97

Parker, R.A. ed. (1980) *Caring for Separated Children*, Macmillan, London

Parker,H. and Parker, S (1986) 'Father-daughter sexual abuse: an emerging perspective', *American Journal of Orthopsychiatry*, 56, 4, Pp.531-549

Parsloe, P. and Stevenson, O. (1978) *Social Services Teams: The Practitioners View*, HMSO, London

Parton, C. and Parton, N. (1989a) 'Women, the family and child protection' *Critical Social Policy*, 8, 3, Pp.431-452

Parton, C. and Parton, N. (1989b) 'Child protection, the law and dangerousness', in Stevenson, O. ed. *Child Abuse: Public Policy and Professional Practice*, Harvester Wheatsheaf, London

Parton, N. (1985) *The Politics of Child Abuse*, Macmillan, Basingstoke

Parton, N. (1991) *Governing the Family: Child Care, Child Protection and the State*, Macmillan, London

Parton, N. ed. (1997) *Child Protection and Family Support: Tensions, Contradictions and Possibilities*, Routledge, London

Parton, N. (1997) 'Child protection and family support: current debates and future prospects', in Parton, N. ed. *Child Protection and Family Support: Tensions, Contradictions and Possibilities*, Routledge, London

Parton, N., Thorpe, D. and Wattam, C. (1997) *Child Protection, Risk and the Moral Order*, Macmillan, London

Patton, M.(1990) *Qualitative Evaluation and Research Methods*, Sage, London

Payne, C. and Scott, T. (1982) *Developing supervision of teams in Field and Residential Social Work (part 1)*, National Institute of Social Work Papers (12)

Payne, M. (1979) *Power, Authority and Responsibility in Social Services, Social Work in Area Teams*, Macmillan, London

Perrow, C. (1979) *Complex Organisations, 2nd Edition*, Glenview, Illinois

Peters, S.D., Wyatt, G.E. and Finkelhor, D. (1986) 'Prevalence', in Finkelhor, D. and Associates, *A Source book on Child Sexual Abuse*, Sage, Beverly Hills, Ca.

Pfohl, S. (1977) 'The "Discovery" of child abuse' *Social Problems* 24, 2, Pp.310-323

Phoenix, A (1991) *Young Mothers*, Polity Press, London

Pinker, R. (1990) *Social Work in an Enterprise Society*, Routledge, London

Pithouse, A. (1987) *Social Work: The Social Organisation of an Invisible Trade*, Avebury, Aldershot

Pithouse, A. (1990) 'Guardians of autonomy: work orientations in a social work office' in Carter, P., Jeffs, T. and Smith, M. eds. *Social Work and Social Welfare, Yearbook 2*, Open University Press, Milton Keynes

Pretky, R. and Burgess, A.W. (1990) 'Rehabilitation of child molesters: a cost benefit analysis', *American Journal of Orthopsychiatry*, 60, (19), Pp.108-117

Pringle, K. (1993) 'Child sexual abuse committed by welfare personnel: British and European perspectives', Paper presented at Fourth European Conference on Child Abuse and Neglect, Padova, Italy

Pringle, K. (1995) *Men, Masculinities and Social Welfare*, UCL Press, London

Prior, V., Glaser, D. and Lynch, M.A. (1997) 'Responding to Child Sexual Abuse: The Criminal Justice System', *Child Abuse Review*, Vol.6 Pp.128-140

Radford, J. and Stanko, E.A. (1996) 'Violence against women and children: the contradictions of crime control under patriarchy', in Hester, M., Kelly, L and Radford, J. eds. *Women, Violence and Male Power*, Open University Press, Buckingham

Renvoize, J. (1993) *Innocence Destroyed: a study of child sexual abuse*, Routledge, London

Rhodes, R.A.W. (1981) *Control and Power in central-local government relations*, Gower, Aldershot

Rhodes, R.A.W. (1986) *The national world of local government*, Allen and Unwin, London

Rhodes, R.A.W. (1988) *Beyond Westminster and Whitehall*, Unwin Hyman, London

Rhodes, R.A.W. (1990) 'Policy networks: a British perspective', *Journal of Theoretical Politics*, 2, 3, Pp.293-317

Rich, A. (1977) *Of Woman Born: Motherhood as Experience and Institution*, Virago, London

Richardson, S. (1989) 'Child sexual abuse: the challenge for the organisation' in Carter, P., Jeffs, T. and Smith, M. eds. *Social Work and Social Welfare, Yearbook 1*, Open University Press, Milton Keynes

Rickford, F. (1993) 'No room for doubt' *Community Care*, (1989), 21 Oct. Pp.18-19

Roberts, J. and Taylor, C. (1993) 'Sexually abused children and young people speak out', in Waterhouse, L. ed. *Child Abuse and Child Abusers: Protection and Prevention*, Jessica Kingsley, London

Rock, P. (1979) *The Making of Symbolic Interactionism*, Macmillan, London

Roche, J. (1989) 'Children's Rights and the Welfare of the Child' in Stainton Rogers, W *et al Child Abuse and Neglect: Facing the Challenge*, Batsford/Open University Press, London

Roper, M. and Tosh, J. (1991) 'Introduction: Historians and the Politics of Masculinity', in Roper, M. and Tosh, J. ed. *Manful Assertions: Masculinities in Britain since 1800*, Routledge, London

Ruane, J.M. (1993) 'Tolerating force: a contextual analysis of the meaning of tolerance' *Sociological Inquiry*, 63 (3) Pp.293-304

Ruddick, S. (1984) 'Maternal Thinking', in Trblicot, J. ed. *Mothering: Essays in Feminist Theory*, Rowman and Allanheld, Towota, NJ.

Runyan, D.K. et al (1988) 'Impact of legal interventions on sexually abused children', *The Journal of Paediatrics*, 113, 4, Pp.647-653

Russell, D. (1984) *Sexual Exploitation, Rape, Child Sexual Abuse and Workplace Harrassment*, Sage, London

Russell, D.E.H. (1982) *Rape in Marriage*, Macmillan, New York

Russell, D.E.H. (1986) *The Secret Trauma: Incest in the Lives of Girls and Women*, Basic Books, New York

Sack, W., Mason, R. and Higgins, J. (1985) 'The single-parent family and abusive child punishment' *American Journal of Orthopsychiatry*, 55, Pp.253-259

Salmon, P. (1992) 'The Peer Group' in Coleman, J. ed. *The School Years: Current Issues in the Socialization of young People*, Routledge, London

Sampson, A. (1994) *Acts of Abuse: Sex Offenders and the Criminal Justice System*, Routledge, London

Sapir, E. (1966) *Culture, Language and Personality*, University of California Press, Berkeley, Ca.

Satyamurti, C. (1981) *Occupational Survival*, Blackwell, London

Saunders, P. (1984) 'Rethinking local politics' in Boddy, M. and Fudge, C. eds. *Local Socialism*, Macmillan, London

Schmidt, S.M. and Kochan, T.A. (1977), 'Interorganisational relationships: patterns and motivations', *Administrative Science Quarterly*, 22, Pp.220-234

Schutz, A. (1972) *The Phenomenology of the Social World*, Heinemann, London

Scraton. P. ed. *'Childhood' in 'Crisis'*, (1997) University College London Press, London

Seebohm Report (1968) *Report of the Committee on Local Authority and Allied Social Services*, Cmnd 3703, HMSO, London

Sharland, E., Jones, D., Aldgate, J. Seal, H. and Croucher, M. (1993), *Professional Intervention in Child Sexual Abuse: Report to the Department of Health*, Department of Applied Social Studies and Social Research, University of Oxford

Sharland, E., Jones, D., Aldgate, J., Seal, H. and Croucher, M. (1995) *Professional Intervention in Child Sexual Abuse*, HMSO, London

Sharpe, S. (1976) *'Just Like a Girl'*, Penguin, London

Sheldon, B. (1988) 'The psychological sequelae of sexual abuse', paper presented to 7th International Congress on Child Abuse and Neglect, Rio de Janeiro, September

Sibeon, R. (1991a) 'A Contemporary Sociology of Social Work', in Davies, M. ed. *The Sociology of Social Work*, Routledge, London

Sibeon, R. (1991b) 'The Construction of a Contemporary Sociology of Social Work', in Davies, M. (1991), *The Sociology of Social Work*, Routledge, London

Siegal, J.M., Sorenson, S.B., Golding, J.M., Burnham, M.A. and Stein, J.A. (1987) 'The prevalence of childhood sexual assault: The Los Angeles epidemiologic catchment area project', *American Journal of Epidemiology*, 126, 26, Pp.1141-1153

Sirles, E. and Franke, P. (1989) 'Factors influencing mothers' reactions to intrafamily sexual abuse', *Child Abuse and Neglect*, 13, pp. 131-139

Skinner, A., Platts, H. and Jill, B. (1983) *Disaffection from school: issues and interagency reponses*, National Youth Bureau, Leicester

Smart, C. 1989) *Feminism and the Power of Law*, Routledge, London

Smith, G. (1995) 'Assessing protectiveness in cases of child sexual abuse', in Reder, P. and Lucey, C. eds. *Assessment of Parenting*, Routledge, London

Smith, M. and Grocke, M. (1995) *Normal Family Sexuality and Sexual Knowledge in Children*, Royal College of Psychiatrists/Gorkhill Press, London

Social Services Committee (HoC 360) (1984) Children in Care, HMSO, London

Social Services Inspectorate (1992) *The Children Act, 1989: Court Orders Study: a study of local decision making about public court applications*, HMSO, London

Squires, P. (1990), *Anti-Social Policy: Welfare, Ideology and the Disciplinary State*, Harvester Wheatsheaf, London

Stainton Rogers, W., Hevey, D. and Ash, E. (1989) *Child Abuse and Neglect: Facing the Challenge*, Batsford/Open University Press, London

Stanley, L. and Wise, S. (1983) *Breaking Out: Feminist Consciousness and Feminist Research*, Routledge and Kegan Paul, London

Steele, B.F. (1976) 'Experience with an interdisciplinary context' in Helfer, R.E. and Kempe, C.H. eds. *Child Abuse and neglect: the family and the community*, Balinger, Cambridge, Mass.

Steele, B. (1986) 'Notes on the lasting effects of early child abuse throughout the life cycle' *Child Abuse and Neglect*, 10 Pp.283-291

Stein, J.A., Golding, J.M., Siegal, J.M., Burnam, A.M and Sorenson, S.B. (1988) 'Long term psychological sequalae of child sexual abuse: The Los Angeles Epidemiologic Catchment Area Study', in Wyatt, G.E. and Powell, G.J. eds. *Lasting Effects of Child Sexual Abuse*, Sage, Newbury Park

Stevenson, O. (1988) 'Multidisciplinary work - where next?', *Child Abuse Review*, 2,1,Pp.5-9

Stevenson, O. ed. (1989) *Child Abuse: Public Policy and Professional Practice*, Harvester Wheatsheaf, London

Stevenson, O. (1989) 'Reflections on social work practice' in Stevenson, O. ed. *Child Abuse: Public Policy and Professional Practice*, Harvester Wheatsheaf, London

Strauss, A. and Corbin, J. (1994) 'Grounded theory methodology: An overview', in Denzin, N.K. and Lincoln, Y.S. eds. *Handbook of Qualitative Research*, Sage, London

Sullivan, M. (1987) *Sociology and Social Welfare*, Allen and Unwin, London

Taylor, S. and Godfrey, M. (1991) 'Parental Involvement in Child Protection Conferences, an evaluation of the pilot project', North Tyneside Social Services Department

Thorburn, J., Brandon, M. and Lewis, A. (1997) 'Need, risk and significant harm', in Parton, N. ed. *Child Protection and Family Support: Tensions, Contradictions and Possibilities*, Routledge, London

Thorburn, J., Lewis, A., and Shemmings, D. (1995), *Paternalism or Partnership? Family Involvement in the Child Protection Process*, HMSO, London

Thorpe, D. (1991) 'Patterns of child protection intervention and service delivery: report of a pilot project', Research Report No.4, Crime Research Unit, University of Western Australia

Thorpe, D. (1994) *Evaluating Child Protection*, Open University Press, Buckingham

Tibbitt, J. (1983) 'Health and personal social services in the UK: interorganisational behaviour and service development', in Williamson, A. and Room, G. *Welfare States in Britain*, Heinemann, London

Tilley, N. and Burke, R. (1988) 'Acting rationally: child abuse registrations', *Community Care* 8.12 pp16-17

The Times 24,3,94

Toren, N. (1972) *Social Work: The Case of a Semi-Profession*, Sage, London

Twigg, J. ed. (1992) *Carers: Research and Practice*, HMSO, London

Twigg, J. and Atkin, K. (1994) *Carers Perceived: Policy and Practice in Informal Care*, Open University Press, Buckingham

Veerman, P.E. (1992) *The Rights of the Child and the Changing Image of Childhood*, Martinus Nijhoff, Amsterdam

Vizard, E. and Tranter, M. (1988a) 'Helping young children to describe experiences of child sexual abuse' in Bentovim A. et al *Child Sexual Abuse Within the Family: Assessment and Treatment*, Wright, London

Vizard, E. and Tranter, M. (1988b) 'Recognition and assessment of child sexual abuse', in Bentovim A., Elton, A., Hidebrand, J., Tranter, M. and Vizard, E. eds. *Child Sexual Abuse within the Family: Assessment and Treatment*, Wright, London

Vollmer, H.M. and Mills, D.L. (1966), *Professionalization*, Prentice-Hall, Eagelwood Cliffs, NJ

Wakefield, H. and Underwager, R. (1988) *Accusations of Child Sexual Abuse*, Charles H. Thomas, Illinois

Waldby, C. (1985) 'Breaking the silence: a report based upon the findings of the war against incest phone-in survey', Honeysett, Sydney

Warren, R. (1973) 'Comprehensive planning and coordination – some functional aspects' *Social Problems*, 20 Pp.396-419

Warren, R. (1973) 'Comprehensive planning and coordination – some functional aspects', *Social Problems*, 20, Pp.355-364

Warren, R., Rose, S. and Bergunder, A. (1974) *The structure of urban reform*, Lexington Books, Lexington, Mass.

Waterhouse, L. ed. (1993) Child Abuse and Child Abusers: Protection and Prevention, Jessica Kingsley, London

Waterhouse, L. and Carnie, J. (1992) 'Assessing child protection risk', *British Journal of Social Work*, 22, pp. 47-60

Waterhouse, L. and Pitcairn, T. (1991) The Effect of Social Worker/Family Relationships on Child Abuse Case Outcome, ESRC Report R000231436 November

Wattam, C. (1991) 'Disclosure: the child's perspective, A research study', NSPCC evaluation (unpublished)

Wattam, C. (1992) *Making a Case in Child Protection*, NSPCC/Longman, London

Wattam, C. (1997a) 'Can filtering processes be rationalised?', in Parton, N. ed. *Child Protection and Family Support: Tensions, Contradictions and Posibilities*, Routledge, London

Wattam, C. (1997b) 'Is Criminalisation of Child Harm and Injury in the Interests of the Child?', *Children and Society*, Vol.11, Pp.97-107

Wattenberg, E. (1985) 'In a different light: A feminist perspective on the role of mothers in father-daughter incest', *Child Welfare*, 64, pp. 203-211

Webb, A. (1991) 'Coordination: a problem in public sector management', *Policy and Politics*, 19, 4, Pp.229-241

Weber, M. (1964) *The Theory of Social and Economic Organization*, The Free Press, New York

Weber, M. (1978) *Economy and Society: An Outline of Interpretive Sociology*, University of California Press, Berkeley, Ca.

Weiss, J.(1981) 'Substance vs symbol in administrative reform: the case of human services coordination', *Policy Analysis*, 7,1,Pp.21-45

Westheimer, I. (1977) *The Practice of Supervision in Social Work: A Guide for Staff Supervisors*, Ward Lock Educational, London

Westrin, C-G. (1987) 'Primary health care: cooperation between health and welfare personnel' *Scandinavian Journal of Social Medicine*, Supplement 38

Westwood, S. (1984) *All Day and Every Day: Factory and Family in the Making of Women's Lives*, Pluto, London

Williams, L.M. and Finkelhor, D. (1990) 'The characteristics of incestuous fathers', in Marshall *et al* eds. *Handbook of Sexual Assault: Issues, Theories and Treatment of the Offender*, Plenum, New York

Williams, S. (1986) 'Case studies in collaboration', *Family Practitioner Services*, 13, 3, Pp.39-43

Williamson, H. and Butler, I. (1995) 'No one ever listens to us: interviewing children and young people' in Cloke, C. and Davies, M. *Participation and Empowerment in Child Protection*, Pitman Publishing, London

Wilson, E. (1977) *Women and the Welfare State*, Tavistock, London

Winch. P. (1958) *The Idea of a Social Science and its Relation to Philosophy*, Routledge and Kegan Paul, London

Wise, S. (1991) *Child Abuse: The NSPCC Version*, Feminist Praxis, London

Wistow, (1982) 'Collaboration between health and local authorities: why is it necessary? *Journal of Social Policy and Administration*, 16, 1, Pp.44-62

Wolfe, D.A., (1993) 'Child abuse prevention: blending research and practice' *Abuse Review*, 2 (3) Sep. Pp.153-165

Women's Resource Centre (1989) *Recollecting Our Lives: Women's Experience of Childhood Sexual Abuse*, Press Gang Publishers, Vancouver

Woodhill, R. and Ashworth, P. (1989) *Parental Participation at Case Conferences*, Sheffield Hallam University

Woodhouse, D. and Pengelly, P. (1991) *Anxiety and the Dynamics of Collaboration*, Aberdeen University Press, Aberdeen

Wyatt, G.E. and Mickey, M.R. (1988) 'The support by parents and others as it mediates the effects of child sexual abuse: an exploratory study', in Wyatt, G.E. and Powell, G.J. eds. *Lasting Effects of Child Sexual Abuse*, Sage, London

Wyatt, G.E. and Newcombe, M. (1990) 'Internal and external mediators of women's sexual abuse in childhood', *Journal of Consulting and Clinical Psychology*, 58, (6), Pp.758-767

Zaretsky, E. (1976) *The Family, Personal Life and Capitalism*, Pluto Press, London

Zurvain, S.J., Benedict, M. and Somerfield, M. (1993) 'Child maltreatment in family foster care' *American Journal of Orthopsychiatry*, 63 (4) Oct. Pp.589-596

Index